A scientist, who is also a wife and mother of two daughters, has an epiphany on a hot July morning. Her children are bored and frustrated, complaining they have nothing to do. Mom decides to make a cake to cheer them up, concluding that hope abounds wherever there is cake. The younger daughter suggests they make a cake every weekend. Saturday becomes Cake Day, the family's newest tradition. This charming and witty chronicle of a year in the life of a Midwestern family includes a wonderful array of cake recipes. But it is also reveals the rich interior life of a delightful and fearless woman who is trying to identify and hold onto what matters most to her: family, friends, community, love, hope, and cake.

the cake chronicles

Lois —
Lovely to meet you!
Remember: when life throws
eggs, make cake!
Sweet regards,
Jynne

the cake chronicles

finding sweet hope in this crazy world

jayne b. robinson

Dandelion Seed Press

Illustrations by Erin Johnson
Design by Ellyn Miller
Back Cover Quote by Dean Koontz, author of *Life Expectancy*, with his permission

Dandelion Seed Press, Dayton, OH 45419

ISBN: 978-0-9830850-0-3
LCCN: 2010939838

Printed in the United States of America.

To my daughters, Lizzie and Kat, who are both lovely and amazing.

contents

Summer Reprise

Cake Day

"Where there's cake there's hope. And there's always cake." —Rudy Tock, from *Life Expectancy*, by Dean Koontz

The saunalike days of summer had come to southwest Ohio. My husband, Wayne; our two daughters, Lizzie and Kat; and I were moaning and groaning about one thing or another, all of our complaints made worse by heat and humidity. Suddenly I heard myself reciting the above quote. Kat's face lit up. "Let's have cake day," she said. "Saturday should be cake day—every Saturday. Can we, can we, can weeee?" And so, Cake Day was born at our house. The following Saturday I made the Perfect Chocolate Cake, a three-layer confection with a whipped cream heart and a coating of chocolate ganache. This cake has been a family favorite for twenty years (well, it was my favorite anyway). That old cliché, "When life throws lemons at you, make lemonade" is not for me. I am a cake girl. I believe that when life throws eggs at you, you should make a cake.

After reading Dean Koontz's gripping novel *Life Expectancy*, I had concluded that cake is the true antidote to the craziness of life and its uncertainties. Koontz's book is the story of a father and son, Rudy and Jimmy Tock, bakers both. They battle evil clowns and the fateful predictions of the grandfather, who dies at the exact moment of Jimmy's birth. The Tocks know in advance, thanks to the grandfather, five days in Jimmy's life that will be terrible. And they are terrible days, but the Tocks survive and prosper. The Tock family motto "Where there is cake there is hope, and there is always cake" was inspired by their profession. But it also speaks to the of love and family and the greatness of small things. It is not necessary to be a domestic diva to create a happy and hopeful home. Cake is my favorite retreat from the low-carb life. I can always bake a cake.

Wayne and I decided long ago that dinner at our house would be sacrosanct. The rule is that we prepare dinner and eat it together at home. Our kids know they need an excuse from us—or from God—to miss dinner, especially Sunday dinner. We don't have family close by, so we've had to create our own traditions. Over the years this has served us well. Most nights we start with the high-low game, which is a good way to connect or vent. We go around the table and everyone, including guests, has to tell the high and low point of their day. When Lizzie went off to college, it seemed silly to continue to cook dinner every night just for the three of us. But we managed to hang tough and do it.

Still, there comes a time when it is a good—even necessary—idea to start new traditions. In Elizabeth Berg's excellent book *Family Traditions: Celebrations for Holidays and Everyday*, she makes the case for families of all kinds creating and maintaining traditions. Berg believes that our health, happiness, and well-being may depend on this.

I am not sure where in the process of evolution traditions arose. Perhaps when early humans figured out how to make and maintain fires they began a tradition of literally passing the torch. The ancient African child's song tradition is one of the most powerful traditions I know. Each child has a song, created before conception, that is learned by all members of the tribe and sung on important occasions throughout the child's life and at their death.

Of course, many traditions involve food. Everyone believes that what their family puts on the Thanksgiving table is the definitive holiday food. I'm certain fights have broken out, and families have even split, after yams with a marshmallow hat are supplanted by a roasted vegetable medley at a Thanksgiving celebration. Berg makes the point that traditions need not be stultifying, rigid, and lacking in personal connection. She believes that new traditions help to shape and express us, bringing order, stability, and joy to our lives. I know she is right. Joy and stability leaked out of my own childhood as alcoholism claimed and consumed my parents, traditions small and large slipping away. I'm lucky I'm not battling that demon. And lucky, too, that I've been free to make my own way, to create my own traditions.

So, at our house a new tradition was born. We argued about the rules and we debated the virtues of different types of cakes. In the end, we kept it as simple as possible. We weren't sure if this tradition was going to stick. And who says traditions must be forever? Some traditions, I believe, have a natural cycle of birth, life, and death.

As we confront life's many choices, how or what we choose defines us and hopefully saves us. Heather Mallick's darkly funny book *Cake or Death: The Excruciating Choices of Everyday Life* posits that we must often make excruciating choices. I, for one, choose cake. And while life is not all cake and champagne—and certainly cake will never save the planet—it might just save the day. Cake can add a festive touch to a ho-hum week or elevate a day when you are feeling down and discouraged. Who doesn't relish a three-layer slice of chocolate hope from time to time? And cake brings folks together like few other things do. As a scientist, I am always checking my assumptions and looking for the GUF (grand unifying force) that will explain and unify all actions and reactions in life. Is it cake? I decided to test this theory.

On that hot day in July 2005 when my family began its Cake Day tradition, it was not a good time in our country's history. Gas prices were at a record high, with no cap in sight; global warming was sparking heated debates everywhere; and the war in Iraq continued to take its toll on U.S. and Iraqi soldiers and citizens.

Our hearts were heavy and in need of leavening. Cake! Every Saturday! Yes, we could do that.

What we didn't realize when we started was how many friends and family would gather with us over a year's time to eat cake and to celebrate life, liberty, and hope. Everyone seems to be searching for the sweet and simple parts of life—the things that cost little and provide a slice of hope. A slice of cake might be the wedge that holds open our hearts.

Why Cake?

What is cake? It is both a noun and a verb—it is a thing and an action. To me this means that maybe you really can have your cake and eat it, too.

Cakes are made from various combinations of flour, shortening, sweeteners, eggs, milk, a leavening agent, and flavoring. Cookies and biscuits are what early cakes looked like—flat and cooked over a fire. Literally thousands of cakes recipes exist (some are simple and breadlike, some rich and elaborate) and many are centuries old. When is this mixture of ingredients bread rather than cake? It is bread when it is denser and less sweet, but the line is a fine one and I tend to like cakes that are breadlike and breads that are cake-like. To each his own. One person's bread is another person's cake.

Cakes come in many styles: angel, sponge, chiffon, pound, and griddle (being a scientist, I tend to start any exploration by learning the taxonomy). After reviewing the history and the why of cake, I have concluded that cakes are the peak of pastrydom. Many pastries, while luscious to look at and delicious to eat, can't do what a cake can do. A cheese Danish cannot be fashioned into an armadillo or made to look like Barbie in order to stun and amaze its audience.

Cake is one of the cheapest forms of happiness I know, but there are expensive and even dangerous cakes. According to Wikipedia, the most expensive one ever made was a wedding cake studded with diamonds and valued at $20 million. Dangerous cakes are wedding cakes, prison cakes (with files as fillings), and gunpowder cakes. Some cakes are so special that mothers-in-law lie about the recipe so you won't be able to make one exactly like hers (more on that later).

Cakes are consumed in solace and celebration, in good times and in bad. At weddings, for example, cake is always the main event. Pies, pastries, and cookies don't fill the bill. For one thing, pies can't be stacked to make seven layers. The lines in the typical wedding ceremony warn about good times and bad but say nothing about cake. I infer from this that there should never be cakeless times in a marriage. And who prefers pie for their birthday? Cake is usually all about sharing. But cupcakes are for those times when you really don't want to share or when you want to take it with you.

Whatever your own reasons for eating cake, and whether you prefer chocolate or white, I urge you to eat cake. Eat it for dinner, lunch, and even breakfast. Eat it until your spirits are as light as an angel food cake. If it were up to me, I would rewrite the Declaration of Independence to proclaim "Life, liberty, and the pursuit of cake."

The Rules

Disclaimer: This story is not about making perfect pastries, it is about sharing cake and satisfying one's soul.

1. Only cakes are allowed on Cake Day (no pies,

cookies, or Jello concoctions—this is not Jello Day!).

2. Cake Day can be any day of the week. It can be whenever cake is called for: every week, every other week, or once a month.

3. The person who offers to make the cake gets to pick the type of cake.

4. No one is allowed to complain about the cake. No one, not ever.

5. Before eating the cake, take a minute to reflect on hope or utter the Cake Day motto "Where there's cake there's hope. And there's always cake."

6. Share the cake! Once people found out that every Saturday around 7 PM there would be cake at our house, we often had visitors.

7. Enjoy every bite. Be grateful for the simple and sweet things in life, like the chance to eat cake with your family and friends (and, late at night, all by yourself).

Summer

Dog Days of July...Birthing a Tradition

"A love for tradition has never weakened a nation, indeed it has strengthened nations in their hour of peril." —Winston Churchill

Saturday. The first of our Cake Days has dawned hot and humid. This is not a day for meringues or angel food cake.

Vacation is over and the tomatoes are not yet in, an awkward time of summer. Kat is moaning about losing yet another swim race and Lizzie is complaining about her babysitting charges and the state of the world (both rude and unruly). Wayne, who works at home, is just trying to keep his cool until we all return to school or work. I enter the kitchen determined to find the perfect cake recipe. Instead I start griping about the state of my kitchen—too small, too out of date. But with one daughter in college and one in braces, now is not the time to transform it into the kitchen of my dreams.

We're all feeling the weight of the world and the words of English poet William Wordsworth have been circling my brain: "The world is too much with us; late and soon, getting and spending, we lay waste our powers." Too true. I have always told my daughters that life is not about having and spending; it is about doing and being. Our only hope of being happy in this world is to find joy in small things while we are working toward big things. I have come to think that happiness is a duty. There is no way to happiness. Happiness is the way.

It is clearly a day for a chocolate cake. The chemicals in chocolate are known to induce a happier, more content state of mind. I decide it is my duty to make a delicious cake. And so we embark on our new tradition: A day every week dedicated to cake.

The Perfect Chocolate Cake

I choose this cake because it is chocolate and it is perfect. Chocolate is chock full of feel-good chemicals and I am in the mood to be in a better mood.

I made this cake for the first time the year Wayne and I got married. It appeared in the *New McCalls Cookbook* I received as a wedding present. The photograph of the cake made my chocolate-loving soul swoon. I was not an experienced cook at the time and making this cake took me all day. I continued to make it every year for Wayne's birthday until he finally confessed, years later, that chocolate cake is not his favorite. I wish I could say I accepted this news gracefully (I didn't). But soon Wayne started making it for my birthday and all was forgiven (on both sides). For his birthday, I now make him his mother's famous all-white cake.

Here is the original, from scratch, recipe. It is worth the effort. Baking from scratch is a form of meditation. Gathering the ingredients—eggs, butter, sugar, flour, flavorings—takes mere minutes but provides time to contemplate where our foods come from and how easy it is to transform them into love in its edible form for family and friends. In her delightful and useful book *Simple Abundance*, Sara Ban Breathnach says of creativity, "You may not draw, paint, sculpt, knit, sing, dance, or act, but baking a cake could be as much a work of art as choreographing a ballet, if you approach it with as much dedication." Sift the flour, crack and beat the eggs, cream the butter and sugar, all the while concentrating on the craft. Craft becomes art and the craziness of the world recedes.

Preheat oven to 350° F.
Butter and flour three 9" layer-cake pans.

Cake

1 cup unsifted unsweetened cocoa
2 cups boiling water
2 ¾ cups sifted all-purpose flour
2 teaspoon baking soda
½ teaspoon salt
½ teaspoon baking powder
1 cup (2 sticks) room temperature unsalted butter
2 ½ cups sugar
4 eggs
1 ½ teaspoons vanilla extract

1. In a medium mixing bowl combine cocoa with boiling water and mix with a wire whisk until smooth. Cool completely.

2. In the medium bowl of an electric mixer combine flour, baking soda, baking powder and salt. Mix on low speed for 30 seconds and set aside.

3. In the large bowl of an electric mixer cream butter, sugar, eggs, and vanilla on high speed, scraping bowl occasionally, until light (about 5 minutes).

4. At low speed, beat in flour mixture in four batches, alternating with cocoa mixture (do not over beat).

5. Divide batter evenly in prepared pans.

6. Bake 20 to 30 minutes, or until the surface springs back when lightly touched with a fingertip.

7. Cool in pans for 10 minutes.

8. Remove from pans to racks and allow to cool completely before frosting.

Frosting

6 ounces semisweet chocolate chips
½ cup light cream
1 cup (2 sticks) butter
2 ½ cups unsifted confectioners' sugar

1. In a medium saucepan combine chocolate chips, cream, butter; stir over medium heat until smooth.

2. Remove from heat. Whisk in confectioners' sugar.

3. In a bowl set over ice beat until mixture holds shape. (Or chill for about 20 minutes in the refrigerator, and then beat without the bowl of ice.)

Whipped-Cream Filling

1 cup heavy cream, chilled
¼ cup unsifted confectioners' sugar
1 teaspoon vanilla extract

1. Chill beaters and cream in the freezer for 10 minutes before beating.

2. Whip chilled cream with sugar and vanilla until it holds soft peaks when beater is slowly withdrawn.

Cake Assembly

1. Place one layer of the cake on a cake plate, top side down, spread with half of the cream filling.

2. Place the second layer top side down and spread with the rest of the cream filling.

3. Place the last layer on top, top side up.

4. Frost sides first, covering the whipped cream, and swirl the rest of the frosting decoratively on top.

Refrigerate for at least 1 hour before serving.

Making Memories

"And even if you were in some prison, the walls of which let none of the sounds of the world come to your senses—would you not then still have your childhood, that precious, kingly possession, that treasure house of memories?"
—Rainer Maria Rilke

It's another hot week. But less than two miles from our house is a gem of an outdoor amphitheater and it's offering cool music from Elvis Costello, Emmylou Harris, and the Imposters. I'd heard that Costello was coming and, though I can't claim to be a fan of the man, I am a fan of live music spun out under the stars. So when Friday dawned clear and hot, although not sauna-like, I decided we should go. We picked up our lawn quilt and the four of us headed for the concert. And what an unexpectedly amazing concert it was. I was remembering some songs, and just experiencing others, when Costello struck up "The Scarlet Tide" from the movie *Cold Mountain*. In this conservative city in the shadow of an air force base the crowd went wild when Costello sang, "Because you lied, men died... bring the boys back home."

I am a mom who is all about making memories and I am hoping this is one that Lizzie and Kat will long remember: sharing a quilt on the grass on a summer night while listening to great music. I realized we were experiencing the music separately, if not equally, when during one of my favorite songs, Kat, known for interrupting the end of every movie or TV show, leaned toward me and said, "Mom, feel my hand—isn't it soft?"

We left the amphitheater floating on the afterglow of a great performance.

On the way home, we stopped at our local market for a peach pie. Cake Day wasn't until tomorrow, so pie was perfectly permissible. While Wayne and Kat went inside, Lizzie and I took a detour down the alley to pick up a cast-off mullioned window that she had spied earlier. Its glass panes were tinted blue and adorned with clouds, which made up for the chipped paint on the frame. We dragged it home and the next morning I installed it in our garden. Stepping back from my first art installation work I caught a reflection of real clouds superimposed on the painted ones and smiled at art reflecting life. I began to think about what cake I would bake for our second Cake Day.

I'd procured a bounty of red, ripe raspberries earlier in the week from our local farm market. All I needed was the cream, or so I thought. I rode my bicycle to the Dorothy Lane Market, five blocks from my house—the best market in the world. I bought some organic whipping cream to appease Lizzie's interest in all things organic. I rode home in the sweltering heat and put the whipping cream and mixing bowl into the refrigerator. I wrapped the beaters in foil and put them in the freezer, mindful that cream whips best when very cold. I made the cake and let it cool. I took the whipping cream and bowl out of the refrigerator and the beaters out of the freezer and started to whip. Nothing happened. Nothing.

As a scientist I understand the chemistry behind whipping cream. But neither my specialized knowledge nor chanting incantations over the bowl had any measurable effect on the creamy liquid. I sent the bowl and utensils back into the refrigerator and freezer. An hour later I tried again, with the same dismal result. Back on my bike, I noticed it was even hotter outside. I returned the empty organic whipping cream container for some of the non-organic stuff. Arriving back home, I began to whip it straight away, skipping the refrigerator-freezer step. Miracle of miracles, white peaks of perfect whipped cream rose in the bowl. Finishing the cake, I slipped it into the refrigerator and headed to the community pool.

When we gathered after dinner for cake, Lizzie's friend Zoe joined us. Zoe was leaving soon for her freshman year at McGill University in Montreal. Happy to see her, we nevertheless knew she was nervous about going off to college, so we didn't bring it up. Instead, we talked about shared childhood memories and raspberries and cake and how summer in Ohio is unbearably hot (we never mentioned how winter in Montreal might be unbearably cold).

Raspberries and Cream Cloud Cake

This is really a gourmet raspberry shortcake; a perfect use of fresh raspberries. The recipe comes from the *CookWise* cookbook by Shirley Corriher. If forced to give up all cookbooks but one, a terrifying thought, this is the one I would keep. It is a cookbook fit for scientists, so explicit and perfect are the directions, or anyone who wants to avoid culinary failure.

Preheat oven to 350° F.
Butter and flour a 9" round cake pan, then line the pan with a parchment or waxpaper circle and lightly butter and flour that also.

Pay attention to the instructions about the temperature of the ingredients. Shirley assures us that this is crucial to ending up with a light cake with an even texture.

Cake

1⅓ cups sugar
1½ cups cake flour
1½ teaspoons baking powder
½ teaspoon salt
½ cup buttermilk at room temperature
1 teaspoon vanilla extract
½ cup (1 stick) unsalted butter at room temperature
2 large eggs, at room temperature
3 large egg yolks at room temperature
⅓ cup vegetable oil

Note: Substitute walnut, hazelnut or almond oil if you would like a subtle flavor note. Just be sure the oil is fresh as nut oils turn rancid faster than other oils.

1. Place the mixer bowl and beaters in the freezer. Measure the sugar into a zip-top plastic bag, seal, and place in the freezer to chill. Chill all for about 20 minutes.

2. Sift flour, baking powder and salt onto a sheet of wax paper. Resift at least one more time onto another piece of wax paper.

3. Measure the buttermilk into a glass measuring cup and add the vanilla. Let this sit.

4. In the large bowl of an electric mixer, cream the butter on medium speed until light in color, about 5 minutes. Add the sugar in a steady stream with mixer running. Continue beating for 3–4 minutes, scraping down the bowl once.

5. Add the eggs and yolks one at a time, beating on medium speed for about 30 seconds after each addition. Continue to beat another 1–2 minutes or until the mixture is light and airy looking.

6. Remove the bowl from the mixer and stir in the oil. Fold in half of the flour mixture with a large rubber spatula. Scrap down the sides of the bowl and then fold in half of the buttermilk-vanilla mixture. Fold in the remaining flour and scrape down, then the remaining buttermilk-vanilla mixture.

7. Pour the batter into the prepared pan. Smooth the batter with the rubber spatula, leaving the edges a breath higher than the center.

8. Bake until a toothpick inserted an inch from the center comes out clean—about 35 minutes. The sides should just begin to pull away from the pan when you place the cake on the rack to cool.

9. Let the cake cook in the pan for 10–20 minutes. Tap the sides of the pan on the counter to loosen the cake (or run a small spatula around the edge). Spray the cooling rack lightly with nonstick spray (or rub oil onto it). Invert cake onto the greased rack.

10. Peel off the parchment paper and then place the liner on the cake with the sticky side up. Invert cake back onto the original cooking rack so the cake is now right side up.

11. Cool completely before assembling with raspberries and cream.

Mascarpone Cream Filling

½ cup mascarpone cheese
2 tablespoons honey
1 cup heavy or whipping cream

1. Place the cream, medium bowl of an electric mixer and beaters in the freezer for 10 minutes.

2. In a small bowl, whisk together the mascarpone and honey.

3. Whip the cream into soft peaks in the cold bowl with the cold beaters.

4. Fold the mascarpone mixture into the whipped cream.

5. Chill until ready to use.

Raspberry Sauce

2 pints fresh raspberries or 2 packages (10 ounces each) frozen raspberries, defrosted but not drained
3 tablespoons raspberry liquor (or Grand Marnier)

Stir 1½ pints of the fresh (save the rest for decoration) or defrosted raspberries and liquor together in the medium bowl of an electric mixer.

Cake Assembly

1. When the cake has cooled slice horizontally into 3 layers.

2. Place the bottom layer, cut side up, on a cake plate or stand.

3. Spoon half the raspberry mixture, including the liquor, onto the layer. Spoon about a quarter of the Mascarpone cream on top in large blobs and spread out carefully.

4. Place another layer on top of the iced bottom layer. Spoon on the remaining raspberry mixture and ice as before.

5. Place the top layer, cut side down on the cake and ice generously with the remaining Mascarpone Cream.

6. Refrigerate for at least 2 hours before serving. Best if refrigerated overnight.

7. When ready to serve, arrange fresh raspberries on top.

8. Serve cold.

How to Rescue a Week

"You can't wait for inspiration. You have to go after it with a club."
—Jack London

All week Lizzie has debated whether to make Cake Day a surprise birthday party for two of her closest friends. All week I have tried to find out what kind of cake her friends might like. I got nowhere. It seems she cannot quite figure out how to surprise her friends and make them happy about being surprised. Sometimes I forget that being nineteen is not all that easy. The last age I remember being easy was ten. That's it, we get one year that is dead solid perfect.

The heat wave has yet to relent. My free days of doing research unfettered by teaching and committee meetings are melting away like ice cream on a sizzling sidewalk. I have several crucial experiments awaiting the right reagents and pair of hands; it seems that never the twain shall meet.

Laboratory research—in-the-trenches research, versus theoretical research à la Einstein—is chock full of unique joys and challenges. And it is the most creative endeavor I have known. But it is just downright frustrating sometimes, in the way that not being able to get your car fixed and your body back on the road to that special event you've planned for months (and paid big bucks for) is frustrating. This has been that kind of week. Apparently I need a new club to wrest inspiration from the titanium jaws of unyielding frustration.

So I devote myself to this week's cake. I decide that it will make me forget the woes of research going nowhere at the speed of light and provide my family and friends with a few moments of pleasure. Craft is the cure. I sift the flour three times, cream the room-temperature butter with the sparkling sugar until it is fluffy, and beat in the eggs one at a time, until the batter is the color of lemons. I pour the mixture into the pans I took the time to prepare perfectly and pop them into the preheated oven. I sit back and sip my iced tea in sweet anticipation. A cake, made with love, elevates craft to art.

Lizzie enters the kitchen and announces her decision. She has given up on surprising her friends and invites them for Cake Night, which she thinks is more than good enough. I am happy to report that one and all loved the cake and the problems of the lab were far from my mind on this Saturday night.

Lemon Poppyseed Cake

Lizzie's friend Zoe said this is her favorite cake. Since

she is about to leave for her first year of college, it is gratifying to have picked a cake she adores. This recipe is a compilation of several I found on the Internet.

Preheat oven to 350° F.
Butter an 8" square pan.

1 cup vegetable oil
1 cup honey
3 eggs
3 cups whole wheat flour
¼ package lemon Jello
¾ cup poppy seeds
3 tablespoons baking powder
1½ cups buttermilk
½ teaspoon salt

Cake

1. Mix all ingredients together, and pour into prepared pan.

2. Bake for 35–40 minutes or until done. Cool cake on a rack for 10 minutes, and then release it from the pan onto a plate. Drizzle with icing.

Glaze

½ box confectioners' sugar
2–3 tablespoons warm water
Juice and grated rind of one lemon

Mix ingredients together and pour over cake.

The Goodbye Girl

"She went her unremembering way, she went and left in me the pang of all the partings gone, and partings yet to be."
—Francis Thompson, from her poem "Daisy"

When my daughters were small, I was always the one saying goodbye as I went off to work or meetings. I did not account for the day that they would start to say goodbye to me. When Lizzie came home at the end of April after her first year of college, the summer had seemed like an extravagant gift of time. We would have time to garden and cook together, time for movies and concerts, and time for our trek to northern Michigan, a vacation we have taken every summer since Lizzie's birth in 1985. We would also have time to argue about which movie to watch and what to have for dinner. Quickly we raced through the time that had once stretched so far ahead of us. It has been a great summer, but it has also been way too short.

Before we know it, Lizzie is returning for her second year at Pitt. Wayne takes on the onerous job of driving, moving, and then leaving Lizzie behind. Back home, after catching up on his sleep, Wayne and Kat finish reading the sixth Harry Potter book. The two of them have stretched it out as long as possible, savoring every page and worrying that someone will reveal the ending before they are done. When the adventure finally concludes with Professor Dumbledore's death, it is heartbreaking for eleven-year-old Kat. The professor has been her favorite character and she swears she will never get over it. Her wiser mother knows that she will get over it, but only when something even bigger breaks her heart again.

This is the pain of parenting: knowing ahead of time that our children's hearts are destined to be broken. The books we read, the movies we watch, and the relationships we enter into are all potential emotional minefields. But we can't help ourselves because it is human to seek connection and meaning, even if ultimately our hearts develop faults the size of the Grand Canyon. The Harry Potter books have resurrected the romance of magic (Kat wants to be a magic witch like Hermione). I tell Lizzie and Kat that love is the only magic that is real. And I tell them to use it wisely and well.

Saying goodbye to those we love—real or fictional—is the greatest pain we can know. But anticipating their return is the greatest joy.

North Coast Cheesecake

We need comfort food this week. Wayne picks up the reins and makes his mother's famous cheesecake, a canyon of comfort in every bite.

This recipe abounds in the church cookbooks of the 1960s, when my mother-in-law, Bernie, was asked to bring it to every church event. After a brief affair with fancy cheesecakes like chocolate fudge, better-than-sex, and amazing amaretto, I decided that this cheesecake will always be my favorite. I love to eat it slowly to savor every delicious molecule.

Preheat oven to 300° F.
Take out a 13" x 9" pan or 10" round springform pan.

Crust

12 graham crackers, crushed (do this on a food processor or put inside a double thick, clean plastic bag and roll with a rolling pin)
3 tablespoons butter
1 tablespoon sugar

Mix together in a bowl and pat into the bottom of the pan.

Filling

3 eight-ounce packages of room-temperature cream cheese (but not the soft type)
5 eggs
1 cup sugar
1 ½ teaspoons vanilla

Topping

1 ½ pints sour cream
½ cup sugar
1 ½ teaspoons vanilla

1. In the large bowl of an electric mixer, beat the cream cheese with the sugar and vanilla until light.

2. Add the eggs, one at a time, beating well after each addition.

3. Pour over crust and bake 1 hour until the cake is set in the middle.

4. Remove the cake from the oven and cool for 5 minutes. Prepare topping and spread over cake.

5. Return to the oven and bake 5 more minutes.

6. Cool completely before refrigerating.

This cheesecake is best served the following day. In fact, I will not touch it until it has spent a night in the refrigerator—it is that much better.

Tom-ahhh-toes!

"You know, when you get your first asparagus, or your first acorn squash, or your first really good tomato of the season, those are the moments that define the cook's year. I get more excited by that than anything else."
—Mario Batali, chef

We are crazy about tomatoes. Lizzie even devoted her college-application essay to this royal fruit disguised as a vegetable. For years Kat referred to tornadoes as "tomatoes."

The last week of August in Ohio brings with it tomatoes, a gardener's greatest triumph. And if you've been diligent and are lucky, you will have lots of them. For me, this year is particularly rewarding because it is our first tomato harvest in over ten years. My tomato garden is where a thirty-foot-tall mulberry tree stood until this past June. It was not an easy decision to cut down that tree. Both of my daughters had climbed it and plucked and eaten mulberries until their hands and mouths turned purple for weeks on end. The birds also loved the mulberry tree, so much so that our cars—and our neighbor's cars—were dotted with purple goo every summer. And the tree had rendered a huge corner of our yard unable to sustain any other plant life. We had no place to plant a vegetable garden on our tiny city lot, so I had resorted to growing tomatoes in pots on the front porch. Although this seemed appealingly European to me, the harvest had failed to match my tomato dreams.

Full disclosure: I attempted to get rid of the mulberry tree when the kids were young, before they could develop an attachment to it. But alas, Wayne rallied Lizzie and Kat—and the rest of the kids in the neighborhood—with a campaign to Save the Mulberry Tree. They did everything but print bumper stickers. My neighbors supported the campaign, perhaps out of nostalgia for the mulberry trees of their own childhoods and perhaps because their grandchildren visit often. So for the past ten years the kids went around and around the mulberry tree all spring and summer, leaving purple-stained footprints behind.

I thought I could wait until Kat went to college, but that was seven years off and I wanted tomatoes and sunflowers and morning glories and roses now! It helped that our lovely neighbors seemed to be losing their affection for the tree as well, although they never complained. So down came the tree and as the branches fell so did the tears on my eleven-year-old's face.

After the remains of the tree had been cleared I set out the tomato plants: Early girl, Brandywine, Brandy boy (son of Brandywine and our personal favorite), Better boy, Lemon boy, Beefmaster, Green zebra, and Santa (grape) tomatoes. I planted heavenly blue morning glories to climb the arbor that was now in the sun and I planted sunflowers. I installed a marigold moat around the tomatoes to keep away pests and I even watered—something I am loathe to do—when July arrived along with a three-week drought.

I waited. Then one day I noticed a tinge of pink on a tomato that was dangling in that provocative way tomatoes have perfected. Every night when I arrived home from work I would examine the tomato and estimate the time left until it would be fully ripe. In my dreams I plucked it and carried it to the kitchen to cut into four equal pieces, one for each of us. Finally the big day arrived. I left for work that morning certain that we would be eating the first tomato of the season for dinner.

Riding my bike home that evening I fantasized about the juiciness of the tomato and its sweet taste. I even momentarily considered devouring the tomato all by myself—as far as I could tell, I was the only person who knew of its existence. I swooped into the driveway and looked to my left. The tomato was gone. My emotions ran the gamut from shock to fury. I ran into the house screaming, "Katherine, did you eat the tomato?" "No," she called out. "Lizzie, did you eat the tomato?" Lizzie proclaimed her innocence. Then Wayne's voice drifted down from his upstairs office. "I think I know who ate your tomato and he's in the tree out front." Sure enough, perched in the crook of the big tree in the front yard was a squirrel clutching the tomato with both paws and staring straight at us. He took a few more bites before throwing it on the ground half-eaten.

My friend Albert calls squirrels "rats with tails" and traps them in his yard. He tells his wife that he releases them down by the river but he actually drowns them in a garbage can full of water. Finally I understood his impulse. If I owned a gun, my garbage bins would be full of squirrel carcasses.

I went back to watering and waiting. Now I cannot keep up with the harvest of yellow-, red-, pink-, and green-striped globes decorating the tomato vines. My morning glories greet me as I walk through the arbor and a hummingbird—rare in our neck of the urban woods—has decided we are the place to be. I couldn't be happier.

Garrison Keillor did a great riff on tomatoes in his monologue of June 2003 broadcast from Kalamazoo, Michigan, my hometown. The tomatoes of Lake Wobegon (or Kalamazoo or Timbuktu) are works of art, true tomatoes (not the store- bought kind). Keillor claims that a fresh tomato is a beautiful thing that any kid can grow. It will be his own and as good as any in the world. That tomato, undressed, or maybe with a little fresh basil or a little sugar, will be as fine as one from Milan, Italy. And the best that any chef in New York, London, or Paris could do with it would be simply orthopedic in nature. You can produce the best of something in your own garden. What a lesson.

So what are we doing with our crop of perfection? Well, the first tomato we shared, cutting it into quarters, grabbing a slice, making a wish, and popping it into our mouths. We are eating our tomatoes out of hand like apples or sliced or in salads and stir-frys. We've transformed them into gazpacho, eggplant parmigiana, lasagna, and countless grilled cheese sandwiches.

This week I went hunting for a recipe for fresh tomato cake. (Along the way I discovered a great recipe for Green Tomato Pie that I plan to make in late October.) I found old recipes calling for canned tomato soup, but only one recipe that features fresh tomatoes. It was published in the *Old Farmer's Almanac Hearth & Home 1993 Companion*. I also found a recipe for fresh tomato ice cream but that, too, is for another time.

Last week we sent Lizzie back to college with a bag of tomatoes and a smile on her face. We took photos of ourselves early that morning in front of the sunflower-tomato-morning glory patch. Tonight, the last Saturday of summer vacation we ate a feast of oven-fried chicken, steamed asparagus, mashed potatoes, and sliced tomatoes. Two of Kat's friends joined us for dinner. I noticed that neither took anything from the plate of sliced red-, yellow-, and green-striped tomatoes. But both ate their fill of Fresh Tomato Cake.

It has been a very good summer. I hate saying goodbye to summer with its laid-back days and the opportunities it offers us to hang out together as a family—to argue about what to have for dinner at a more leisurely pace. As Kat prepares to begin her last year of elementary school, I am reminded that the end of summer also means that the kids are another year older and closer to moving out of the nuclear-family orbit.

Fresh Tomato Cake

Whether you say Tuh-MAY-toh or Tuh-MAH-to, I hope you get a chance to enjoy your own tomatoes in whatever form you choose. Once your tomatoes start rolling in, you may find yourself with more than you can eat out of hand or in grilled cheese sandwiches, as happened to us this week. I advise you to use up your fresh tomatoes by making this cake. And when the fresh tomatoes have become a rosy memory, you can try tomato-soup cake.

Preheat oven to 350° F.
Butter and flour two 8" round cake pans.

Cake

1 cup dark brown sugar
½ cup room-temperature unsalted butter
2 eggs
3 cups flour
2 teaspoons baking powder 1 teaspoon baking soda
1 teaspoon nutmeg
1 teaspoon salt
2 cups ripe garden tomatoes, peeled and chopped with seeds removed (to remove skins easily, plop into boiling water for 1 minute)
½ cup chopped nuts
½ cup chopped dates (optional)
½ cup chopped raisins (optional)

1. In the large bowl of an electric mixer, cream butter and sugar until light—about 5 minutes.

2. Add eggs and beat well.

3. Sift dry ingredients, add, and mix well.

4. Stir in tomatoes, nuts, dates, and raisins. Divide evenly into two prepared pans.

5. Bake for 25 minutes or until tester comes out clean but not dry—do not overbake.

6. Place cake pans on wire racks until cakes are completely cooled, remove from pans, and frost.

Cream Cheese Frosting

8 ounce package of room-temperature cream cheese
½ cup room-temperature butter
2 teaspoons vanilla extract
2 cups powdered sugar

Whip cream cheese and butter until light.

Add vanilla and powdered sugar and mix well.

A Titanium Anniversary

"The most dangerous cake is wedding cake." —James Thurber

Order was restored when Kat started back to school this week. Well, almost. I managed to snag a wicked virus just as the aftermath of Hurricane Katrina made its way to Ohio. The images of the devastation wrought by Katrina began to hit the television screen and the papers and none of us could easily get past the tragedy. How do we comprehend a disaster of such proportions? How do we respond? How can we do homework or prepare a lecture when people are dying? Our community is home to a major air force base and we witnessed convoys of trucks and planes heading south while blue skies reigned above. It seemed unreal.

The week rolled on and the images grew worse but we turned away long enough to ready ourselves for a trip to the north coast of Ohio to celebrate my in-laws' sixty-third wedding anniversary. How do we celebrate a marriage of such longevity? What do we give a couple that has endured over so many years the inevitable challenges and surprising joys of marriage? This is not considered one of the special anniversaries. It isn't silver, ruby, sapphire, gold, or emerald—and it goes beyond even the diamond that is supposed to mark a sixtieth year of marriage. A sixty-third wedding anniversary is a No Man's Land between diamonds and the end of time. Perhaps a titanium anniversary? But this year was as special as any. All of us were well and none of our lives disturbed by natural or man-made disasters. We were feeling very lucky indeed.

Wayne, Kat, and I traveled north and Wayne's brother, his wife, and their son drove west from their home in Washington D.C., stopping to pick up Lizzie at Pitt along the way. We all arrived shortly after sunset at my in-laws' stately colonial high on the bluffs overlooking Lake Erie. Turning into the long driveway, we saw the house lit up as if for a fantastic party. This house has looked the same every Thanksgiving, Christmas, and Easter eve as we arrived toting grandchildren and all the paraphernalia associated with them. My children love to describe their grandparents' house to anyone who will listen. "It's humongous, it has a three-story lighthouse attached, it sits high above the lake and the waves are huge, and my grandma makes the best cookies and cakes." It's all true. My mother-in-law, Bernie, has been the quintessential grandmother and the perfect mother-in-law. I do not personally know a finer human being.

We stayed up late catching up and awoke the next

morning to a perfect day, with azure skies and a hint of autumn crispness in the breeze coming off the lake.

At the breakfast table we asked the happy couple to describe their wedding day, September 4, 1942. My mother-in-law recalled it as a day as lovely as this one. When asked the color of her wedding suit, she replied, "Beige," as my father-in-law simultaneously said, "Blue." Giggles that built into belly laughs swept around the table. Wayne and I have been married for almost twenty-eight years and my brother-in-law and his wife for almost thirty-four years, so all of us were in sync with this marital moment. A total of 125 years of marriage was represented around that breakfast table.

The issue of how to manage Cake Day this week had resolved with my mother-in-law insisting that she would make the cake. We knew it would be the simple white cake with white icing that has defined all celebrations in this family for four decades. It is the same cake she has made for every birthday, Easter, Christmas, and Thanksgiving. We all start out believing we won't gorge ourselves, but then find ourselves going back for one more piece of cake. Being an avowed devotee of chocolate cake, I had never bothered with white cake until this one. Years ago Wayne and I asked for the recipe, but it never tasted the same when we made it at our house, so we gave up making it.

This weekend we discovered that my mother-in-law had given us a recipe decades ago that was on purpose not quite right. When I told her that I wanted to include her recipe in this book, she quickly produced without comment the original recipe. Wayne and I looked it over and noticed the one stunning difference between the recipes. The original one had Crisco listed instead of butter. Mon Dieu! Wayne asked if this was like the time that her own mother at age 102 had adamantly denied that she added vinegar to her highly regarded piecrust (Wayne's grandmother was taking her secret recipe to the grave). My mother-in-law nodded, "Yes." So here it is folks, the true recipe for my mother-in-law's famous and much-loved white cake. I suggest that you do as my fine mother-in-law has done and save it for yourselves. You have my permission.

The White Cake

This cake is courtesy of my fabulous mother-in-law, Bernie, who has made it famous in her corner of the world. She made it herself this week to celebrate sixty-three years of marriage.

Preheat oven to 350° F.
Prepare two 9" layer-cake pans or one 9" x 13" pan: grease with Crisco, line with wax or parchment paper, grease the paper and dust with flour (if you don't prepare the pans properly, the cake will not come out in one piece).

Cake

1. Measure into mixing bowl:

2 cups sifted cake flour
1⅓ cups sugar
½ cup Crisco (do not use butter)
1 teaspoons salt
⅔ cup milk

2. Stir vigorously by hand or in mixer (medium speed) for two minutes. Next stir in:

3 ½ teaspoons baking powder
4 unbeaten egg whites
⅓ cup milk
1 teaspoon vanilla

The batter will be smooth and thin. Pour it into prepared pans and bake for 25 minutes or until a toothpick inserted into the center comes out clean.

Frosting

1 pound confectioners' sugar
1 ½ sticks room-temperature unsalted butter
2 teaspoons vanilla
whole milk

1. In the large bowl of an electric mixer combine sugar and butter. Beat on medium speed at least 5 minutes, until light and fluffy.

2. Add vanilla and just enough milk to obtain the right consistency. The frosting should be thick but spreadable.

New Orleans Blues

"Thank the Good Lord for a job."
—Wynton Marsalis, jazz musician

This morning there were over 100 Heavenly Blue morning glory blooms on the arbor in my backyard. I paused before heading to work to take a photo just as the morning sun began to light them up on the edges. On the way to work I heard that the deaths attributed to Hurricane Katrina, which has laid waste to New Orleans and other parts of Louisiana and Mississippi, were more than four times the number of heavenly blue blooms, and climbing. I said a prayer for the lost souls and vowed to send more money to help the surviving souls. I gave thanks for the safety of my own family.

Today wasn't Monday but it sure felt like it. I dragged myself to my office before looking at what lay ahead for the day. I had a relatively clear slate and yet I was under pressure to reconstruct the last five years of my professional life, to make a case for my promotion to full professor ("Full of what?" you might ask).

I had to face all the things that I had not accomplished: the less-than-perfect reviews of my teaching, the papers not yet published, and the accomplishments deferred while I fixed aging equipment and listened to students sort through their lives. Truth is I enjoy discussing with young people what they want to do with their lives. I enjoy taking them by the hand and teaching them the unique joys and frustrations of research—challenging them with a reminder that, "Research is not for cowards or slackers"; encouraging them with a quick, "Wow, that's great. Now repeat it...Yes, again"; and, finally, when I think they've gotten it, celebrating with a, "Yes, that's it! Cut, print, publish." Only there are no cameras filming their triumphs. It is a lot like parenting and I adore it. I will be sad when that part of my life is over.

I have a folder in my file cabinet made by the very first undergraduate student who worked in my lab. Her name is Kate. I have no talent for filing, and Kate helped me organize my office the first year I landed on campus. Wisely, she started by making a file with a bunch of smiley faces adorning the tab. And so, for the past eleven years I have thrown into that file anything that made me smile: comics, quotes, notes from students, and even notes from parents of students. Over the years the file has grown thick and threatened to burst.

It had been many years since I'd read this notes. Today I sat down and read them all again. I was very touched. The letters and notes reminded me of why I chose the life of an academic researcher over the corporate researcher I was in a previous life. One of my favorite students, Ian, worked in my lab and then in a lab at the Centers for Disease Control and Prevention in Atlanta. He followed this up with a two-year stint in the Peace Corps in Namibia, Africa, teaching biology. I prayed every day for his safety. Ian is now back in the U.S. to pursue a master's degree in teaching. He was originally part of an experimental program that brings at-risk high school students from the city to the campus of the University of Dayton to learn along-side college students. I have many such inspiring stories. Often people say that if they had to evacuate their homes in a hurry because of a hurricane or an approaching flood, they would grab the photo albums first. I suspect I would want to take this file with me if I knew my office was about to be destroyed. (I might also grab my PhD dissertation and a few lab books with as yet unpublished data.)

I took a break from this exercise to have lunch with my friend Steve, a man who has been my boss for the past four years in a program that brings to campus the best and brightest students at my university. I chose to serve in this program because the students here are not only bright but also dedicated to the concept of community: the university community, the surrounding city, and all that lies beyond. The University of Dayton, which is a private Catholic university, has promoted community service for 150 years, long before it was the popular thing to do. Our students serve the dis-advantaged in our aging industrial city as well as in Cameroon, Africa; Bangalor, India; and in Central and South America. The University of Dayton has been ranked third in the nation for the extraordinary efforts it makes on behalf of the renewal and revitalization of its surrounding community.

Steve and I had our usual conversation, ranging widely from the posts and pillars that make up our university to the inanity of politics in the U.S. to the tragedy that has befallen Louisiana. When we had exhausted the subject of the tragedy, we began to talk about cake. Steve told me that his sons, ages ten and five, say the word "cake" with a special reverence, adding an extra syllable not quite articulated—a ghost syllable—that speaks to the special nature of cake. Steve's boys do not develop the same twinkle in their eyes when speaking of cookies or candy.

The conversation next veered to issues of black and white. A sociologist of note, Steve and I often discuss issues of race and culture, but today our conversa-tion turned to chocolate versus vanilla. My friend be-lieves that white cake is elegant—redolent of special occasions like weddings and coronations—and that it goes well with champagne. But chocolate cake is what he wants to eat. He also challenged me to examine the philosophical question "What is cake?" I declined.

This weekend Steve will begin his forty-second year in this world that we both yearn to study and under-stand. I am throwing him a surprise birthday party on Friday afternoon to which all of his favorite colleagues are invited (Shhh). I hope this small celebration, with chocolate cake and champagne, will bring this week to an end with a certain joyousness that I suspect none of us feel on this Tuesday in early September in the year 2005.

New Orleans Blues Chocolate Layer Cake

I chose a cake with a name—New Orleans Cake—

that has special meaning this week in the aftermath of Hurricane Katrina. I felt the urge to celebrate the city and its contributions to American cuisine. I have taken the recipe from *Maida Heatter's Book of Great Chocolate Desserts*. Heatter tells the story of how this recipe came to be included in her great cookbook. She and her husband were dining at a seafood restaurant in New Orleans and struck up a conversation with a couple at the next table. The couple invited them back to their home for dessert. The house was an elegant one that had been in the family for generations. And, so too, the cake recipe, which they claim never to have given out before. I made this cake in honor of the great city of New Orleans and its unique culture and cuisine.

This is a dense, moist sour cream chocolate cake with a rich dark chocolate pudding-like filling and whipped-cream icing. Heatter says this cake is best filled and iced on the day it is to be served. I made the cake and the filling the night before, storing the filling in the refrigerator. In the morning I simply had to assemble and fill the layers and whip the cream. While attempting to frost the cake with the whipped cream (a messy job), Kat came bursting into the kitchen announcing that she needed me to drive her to school immediately so she wouldn't be late for Camera Club. I hastily finished frosting the cake and transferred it to the refrigerator in the basement. My aim was to keep the dog from eating it (Tula once ate fourteen red-velvet cupcakes). I threw a coat over my pajamas and drove Kat to school.

The cake was delicious and worth the extra time. You could use store-bought dark chocolate pudding for the filling, the cook-and-serve variety, and save a little time without sacrificing the essence of the cake.

Preheat oven to 350° F and adjust rack to the center of the oven.

Butter two 9" round cake pans and line them with parchment or wax paper cut to fit. Butter the paper and dust the inside of the pan with flour; tap out excess. Set the pans aside.

Cake

4 ounces (4 squares) unsweetened chocolate
¼ pound (1 stick) butter
½ cup sour cream
1½ teaspoons baking soda
2 cup sugar
½ teaspoon vanilla extract
¼ teaspoon salt
2 eggs
2 cups sifted all-purpose flour
1 cup boiling water

1. Place chocolate and butter in a small saucepan over low heat and stir frequently until melted and smooth.

2. When the chocolate mix is almost melted, stir the sour cream and baking soda together in a small bowl and set aside.

3. When the chocolate mix is melted, transfer to the large bowl of an electric mixer. Add sugar, vanilla, and salt and beat just to mix.

4. Add the eggs, one at a time, mixing well after each addition.

5. Mix in the sour cream and baking soda and, on low speed, add the flour, scraping the bowl with a rubber spatula and beating only until smooth.

6. With the mixer on the lowest speed, gradually add

the boiling water, scraping the bowl and beating only until smooth.

7. The mixture will be thin. Divide between the prepared pans.

8. Bake for 25 to 28 minutes, until the top springs back lightly when gently pressed with a fingertip.

9. Cool the layers in the pans for 10 minutes. The cake may not release on its own, so insert a small, sharp knife between the cake and the side of the pan and run it around the outside of the cake. Cover with a rack, invert, remove pan and paper lining; cover with another rack and invert again so that it is right-side up. Allow the layers to completely cool. In the meantime, prepare the pudding below.

Chocolate Filling

(You can substitute any good chocolate pudding or mousse from a mix.)

2 cups milk
2 ounces (2 squares) unsweetened chocolate
1 tablespoon (1 envelope) unflavored gelatin
¼ cup cold water
⅓ cup sifted all-purpose flour
1 cup (less 2 tablespoons) sugar
2 egg yolks
½ teaspoon vanilla extract
Pinch of salt

1. Scald milk in a small saucepan over moderate heat.

2. Melt chocolate on low heat in the top of a double boiler. When the chocolate is melted, remove it from the hot water and set aside uncovered.

3. Sprinkle gelatin over the cold water in a small custard cup; set aside.

4. In the top of another double boiler, off the heat, stir together the flour and sugar.

5. Gradually add the scalded milk to the flour and sugar mixture, stirring well to keep it smooth.

6. Place over hot water on moderate heat. Stir constantly, scraping around the bottom and sides of the pot with a rubber spatula until the mixture is the consistency of a thick cream sauce.

7. Continue cooking and stirring for about 2 minutes.

8. Remove from heat. Add softened gelatin and stir to melt it; next stir in the chocolate, vanilla, and salt. (The mixture can be strained, but it is not essential.)

9. Place the double boiler into a large bowl of ice water, stirring occasionally until cool; begin to stir more frequently until the filling is thick enough to spread—it should be like a very think mayonnaise, so that it does not run when spread on the cake.

10. While the filling is chilling, prepare a large flat cake plate or stand by placing four strips of wax paper around the outer edges.

11. Place one layer upside down on the prepared plate, checking to be sure the paper is touching the cake all the way around.

12. Spread the thick filling smoothly over the cake, but not beyond the edges; it will be almost 1" thick.

13. Place the other layer right-side-up over the filling.

14. Refrigerate while preparing the whipped cream icing below.

Whipped Cream Icing

2 cups heavy or whipping cream
⅓ cup sifted confectioners' sugar
1 teaspoon vanilla extract

1. Place small bowl of electric mixer, beaters, and cream into freezer for 10 minutes.

2. Whip the ingredients until they are thick enough to spread—do not over beat.

3. Spread cream over the sides and top of the cake—it will be a thick layer.

4. Decorate (optional) with chocolate curls.

5. Refrigerate for at least one hour before serving, but not overnight, as the whipped cream icing will not be as light and delicious.

Camp Survivor, Girl Scout Style

"Grown-ups never understand anything for themselves, and it is tiresome for children to be always and forever explaining things to them." —Antoine de Saint-Exupery

September is the hottest month in my corner of Ohio, and this one is no exception. I am headed to Camp Whip-Poor-Will with Kat, for the last Girl Scout camp-out of the year, and of her GS career.

The theme: "Survivor: Camp Whip-Poor-Will." The goal, of course, is to Outwit, Outplay, and Outlast. To me this seems a bit at odds with the Girl Scout Law: to be honest and fair, friendly and helpful, considerate and caring. I guess even the Girl Scouts are bending to pop culture. Still, a little competition seems like a good thing. (Full disclosure: I have never watched the popular TV show "Survivor", so I have no idea what is about to happen.)

We arrive in time to set up camp before heading to the lodge for phase one of GS Survivor: picking names for the tribes. Soon they are no longer young girls from the suburbs of southwestern Ohio but members of different tribes: the Lakeeda, Snake Charmer, Los Tres Amigos, Pinkalicious, Tropicana, Sushame, Cow-moo-moo, Chimalecee-blam, and Mahi-Mahi.

Kat has named and belongs to the Mahi-Mahi tribe. (When asked later why she chose this name, she replied that they were very large fish, from Hawaii—'nuf said.) Then it is into the darkening woods, armed with clues, to find previously hidden caches to make their banners and bandanas. It turns into a free-for-all, and only the lucky ones find their supplies. Finally, they are forced to eat cat "poop" (tootsie rolls masquerading as cat poop) from kitty litter boxes before they are given the supplies to make their immunity necklaces. I eat huge quantities of cat poop in hopes it will help me be a survivor.

Back at our own campsite, the Mahi-Mahi, fueled by cat poop and s'mores, regale us with skits and silliness around the campfire. Finally, and only after many trips to the latrine down the forest lane, the girls settle and sleep.

It is time for the moms to hold campfire court. We discuss the girls, their futures, and our pasts. As the talk bounces around the fire, my mind wanders off into the shadows of this forest fortress imbued with decades of feminine spirits. I am well into a previous century, when

I am called back. I hear one of the women, the mother of several highly successful children, pose a question that brings me up short. She asks whether, if we, as mothers, knew we could do something to help our offspring get into Harvard, would we do it? I ask what she means, envisioning altering SAT scores or other illegal or immoral acts. She verbally sketches, with waving hands, what she means: orchestrating volunteer and service activities and keeping a scrapbook of all our children's accomplishments so that when they apply to colleges the eyes in admissions' offices will pop out of their jaded sockets. I foolishly jump in and say that, while I would support my children and, if asked, offer help, I would not orchestrate their way into the Ivy League. I venture forth with the opinion that getting in is only the first step, and if a kid doesn't have the drive and the fire inside then that kid just isn't going to succeed. Around me I see looks of pity and astonishment—no one, it seems, agrees with me. The only comment is a crackle from the fire, which I take as the feminine almighty taking my side. Clearly, I am not a mother who will outwit, outsmart, or outlast these Survivor mothers.

We all head off to our tents. I toss and turn all night, as well as one can toss and turn in the cocoon of a sleeping bag (how do caterpillars stand it?). My dreams are filled with the sounds of giggling girls, the soundtrack for a failed Ivy League college trip in which my daughters, pale and pinched, seemed more like prisoners than the flowering peonies they are.

With first light, I give up on a good night's sleep. I join the group building the campfire in hopes I can score some hot water for a badly needed cup of tea. We breathe life into last night's fire, and I get that cup of tea just in time for the day's activities.

By lunchtime I am exhausted, but it is my turn to teach the girls how to make dump cake. I bring out the ingredients for the cake, a GS tradition that involves dumping ingredients into an iron kettle to be placed in the campfire. My helpers do the dumping and drag the kettle to the fire.

We bank the coals around the kettle and stand watch. A campfire in a sauna could not be hotter.

An hour later we recover the pan from the fire. With great drama I remove the cover, using GS-approved oven mitts. Oohs and aahs greet the slightly crisp looking "cake"—every bit as elegant as its name advertises. Surrounded by girls glistening with sweat, I dish generous portions into cups and let them have at it with aerosol cans of whipped cream straight from the cooler. Ten minutes later there is not a speck of cake or whipped cream in sight.

A ringing bell interrupts our cake reverie. The five Survivor challenges are about to begin: gross food, survivor puzzle, bull's-eye, slingshot, and the tribal trust. I am assigned to the tribal trust challenge along with the Ivy League groupie mom. In this challenge, two tribes compete to be the first to carry piranhas (the inflatable kind) through a challenging course in which all but the leader are blindfolded. The leader has to talk the rest of the girls through the course, avoiding pitfalls and obstacles strewn in their way. Many are outwitted by the plastic piranhas and outlasted due to the failure of their members to follow directions. Each group has a unique leadership style, and I find this fascinating.

The Mahi-Mahi win the event easily without breaking a single GS law. I note, with pride, how helpful and respectful they are with members of their own tribe and challengers alike. To my delight, the girls in all the tribes do a wonderful job of rising to the difficult task at hand.

Unfortunately, several of the mothers do not. Some actually complain and cheat on behalf of their daughters. These women clearly do not know or live by the GS laws. One mother told the talented, sincere, and hardworking organizer that her daughter had been "scarred for life." Proof that if you build it they will come, and they also will complain.

Soon we are off to the final campfire, where the winner, the tribe that outwitted, outsmarted, and outlasted all the others, will be announced. I see torches and hear wild music, and girls are running everywhere. I am supremely confident because I know the Mahi-Mahi are the only undefeated tribe. I feel like a mother who is sending her kid off to Harvard, a kid who has gotten in on her own sweat and smarts. I cannot wait for that moment when the mighty Mahi-Mahi take their rightful place in the tribal circle and, surrounded by fire and drum music, are proclaimed the rightful winners. My tush is turning to stone and my eyes are filled with smoke, but I do not move. And then something weird happens. I hear the Mahi-Mahi tribe being called up along with the Lakeedas, signaling a tie. What? I am tempted to pop up to my feet and protest, but my fossilized fanny won't let me.

The Mahi-Mahi tribe is taking it well, appearing dazed but happy. When reunited with their offspring, the Mahi-Mahi moms are full of congratulations, saying nothing about how the kids were robbed. But I cannot help thinking that in their little Survivor hearts, they know this. Still, they leave camp feeling strong and capable, which is surely the goal of GS. As we drive out of Camp Whip-Poor-Will, I feel as though I am leaving behind both Kat's childhood and my own.

But once again, as Antoine de Saint-Exupery reminds us, it is the children who have taught me what is truly important.

Dump Cake

"Dump cake. A cake made by 'dumping' the ingredients directly into the baking pan, mixing them, and baking the batter." —John F. Mariani, *Encyclopedia of American Food and Drink*

This week's cake was really a no-brainer. It is the only cake I know that can be made in a campfire and the only official GS-sanctioned cake. What follows are two versions of dump cake. The first is the official GS recipe, to be made in the cast iron kettles that are provided in GS campgrounds around the country and to be baked in a campfire. The second is a version you can make at home and bake in your very own oven.

Girl Scout Style

Build a campfire and let it burn until there are coals.

This takes quite a long time, as any Girl Scout (or GS leader) can tell you. This recipe requires a standard GS issue cast iron Dutch oven.

Cake

3 (29 ounce) cans fruit cocktail or other canned fruit
2 boxes white or yellow cake mix, dry
1 ½ cups (3 sticks) unsalted butter

1. Pour fruit in cast iron Dutch oven.

2. Sprinkle dry cake mix over fruit. Dot butter on top of cake mix.

3. Cover tightly, set in coals of a campfire, putting coals on lid also, and let cook until cake is lightly browned. Rotate Dutch oven one quarter turn every 15 minutes for even cooking, especially if the active fire is only on one side of the Dutch oven. Recipe can be halved easily.

Home Style

Preheat oven to 350° F; 9" x 13" pan.

Cake

2 (15 ounce) cans fruit cocktail or other canned fruit
1 box white or yellow cake mix, dry
¾ cups (1 ½ sticks) unsalted butter

1. Dump fruit into the baking pan.

2. Sprinkle cake mix over fruit.

3. Dot all over with butter.

4. Bake until brown, approximately 1 hour.

The Pampered Camper

"Is that weird taking my
Louis Vuitton bag camping?"
—Jessica Simpson

Yes, Jessica, it is. Unless you are going where I am going.

It is Saturday morning and I am headed back to Camp Whip-Poor-Will for the second weekend in a row. This is the weekend that the Girl Scout Council opens up the camp for their Pampered Camper fund-raising event. There will not be a Girl Scout in sight (except for those formerly known as Girl Scouts). The words pamper and camper together would appear to be an oxymoron; I am hoping that on this particular weekend they are not.

A wine tasting is on the schedule. I hope this means I will be able to live out one of my fantasies, which is to drink a glass of wine by the fire circle. This particular fantasy has been fueled by ten years of GS campouts with Lizzie and Kat when wine was not allowed but desperately needed. The illicit does have pull.

I am up early, packed and ready to go by 7:15 AM, when my university co-worker Karen arrives. The forty-minute drive to the camp is helped along by caffeine and conversation. The countryside is just waking up by the time we leave the highway. As I turn onto the misty winding road that takes us to the camp, I swear can I hear voices of little girls asking, "when are we going to beeeee there?" Then the Camp Whip-Poor-Will sign floats out of the mist like an answer in an 8-ball to the question: "where can a woman be pampered and sleep under the stars?"

At the lodge we meet up with Lynda, another one of our co-workers. The three of us squeal like ten-year-old girls and run inside the lodge to get our schedules for the day. I head off to archery, Lynda and Karen to canoeing. After listening to a very long recitation on safety—to make certain that we don't end up with an arrow in our head or butt—I manage to score a few bull's-eyes and also to snap the bow string on my inner wrist, which leaves a nasty purple welt. Next, on to master gardening, where I learn tricks to use next summer in my own garden, followed by Pilates (ouch), and, finally, belly dancing, where my belly definitely moves, even when the rest of me has stopped.

Dinner is a catered affair with shrimp and salmon and more wine than I can consume, even in my craziest campfire dreams. When dinner is over, we move on to karaoke—made better by the wine—and finally back to our cabin where Karen pulls out a Oujia board. I have hated Ouija boards since a sleepover at Heidi Stucki's house in seventh grade. That night the board predicted I would have the biggest boobs in the school by eighth grade. This was the era of flat-chested models, and my chest was getting bigger by the minute. I know the question Karen is going to ask the board: who is going to be the next chairperson of our department? My initials appear. I want to be chairperson like I want an arrow in my butt.

I fall into a sweaty sleep where I dream I do become the chair of the department, hassled by all, until I morph into an actual chair with a saggy seat and broken arms. As I pull out of camp that morning, I resolve to outwit, outplay, and outsmart the Ouija board.

The event raised thousands for the Girl Scout Council. The money will be used to grant scholarships to girls who cannot afford to attend camp. I've added the Pampered Camper fundraiser to my calendar for next year and plan to make it a yearly pilgrimage.

Take-Me-to-a-Picnic Cake

Upon re-entry into the non-pampered world, I remember my promise to take a cake to the departmental picnic. I found this recipe in an old church cookbook, *A Taste of Avon Lake*, and it really fit the bill.

We gather cake, Kat, and friend and head out into the autumn afternoon to the horse farm owned by my friend, John, the current chair of my department. The afternoon dissolves into dusk to the soundtrack of volleyball and horses. Kat is in love with the farm's latest batch of horses and does her usual begging to be allowed to own one. Eventually I pry her away from the horses and out onto the lake for a spin in the rowboat. By this time John has lit the huge bonfire—a mountain of wood and debris stored up the whole year just for this event—sending a fifty-foot column of flame and sparks into the jet blue sky. I can see Kat and her friend in the boat on the lake highlighted by the sparks and ash falling like snowflakes.

We drive home with the top down on our classic convertible. But now it is cold, a reminder that summer has left us behind, and so the girls hunker down in the back under a blanket and I turn on the heat. (I can think of few things more decadent and fun than driving in a convertible with the top down and the heat on). With The Guess Who on the radio and the stars in the heavens, it is the perfect end to a perfect picnic.

Preheat oven to 350° F.
Butter and flour a 15 ½" x 10 ½" x 1" deep jelly roll pan.

Cake

1 cup water
½ cup cocoa powder
1 ¾ cups flour
½ teaspoon salt
¾ cup sour cream
1 cup (2 sticks) room-temperature unsalted butter
2 cups sugar
1 teaspoon baking soda
3 eggs

1. In a medium saucepan, combine water, butter and cocoa. Cook over medium heat, stirring occasionally, until the mixture boils. Boil for 1 minute. Remove from heat; set aside.

In the medium bowl of an electric mixer, stir together sugar, flour, baking soda, and salt. Beat on low for 30 seconds to mix.

3. Add eggs and sour cream; beat until blended.

4. Add cocoa mixture; beat just until blended. Batter will be thin (or not!).

5. Pour into prepared pan and bake for 25–20 minutes or until a wooden toothpick inserted into the center comes out clean but not dry.

6. Cool cake in pan on wire rack. Spread with peanut butter frosting and drizzle chocolate garnish over top.

Peanut Butter Chip Frosting

5 tablespoons butter
⅓ cup milk
12-ounce package of peanut butter chips
1 cup confectioners' sugar

In medium saucepan, combine butter, milk, and peanut butter chips. Cook over low heat, stirring constantly, until chips have melted and the mixture is smooth. Remove from the heat and stir in vanilla extract. Put sugar in a small bowl and gradually add the chip mixture, beating until well blended (add more sugar if it is too thin). Spread over cake.

Chocolate Garnish

½ cup semi-sweet chocolate chips
1 teaspoon butter

Melt chocolate chips and butter in the microwave for 1 minute, until the chips are melted and mixture is smooth. Drizzle over peanut butter frosting.

Fall

I Really Should Be Making a Halloween Costume

"A cake's no good if you don't mix the batter and bake it."
—June Carter, from her song "Time's A Wastin'"

For eighteen years I have made Halloween costumes. Every year since Lizzie hit the big age one. The Halloween itch would start sometime in August, when summer was stifling and I was longing to wake up to cool air and pumpkins on the vine. When my kids grew old enough to understand—or even before they were old enough—I would start probing: "What do you want to be for Halloween?" I told myself and others that I was just planning ahead so that I didn't have to be up the whole night before Halloween hoping that "part A" would match up with "part B" and seamlessly become "Eowin" by dawn. The truth was that I couldn't wait to get started.

Last year was the first time a store-bought costume made its way into our house. Lizzie was away at college and Kat decided she wanted to be a "Vampiress." I was not interested in spending my time making a vampire costume that would be black in both fabric and spirit. So out we ventured to the recently opened Halloween Express store. What a horrifying experience. There were the usual costumes-in-a-bag for young children. To my utter disgust, though, the not-for-prime-time adult costumes were intermingled with the rest. Several eternities later I left the shop with an acceptably modest vampiress costume and a four-aspirin headache. Never again. This was not an empty threat, as you will soon find out.

Now that I was no longer going to be a Halloween seamstress, the only question that remained was what was to become of the really expensive sewing machine I had bought just three months before? What can I say? I felt I owed it to myself after the years of making Halloween and ballet costumes.

I knew I had only one choice. I must end the twenty-eight-year quilt "thought project." Thought projects—or those who are not familiar with the term—are those you "think" about doing but never actually do. I had thought about making a quilt for the previous twenty-eight years. But a cake ain't a cake until you bake it. In the very hot summer of 1977 I had cut out 300 tiny fabric pieces in hopes of making a wedding quilt. It would be for my own wedding that was going to take place later that year, in October. My attempts to turn those pesky little pieces of fabric into the pattern so deftly described in the book came to naught. They refused to become a double-wedding-ring quilt. Frankly, when I finally gave up, they were on a path to becoming a chaos-of-marriage quilt. I don't recall what happened to all of those tiny pieces. I just remember that at some point I gained enough wisdom and cynicism to ditch them, burying them along with my other failures.

What I am trying to say is that last year I was freed of the obligation, the honor, of making Halloween costumes. I was not happy about it. I, who never liked Halloween, loved making Halloween costumes for my daughters. I, who rarely catered to my children's whims, ("No, you cannot have a hamster, they are stupid, stupid animals!") would agree to make my daughters any costume of their desires, the more difficult the better. (A word of caution to those of you who have yet to embark on parenthood: You cannot predict ahead of time what you will love about being a parent and what you will absolutely abhor.) Now my love affair with making Halloween costumes was over and I was feeling deprived and desolate.

I had to do something to compensate, to fill the gap. I started a quilt. Like a general planning a battle, I took over the ping-pong table and began to formulate my attack. By Thanksgiving pieces of fabric were everywhere, and I had a chronic backache from bending over the table. By two weeks before Christmas I had created forty-nine blocks of blue-and-white squares ready to be fashioned into the Irish Chain quilt of my dreams. Not a Christmas card had been sent, not a present wrapped or even purchased. Could I give each person on my Christmas list a block of the quilt? Nah, they weren't worth it. I finished the top a few days before Christmas and decided to rest. After about twenty minutes, I realized that I still had presents to wrap and packing to finish.

This year Kat took care of her own costume and ended up the most stunning gypsy in the city. Instead of a quilt, I decided to make this cake. The cake is much easier, in case you are deciding between the two.

We had guests coming for Sunday brunch, a friend and her husband Barry. This friend, Ellen, has always been my oracle on all things scientific. We had a long leisurely brunch and then headed to my lab to check on some specimens for a paper we are hoping to publish together one day soon. The brunch and the cake turned out much better than the specimens.

Almond Semolina Cake

My brunch cake was "dessert of the month" in the May 2005 issue of *Martha Stewart Living* magazine. It is dense and not too sweet and good for brunch or dinner (or the middle of the night). It is even better on the second day and keeps well for several more days.

Semolina flour is a grainy yellow flour and it gives this cake its lovely texture. Yellow cornmeal can be substituted without losing the great flavor, but the cake will be a little more crumbly.

Preheat oven to 350° F. Generously butter a 9" springform pan; set aside.

Cake

1 stick (8 tablespoons) room-temperature unsalted butter; plus more for the pan

1 cup all-purpose flour
1 ¼ teaspoons baking powder
¾ teaspoon (plus a pinch) of salt
½ cup finely ground semolina flour
4 large eggs, separated
¾ cup sliced almonds (with skins)
3 tablespoons packed light-brown sugar
1 ¼ cups granulated sugar
⅓ cup almond paste
½ teaspoon vanilla extract
⅔ cup whole milk

1. Sift flour, baking powder, and ¾ teaspoon salt together into a medium bowl; stir in semolina flour; set aside.

2. Beat the egg whites in a small mixing bowl on medium-high speed until foamy. Gradually beat in ¼ cup granulated sugar; beat until soft peaks form (stop before they are dry and stiff).

3. Take out 2 teaspoons of the egg whites and place into a medium bowl. Stir in almonds, brown sugar, and a pinch of salt. Set this mixture aside—it is for the top of the cake and will be added halfway through the baking.

4. Put butter, 1 cup granulated sugar, and the almond paste in large mixer bowl and mix on medium-high speed (with same beaters used for egg whites) until pale and fluffy (3 or 4 minutes). Add egg yolks and vanilla; mix about 2 minutes, until well blended.

5. Using a rubber spatula, fold half of the beaten egg whites into the batter, then gently fold in the other half.

6. Transfer the batter to the buttered pan and smooth the top with the spatula. Bake until the cake starts to turn golden but the center is still wobbly (15 – 20 minutes).

7. Remove cake from oven; scatter reserved almond mixture evenly over the top.

8. Return cake to oven; bake until topping is golden brown and a cake tester inserted into the center comes out clean (about 25 minutes, but check cake after about 15 minutes, and if darkening too quickly, cover loosely with foil and continue baking).

9. Let cake cool completely in pan on a wire rack. Run a thin knife around edges of cake to loosen; remove sides of pan. Using two spatulas transfer cake to a serving platter or cake stand. Cake can be stored in an airtight container at room temperature for up to 4 days.

Appliance Envy

"Oh, Lord, won't you buy me a Mercedes Benz, my friends all drive Porsches, I must make amends." —Janis Joplin

Fall has come to our part of the country and humidity has lost its sweaty grip. The pumpkins on my porch are filled with mums and not yet carved. The morning glories continue to bloom, but their days are numbered, and the paper is full of festival listings—October Fest and the Renaissance Festival may reign but there are apple, garlic, and pumpkin festivals, too.

While I like festivals just fine, it is the cool air and sparkle in the fall sky that I truly love. Even walking the dog this morning was a pleasure. Tula Boo felt it too. She, of husky-border collie origins, with a fantastic fur coat, had a new spring in her step. And I have come out of my usual humidity-induced summer stupor. I am like one of those people portrayed in a current commercial for a fast-food restaurant coffee. Customers drink the coffee for the first time and suddenly wake up to realize to their utter surprise that they have been married for years or have a twin. In my case it is the sudden realization that the stand mixer I own is woefully inadequate. I hate it.

Janis may have wanted a Mercedes Benz, but what I have always wanted is a KitchenAid mixer. As a bride-to-be, I saw them for the first time lined up on the shelf next to the gift registry table. To me they are the Clydesdales of the kitchen, gleaming and strong, with the promise of transporting me, in style, to culinary success. Of course I didn't buy it at the time and when I went back to the store, wedding money in hand, I simply could not afford one. What I bought instead was a good, solid brand-name mixer that gave me its best for twenty-four years, years filled with cakes, cookies, whipped cream, and mashed potatoes. However, it refused to do bread despite the bread hooks that came with it. But I forgave my mixer, appreciating the opportunity to build up my arm muscles. My mother-in-law owned the same mixer and we agreed that it was a good mixer, if not a classy and elegant one.

Still, I could not pass a kitchen store without lingering near the KitchenAid mixers. I imagined how my kitchen would look with one of those babies sitting on the counter. I fretted constantly about which of the luscious colors would look best in my kitchen. I felt a little guilty about being unfaithful to my mixer at home, which had served me so well. It may not have had much style, but it was always loyal and true. But one day my mixer gave up the ghost and I was confronted with the opportunity to finally enter the ranks of kitchen divas. My pulse quickened and my brain flooded with excitement. Which color should I pick? Wayne and I raced to the store to purchase this long-anticipated appliance. We selected a white one on the theory that we would never tire of it. Back at home, Lizzie and Kat did not share in our excitement. They didn't understand. It was just a mixer for God's sake.

Wayne and I lifted the mixer out of the box, set it on the counter, and stood back to admire it. In our tiny, vintage 1920 kitchen it looked huge and shiny—and out of place. But its biggest sin was that it didn't fit under—or in—the cabinets. We lived with it for a day, just looking at it. I'd enter the kitchen quickly, hoping to catch, in a glimpse, the truth. I couldn't make up my mind. Did it look out of place or didn't it? It did. I began picking at its faults: it was too expensive, it came with only one bowl , it was too heavy, too pretentious, too expensive, and it didn't fit under the cabinets. The final straw? The bowl didn't spin. After two days on our kitchen counter, back to the store it went. We replaced it with the current model for the mixer that had died.

Life went on. I found myself not making foods that required the mixer. But when I finally started to use it, I discovered it is quite different from my old faithful in odd ways. It has different latches and requires two hands to operate and it is not at all intuitive. Worst of all, the bowl doesn't spin very well. What? How could this be? My daughters and I had spent many hours happily mesmerized watching our old mixer bowl spin. I had been betrayed but it was too late to return it.

When we visited my in-laws for Thanksgiving, I learned that my mother-in-law's mixer had also recently died and that both of us had bought the same replacement model (same company, same color). And Bernie hated hers too. We cursed the company as we whipped the potatoes.

It is now four years since we bought my "new" old mixer. On three occasions Wayne has brought home another KitchenAid and three times we've taken it back. It's crazy, I know, but it never feels quite right. Wayne likens it to buying a riding mower to mow our small urban plot of grass. Excess is not our style, and we simply have a hard time getting rid of anything before it dies a natural death.

The KitchenAid factory and showroom are an hour's drive from our house. When my current mixer dies, I swear I will take that drive through the charming countryside to the factory. I will take the tour and linger in the showroom. Who knows, maybe I will come away with the perfect mixer and I'll finally stop returning it. But somehow I know my lust for things new for my kitchen won't end there. Soon some other appliance will catch my eye. Oh Lord, won't you buy me a KitchenAid stove.

Irish Buttermilk Bannock

Fortunately some cakes can easily be made without the help of a stand mixer. This week's cake is one of them. Thank the Lord, because I really need a break from kitchen-appliance envy and the engineering mistake that is my mixer.

I chose this recipe for its simplicity and because Cake Day this week fell on September 29, the Feast of St.

Michael. The legend has it that on this day St. Michael drove Lucifer out of heaven, causing him to land in a patch of blackberry brambles. St. Michael is invoked to help us in our fight against and our efforts to rescue souls from Lucifer, especially at the hour of death. It is tradition in England to eat blackberry concoctions on this day—blackberry pies, tarts, and scones. According to an old Irish folktale, blackberries were supposed to have been harvested and used up by this date. It is told to children that Lucifer returns each year to curse and spit on the fruits of the plant he landed on, rendering them inedible thereafter.

This flat cake is a first cousin to the scone. I chose to make it with blackberries, adding them both inside and on top. Add whipped cream or vanilla ice cream, if you are so inspired.

Preheat oven to 375° F, and lightly oil a cookie sheet or pan.

Cake

2 cups all-purpose flour
2 tablespoons white sugar
½ teaspoon baking powder
½ teaspoon baking soda
½ teaspoon salt
2 tablespoons butter
1 cup buttermilk
Blackberries with sugar for topping

1. Combine flour, sugar, baking soda, baking powder, and salt. Cut butter into flour mixture with pastry cutter. Add buttermilk until dough is soft.

2. Turn dough out onto a lightly floured surface. Knead for 5 minutes or until smooth. Form dough into a 7" round. Place on a lightly oiled cake pan or cookie sheet. (Score the top ½" deep, from side-to-side, making a cross.)

3. Bake for 40 minutes.

Goodbye Kitty

"If you want to harvest the honey, you best not destroy the hive."
—Abraham Lincoln

This week Jews around the world will observe Rosh Hashanah, the Jewish New Year, ushering in the year 5766. My family is not Jewish, but I have had the good fortune to live in communities with substantial Jewish populations. I was raised in the Christian faith but have always gravitated to the Judeo side of Judeo-Christian values.

A popular observance during Rosh Hashanah is eating apples dipped in honey, a symbol of the wish for a sweet New Year. Honey cake is often served for the same reason. I confess that, in addition to being envious of Jewish family values, I am envious of the food—the steaming hot potato latkes of Hanukkah, served with sour cream; the bagels and lox eaten all-year round; and the honey cake of Rosh Hashanah.

I've decided to make honey cake for Cake Day this week, but our plans are to visit Lizzie in Pittsburgh. So I ask Lizzie whether she would like to do the honors of making this week's cake. She quickly accepts the challenge, sighing sweetly as she croons, "honey cake…wow." One of her best college friends is Jewish, which may have added to the appeal of making this particular cake. At any rate, I appear to be off the hook for Cake Day. The day we are leaving, Lizzie notifies me by e-mail of the things she needs for us to bring. She also mentions that she is looking forward to food shopping with us, since she has no food on hand. This is my first indication that I may not be off the hook after all.

We arrive late on Friday and meet up for breakfast the next morning. With bellies full of crepes and tea we head to her favorite market, Whole Foods, to stock up for the next few weeks at Mom and Dad's expense. Kat and I take off in one direction, leaving Lizzie, the shopper, to fill her cart in peace. I find myself in the bakery section staring at unbelievably beautiful cakes, and some are even vegan cakes. Since we are scheduled to take Lizzie and friends, several of whom are vegans, to dinner that night, I buy a perfectly lovely "Black and White" vegan cake. Lizzie finds us and says this is the best idea ever. Breaking the rules of Cake Day takes a backseat to having fun and flowing with the reality of the day.

After a leisurely dinner at a local Indian restaurant, the eight of us head back to Lizzie's house for cake. While we eat, the four kittens that Lizzie and her roommates have recently rescued tumble and scamper at our feet. They are adorable to all except the girls' landlord. So tomorrow the kittens are to be handed over to a different friend, one with a clueless landlord. The generation of girls who grew up watching "Hello Kitty" are staging a "Goodbye Kitty" party before the hand-off.

On the trip home, the clouds tinged with occasional bursts of sunlight mirror my mood: gray for the sadness I feel as Lizzie moves further and further away from us and into her own life, sunlight for the happiness I feel because Lizzie is healthy, doing well in her studies, and has great friends. When we arrive home, I decide to make that honey cake. I do this to keep a family tradition, despite our smaller number, and to sweeten the future.

We are all beekeepers, laboring endlessly to keep our hive alive. The honey is the reward.

Honey Cake

There is something about honey that thrills and comforts, and I worship both bees and flowers. Recently reports have been emerging about a strange phenomenon that scientists are calling Colony Collapse Disorder (CCD). Bees are observed to leave the hive in search of pollen but never return, leading to a collapse of the colony. Scientists are on it because they recognize the supreme importance of bees to our own survival. It has been said that if the honey bees of the world perish, so will we. We depend on bee pollination for the crops we eat. Lincoln may not have had this scary thought in mind but the sentiment holds.

I could not find a recipe for honey cake in my many cookbooks, so I turned to the Internet. This recipe is a hybrid of several I found. If you like honey, you will love this cake. It is dense and rich and honeyed to the max. Happy New Year!

Preheat oven to 350° F.
Butter two 9" loaf pans or one 10" tube or bundt pan.

Cake

3 ½ cups all-purpose flour
1 tablespoon baking powder
1 teaspoon baking soda
½ teaspoon kosher salt
4 teaspoons ground cinnamon
½ teaspoon ground cloves
½ teaspoon ground allspice
1 cup vegetable oil
1 cup honey
1 ½ cups granulated sugar
½ cup brown sugar
3 large eggs at room temperature
1 teaspoon vanilla extract
1 cup warm coffee or strong tea
1 tablespoon orange zest
½ cup fresh orange juice
¼ cup bourbon or whiskey

1. In a large bowl, whisk together the flour, baking powder, baking soda, salt, cinnamon, cloves and allspice.

2. Make a well in the center, and add oil, honey, white sugar, brown sugars, eggs, vanilla, coffee or tea, orange juice, orange zest and rye or whiskey, if using. (If you measure your oil before the honey, it will be easier to get all of the honey out.)

3. Using a strong wire whisk or in an electric mixer on slow speed, stir together well to make a thick, well-

blended batter, making sure that no ingredients are stuck to the bottom.

4. Pour or spoon batter into prepared pan(s). Place cake pan(s) on two baking sheets, stacked together (this will ensure the cakes bake properly without the bottom baking faster than the cake interior and top).

5. Bake until cake tests done, that is, it springs back when you gently touch the cake center. For angel and tube cake pans, this will take 60–75 minutes, loaf cakes, about 45–55 minutes. Cake make fall a bit in the middle but this does not detract from its greatness.

6. Let cake stand fifteen minutes before removing from pan.

Glaze

1½ cups honey
2 tablespoons orange juice
½ cup water
½ teaspoon orange zest
2 ounces slivered almonds for topping

1. Boil together honey, orange juice, orange zest, and water.

2. When glaze reaches a thick consistency, remove from heat and drizzle over cakes.

3. Sprinkle with slivered almonds.

The Boys of Summer

"Baseball is a red-blooded sport for red-blooded men. It's no pink tea, and mollycoddles had better stay out. It's a struggle for supremacy, a survival of the fittest."
—Ty Cobb

The World Series starts today. This year's competition is between the Chicago White Sox and the Houston Astros—the Rust Belt versus the Sun Belt. The first game is in Chicago, where showers and a high of only fifty-four degrees are expected. Summer it ain't, but the boys will play.

I grew up in Detroit rooting for the Tigers and so find myself on the rusty side of the belt. We spent every summer at our cottage in Ontario, on a bluff high above Lake Erie. My brother, Steve, would listen to the games on the radio. If the Tigers lost, he would diffuse his anger by hitting golf balls, or rotting apples when balls ran out, into the lake after the game. But several times a summer we would make the trip from the cottage to Tiger Stadium in Detroit to see a game. In my memory the days were always sizzling and the Tigers always lost, or came so close to losing that my brother had to keep up a steady litany of complaints. I came along for the hotdogs and the chance to spend time with my dad. A civil engineer by training, he was adept at explaining things mechanical, from a bunt to why bridges don't fall into rivers (at least, not very often). He could also explain the fly-ball rule. Slowly I started to notice the games and caught the rhythm and grace that was, in some fundamental way, not unlike ballet. I have been a fan ever since.

The years the Tigers won the World Series, 1968 and 1984, were trying years for Steve. He could barely stand to watch a game, convinced he would jinx the team. In this year, the Tigers are twenty under five hundred and have fired their manager, Alan Trammell, because during his three-year tenure they have lost three hundred games. I can hear my brother complaining from two hundred miles away. Somewhere in the 1990s, my fondness for the business of baseball lessened. It includes altogether too much mollycoddling. These days when I feel nostalgic for baseball, I satisfy my craving by watching *Field of Dreams*, *The Natural*, and *For Love of the Game*.

I have found a new game to love, and it is girls' soccer. My brother hates soccer, which both adds to my appreciation of it and means that whenever we talk

I won't have to endure excruciating recitations on the finer points of the game. Today I will be watching Kat's soccer game. The girls of summer are two games away from the end of what has been a tough season. Today the high is expected to reach fifty-four degrees in southwestern Ohio, but the sun and leaves are brilliant. After the game parents will form a hand-to-hand tunnel, and the girls will run through. I had considered staying home, to avoid jinxing the girls, but realized I would be needed for the tunnel. Win or lose, we will come home to cake. Maybe I'll watch a minute or two of the World Series, while I indulge in this famous cake.

Tunnel of Fudge Cake

This week's theme is tunnels: tunnels made by the hands of soccer moms and dads and tunnels of fudge. This cake is warm and indulgent, a good cake for a victory, and an even better one for a defeat on a cold autumn day. Bundt cakes are rich and dense and keep well.

A bit about the pan itself: the aluminum Bundt pan was invented in 1950 by H. David Dalquist at the request of members of the Minneapolis Center of the Hadassah Society. They were interested in a pan that could be used to make kugel, a Jewish side dish made of noodles or potatoes. They had old ceramic cake pans of a somewhat similar design but wanted an aluminum one. Dalquist created a new shape and added regular folds to make it easier to cut the cake. The women from the society called the pans bund pans because "bund" is the German term for a gathering of people. Dalquist added a "t" to the end and trademarked the name.

For years the company sold few of the pans. Then, in 1966, Ella Rita Helfrich from Houston, Texas, won second place (and $5,000) in the Pillsbury Bake-Off for her Tunnel of Fudge Cake made in a Bundt pan. The win prompted a nationwide scramble for the pan. Pillsbury licensed the name in 1970 for a line of cake mixes. When H. David Dalquist died, on January 6, 2005, the company had sold more than fifty million Bundt pans. It is the top-selling cake pan in the world.

Preheat oven to 350° F.
Butter and flour a 12-cup bundt pan.

Cake

1 ¾ cups (3 ½ sticks) room-temperature unsalted butter
1 ¾ cups granulated sugar
6 eggs at room temperature
2 cups confectioners' sugar
2 ¼ cups all-purpose flour
¾ cup cocoa
2 cups chopped walnuts*

1. In the large bowl of an electric mixer cream butter and granulated sugar until light and fluffy—about 5 minutes.

2. Add eggs, one at a time, beating well after each addition. Gradually add powdered sugar; blend well.

3. By hand, stir in remaining cake ingredients until well blended.

4. Spoon batter into prepared pan; spread evenly.

5. Bake for 58–62 minutes.**

6. Cool upright in pan on rack for 1 hour; invert onto serving plate.

7. Cool completely.

Glaze

¾ cup confectioners' sugar

¼ cup cocoa

1½ to 2 tablespoons milk

1. In small bowl combine glaze ingredients until well blended. Spoon over top of cake, allowing some glaze to run down sides.

2. Store tightly covered.

*Nuts are essential to the success of the recipe.

**Since this cake has a soft tunnel of fudge, ordinary doneness test cannot be used. Accurate oven temperature and baking time are critical.

The Girls of Summer

"The spirit, the will to win, and the will to excel are the things that endure. These qualities are so much more important than the events that occur."
—Vince Lombardi

The White Sox carried the series in a four-game sweep of the Astros. Rust Belt redemption. It is the White Sox's first World Series championship since 1917. A sweet, sweet victory for the boys of summer, who today earned the right to a winter basking in the glow of success.

This week Kat's soccer team—the girls of summer—will play their last game of the season. This is their third season together, and they have yet to win a game. This year things were looking good. They had managed to recruit some new players, which meant they could substitute. Still, they lost. They could defend, but they could not score. Not a single goal was scored all this season; it is as if there is a force field around the goal.

Every game, it has been harder and harder to motivate the parents. But the girls themselves are surprisingly calm about their seeming inability to win. Oh, they want to win, and they recognize that perhaps part of the problem is that their coach is too nice. But they like him and they like each other. Of course, at some point during the season the parents jumped into the lurch and started coaching from the sidelines. "Mark-up, mark-up, mark-UP," we all seemed to be yelling at every game. I had always sworn I would never be one of those parents, the ones who yell from the sidelines. Lizzie had trained us well by forbidding us to express ourselves during a game, and with her supersonic hearing she knew when we slipped up. But I've been reduced to yelling, no better than anyone else. In my defense, most of my yelling has been of the encouraging sort: "Nice try…great kick…way to defend." But last week I actually heard myself calling out, "Get in their *face* Oakwood!" Yikes! Had I just said that out loud? I knew the answer was yes when I overheard a father standing a few feet away say, "I cannot believe I just heard the quiet scientist say that."

Which brings me to this day and to the last game of the season. I wake early, and trailing Tula our dog I step onto the porch to retrieve the newspaper. The air is still and cool with a hint of warmth (Indian summer had come on the night air). I head to the kitchen to make the cupcakes I'd promised for the after-game party. I am done and we are out the door well before noon.

Our girls score a goal in the first half, and it is a high, soaring one. We do not hold our breaths and neither do the girls, who continue to pass, block, and mark up. With just ten minutes to go, they still lead 1–0. A very long ten minutes later, they taste victory for the first time. Shocked—and relieved—the parents race to form the tunnel before the referee, or the other parents, can conjure up something to accuse us of having done wrong. We are not about to let this one slip away from us. The other team refuses to do the slap-hands walk with our team. Poor losers, or so it seems.

As a parent, you hope and pray your children will learn the lessons that will help them to do the right thing and to sustain their sense of confidence when they are faced with failure. Our team had learned to be good losers and to work hard, despite repeated losses. Success is instructive, too. And victory, after a prolonged period of losing, is the sweetest of all. Just ask the White Sox or any girl on Kat's team.

Black and White Cupcakes (makes 24)

Few things in real life are black and white, totally good or totally bad. But winning a game after a three-season drought is clearly a good thing. This recipe comes from the *Potato Chip Cookies and Tomato Soup Cake: Recipes of Americana* cookbook.

To be honest, I volunteered to bring the cupcakes thinking the team would need cheering up after losing *again*. I was thrilled when the frosting on the season was winning the game.

Preheat oven to 350° F.
Prepare muffin pans by adding paper liners to 24 wells.

White Batter

1 package cream cheese (8 ounces)
⅓ cup sugar
1 egg
⅛ teaspoon salt
1 package of semi-sweet chocolate chips (6 ounces)

Beat cream cheese, sugar, egg, and salt together until smooth. Stir in chocolate chips and set aside.

Black Batter

2 ¼ cups flour
1½ cups sugar
⅓ cup cocoa
1½ teaspoons baking soda
¾ teaspoon salt
1½ cups water
⅓ cup plus 3 tablespoons vegetable oil
2 teaspoons vanilla

1. Sift together flour, sugar, cocoa, baking soda, and salt in a large mixing bowl. Add water, oil, and vanilla to dry ingredients, beating just until mixed.

2. Fill paper-lined muffin cups ⅓ full with black batter. Top each cupcake with a heaping teaspoon of white batter. Bake 30 minutes or until toothpick comes out clean but not dry.

The Professor and King Alfred

"If you want the rainbow, you gotta put up with the rain."
—Anonymous

Today I found out at exactly 9:21 AM that I have been promoted to full professor. A hope has been fulfilled. I dawdled getting ready this morning, knowing I couldn't pick up the letter at the dean's office until 9 AM. I sure as hell didn't want to be the first one there. I signed for the letter and walked out into the brilliant and cool early November sunshine, traveling about twenty yards before cracking open the envelope. Carefully unfolding the letter, I peeked at the first line with eyes half open: "I am pleased to…" was all I need to read. So, eleven years, three months, and nineteen days after I first set foot on the campus of this university, I have finally arrived at the end of the line. This is the final stop in the academic *tour de farce* that begins with college and continues on through grad school, post-doctoral work, assistant professor, associate professor, and, finally, full professor.

But on this brilliantly sunny day something didn't seem quite right. The truth is that it has rained mercilessly on every important day of my life: my wedding day, the birth days of my two daughters, and on the day of my PhD candidacy exam and defense! It had rained so hard on my wedding day that we were late getting to the church because we'd had to pull off to the side of the road. The skies had continued to pour down on us as we left the church and during the first two hours of our journey. But while crossing the Ambassador Bridge linking Detroit to Canada, the rain had stopped and a double rainbow appeared in the sky. I knew at that moment our marriage was blessed and I never again bemoaned a rainy day.

Since the mid-1990s, nearly 50 percent of all PhDs in the biological sciences have been awarded to women. But only 8 percent of full professors are women and I am the first full professor ever in biology at my university. I've never been first in anything, unless I count a swim race at the end of my sophomore year in college. Like most women I know, I am comfortable not being first, I am resigned to not winning. It has been said that women are more afraid of success than of failure. I don't doubt that (just as I don't doubt that public speaking is the number one fear of most people, trumping death itself).

To celebrate my success, I took the entire day off: no reading of scientific papers, no grading of exams, no preparing of lectures. Instead I planted daffodils. King Alfred is buried all around my yard.

The hours spent digging and planting in the nimbus of November sunshine were followed up with a ride in our classic convertible through the gathering dusk. Dinner was simple because we had lingered a long time on our roofless ride, returning home just as darkness fell. Waiting for us at home was the cake Kat had baked for the occasion. I cannot remember a cake ever tasting sweeter.

Twilight Velvet Crumb Cake

Kat's cake this week is also the first cake I ever made by myself. I found the recipe on the side of the Bisquick box when I was eleven. It' still there in the same place, a fact that is immensely comforting. It's the same great comfort I feel knowing that books I haven't read for decades, as well as books I might never read but hope to read someday, are waiting for me on the shelf at the library.

Preheat oven to 350° F.
Grease and flour an 8" square, or 9" round, pan.

Cake

1½ cups Bisquick
½ cup sugar
½ cup milk or water
2 tablespoons shortening
1 teaspoon vanilla
1 egg

Topping

½ cup flaked coconut
⅓ cup packed brown sugar
¼ cup chopped pecans
3 tablespoons butter, softened
2 tablespoons milk

1. Beat all ingredients except topping in large bowl of mixer on low speed for 30 seconds, scraping bowl constantly. Beat for 4 minutes on medium speed, scraping bowl occasionally.
2. Pour into prepared pan.
3. Bake 30 to 35 minutes or until toothpick comes out clean; cool slightly.
4. Stir together all topping ingredients and spread over cake.
5. Broil on rack 3 inches from the heat for about 3 minutes or until golden brown.

E-lection Day

"A great empire, like a great cake, is most easily diminished at the edges." —Benjamin Franklin

Elections went electronic this year in my state. Touch screens have replaced punch cards, which had previously replaced the lovely old curtained booths with the levers. I still miss the curtained booths where, wrapped in privacy and quiet, we could not help but feel the sacredness of the act of voting. Today it was "touch n' go" under the bright lights of the high school library. I left feeling as if I had just visited an ATM and left without my cash.

Each new technology brings with it unsought and unforeseen consequences. I wish I could say that I cannot wait to see what touch-screen voting adds to our already overly complex world. Will polling places perish altogether as votes are cast from home computers? While that might up the percentage of people who vote (I'm thinking of those who stay home when it rains, or threatens to rain), it will rob us of the public and social act of exercising our franchise.

Last year's election was of the presidential variety and the bloodiest one in my lifetime. We the people are still reeling from that one. And in the one before, in 2000, voting was delayed and derailed and the election delivered, ultimately, to the Supreme Court to decide. It has been a long and desolate five years for over fifty million of us (including those who stayed home).

In this off-year election there were no less than five local initiatives aimed at election reform, all of which lost handily. We are in the desert of political strife and it might be decades—or never—before we return to civility and consensus. I'm not holding my breath.

I awoke early on Election Day to make a Hartford Election Cake. I made two: one for home and one for the office. I put a sign next to the cake that proclaimed "Non-Partisan Election Day Cake." When I returned for a second piece, it was gone. Voting makes people yearn for something sweet and uncomplicated.

Election Day started and Veteran's Day ended the week, lending a certain symmetry to it. While these two days don't always fall in the same week, I think of them as patriotic partners. Both of these days are important in our republic—without men and women willing to defend our country and our ability to hold free elections, our nation would perish.

This year Veteran's Day is particularly meaningful because men and women are serving and dying in Iraq.

I wonder what my late father, a veteran of World War II, would have to say about this particular war. I believe, along with my brother and sister, that he would be opposed to it. But he was not opposed to the Vietnam War.

The only big fight I ever remember having with my father was over the Vietnam War, one he reluctantly supported. The fight occurred when my father came to pick me up at the end of my first semester of college at the University of Michigan, his alma mater and his father's alma mater. The year was 1972 and the war was raging, both at home and in Vietnam. As soon as I climbed into the car, I started to spout antiwar rhetoric, as only a seventeen-year-old college freshman can do. I don't remember exactly what I said, thank goodness, but I am sure I criticized those who were fighting the war. I have no doubt that I was annoying the daylights out of my dad. But he was the strong-and-silent type, and I felt pretty confident that I could get away with raving against the war all the way home.

My father smoked and drove and said nothing. Suddenly the car was careening all over the road and I was sure my father was having the heart attack due an overweight, middle-aged man with a three-pack-a-day cigarette habit. (Losing my father to a heart attack was the single most vivid fear of my childhood.) I was terrified of crashing the car but even more frightened that I might be losing my dear, dear father. The car finally stopped and my perfectly healthy father turned to me, saying very calmly and very slowly, "You don't know what the hell you are talking about." The words stung as if he were spitting acid into my eyes. My father had rarely been angry with me and had never, ever sworn at me or in front of me. This was even more terrifying than the idea of a car crash. We drove the rest of the way home in silence.

It took me many years (and a confirming conversation with him) to understand exactly what had caused him to blow up that day. He believed, I learned, that a person who has never seen combat does not have the right to speak for or to judge those who have. I have concluded that my father, a mid-life convert to conservatism, would never have voted for George W. Bush. He would have seen Bush as a man who evaded serving his country because of his privileged status and personal lack of courage, although Bush seems to have no trouble sending others to hell. I am also sure my father would have detested the same Bush for his role in the slandering of John Kerry, his 2004 opponent who had served with valor in the war my father defended (albeit reluctantly).

And so, thirty-three years later I can tell you that I have learned my lesson. I sit here today even more deeply opposed to this war than the one fought in the rice paddies and jungles of Southeast Asia all those years ago. Perhaps my view of the Iraq War is connected to my feelings for my two children who may yet be asked to fight and die for this country. But I feel nothing but towering gratitude, admiration, and support for those who are fighting it. We owe to these men and women a lifetime of gratitude and a willingness to listen to what they have to say. And we owe every last one of them the best health care our country has to offer for the rest of their lives. I echo Teddy Roosevelt who said, "A man who is good enough to shed his blood for the country is good enough to be given a square deal afterwards." I only wish that Teddy Roosevelt's square deal had been one of the initiatives on the ballot earlier this week.

Hartford Election Cake with Sugar Crackle Topping

While trying to survive the last throes of a tough election, I found myself surfing the Web, where I found this recipe. It comes from *American Home Cooking* by Bill and Cheryl Jamison. Here is their explanation of the cake's origins:

"In the early Republic, Election Day in New England used to be a time for celebrating and feasting. Voters gathered in towns like Hartford and Salem, both associated with this cake, and stayed with family and friends for up to a week, particularly when they had to travel some distance to exercise their democratic rights. Cooks made the yeasted cake in huge loaves that would provide a generous slice to anyone who stopped by for a visit. Despite the patriotic overtones, the cake came from the vanquished British, being one of the surviving great cakes of the colonial era. In light of its distinguished heritage and the time involved in the preparation, we make a double loaf, freezing one for later if we're not feeding a crowd. The cake continues to delight because of its moist richness, still worthy of a vote in Hartford or anywhere else."

Cake

1 cup raisins, preferably half light and half dark
3 tablespoons dark rum
1 package active dry yeast
1 ½ cups lukewarm milk
1 ¼ cups packed light brown sugar
3 ½ cups unbleached all-purpose flour
¾ cup (1 ½ sticks) room-temperature unsalted butter
2 large eggs
1 tablespoon orange-flower water (see Ingredient Tip)
1 teaspoon ground cinnamon
1 teaspoon ground coriander
¾ teaspoon ground allspice
½ teaspoon salt
1 tablespoon minced orange or lemon zest
1 ½ cups chopped walnuts

Sugar Crackle Topping

3 tablespoons unsalted butter, melted
6 tablespoons sugar

1. Butter and flour two 8" x 4" loaf pans. Combine the raisins and rum in a small bowl.

2. Dissolve the yeast in the warm milk in a large mixing bowl. With an electric mixer, beat in the brown sugar and 1 ¾ cups of the flour, followed by the butter, eggs, and orange-flower water. When combined, mix in the remaining 1 ¾ cup of flour and beat for 3 minutes. Cover the bowl with a clean dish towel and set it in a warm, draft-free spot until doubled in size (about 1½ hours). The batter will be sticky, with he consistency of a soft, moist dough.

3. When it has doubled in size, stir down the batter. Mix in the spices and salt, followed by the zest, walnuts, and raisins and rum. Divide the batter between the two pans, smoothing it so that it is mounded on the top. Cover the pans and let the batter rest again in a warm, draft-free spot until it has risen to the top of the pans (about 1 additional hour). Near the end of the

rising time, preheat the oven to 350° F.

4. Top the cakes with the sugar crackle: pour the butter evenly over the dough and sprinkle it thickly with sugar.

5. Bake the cakes in the center of the oven. Cook for 50 to 55 minutes, until the tops are golden and a toothpick inserted in the center of each comes out clean. Cool in the pans for 10 minutes, then unmold and cool for at least 15 additional minutes. Serve warm or at room temperature. Leftovers can be toasted and slathered with sweet butter.

Ingredient Tip: Our common use of vanilla extract to flavor baked goods is largely a twentieth-century development. Before then, cooks scented their dishes with lemon and distillations of orange and rose blossoms. Look for fragrant rose water and orange-flower water in large grocery stores and Middle Eastern or Asian markets. Orange-flower water lends a lighter, more flowery complexity than vanilla to Election Cake.

Apparently Election Cakes have long been popular. I found this very old recipe while researching this book:

Election Cake (from *American Cookery*, by Amelia Simmons, 1706)

Thirty quarts flour, 10 pounds butter, 14 pounds sugar, 12 pounds raisins, 3 dozen eggs, one pint wine, one quart brandy, 4 ounces cinnamon, 4 ounces fine colander seed, 3 ounces ground allspice; wet the flour with milk to the consistency of bread overnight, adding one quart yeast; the next morning work the butter and sugar together for half an hour, which will render the cake much lighter and whiter.

Jamnesty

"The candle burns not for us, but for all those whom we failed to rescue from prison, who were shot on the way to prison, who were tortured, who were kidnapped, who 'disappeared.' That's what the candle is for."
—Peter Benenson, Amnesty International

These days everyone I know feels as though they are holding onto a planet—with both hands—that is spinning way too fast, spinning faster than it ever has before. All this spinning is pulling us apart. The name for this type of force is centrifugal, and it is measured in units of gravity. Standing in line at the grocery store (or at work, at home, or at sports stadium), we experience gravity that is, by definition, a 1g unit. But we can create, artificially, much greater gravity by spinning things at high speeds. For example, to separate the bacterial cells I work with we rotate them in a centrifuge, a spin machine, to generate 10,000 times the force of gravity we normally experience on the surface of earth. Lately I feel more like a microbe in a centrifuge than a human walking the earth.

Way too often I think that once this project, report, paper, budget, lecture is over then things will slow down—the spin machine will glide to a stop. But the minute I complete a task, or often before it's completed, a new one gets added to the top of the pile. And I am pulled in yet another direction.

I was not surprised, although a bit saddened, to learn that Lizzie is also experiencing excessive g-forces. In addition to classes, she is the business manager for the Amnesty International chapter at the University of Pittsburgh. The group is holding their annual fund-raising event, Jamnesty. They have been working on it since August, but this is the week. Over the not-quite-as-good-as advertised cell-phone connection, she sounds a bit wired and rushed. It is late Friday afternoon and she is outside the student union, the site of the event, trying to soak up some of the weak November sun before throwing herself into the eight-hour abyss of the event. She clearly does not want to chat. I hang up and say a quick prayer that things go well, or at least that she and her friends have a good story to tell afterward.

The next day she calls to fill us in on Jamnesty. We

hear that the turnout was better than expected, the bands played, even though the money to pay them had not materialized, and they raised almost $500. When it is my turn to talk, I ask her if she has been inspired enough by this success to become an event planner. The answer is a firm no. Lizzie has learned at a young age that event planning is often ruined by what other people forget or fail to do. But she is quite pleased with the amount raised and tells me the proceeds will go to students who tutor the children of Sudanese refugees who have recently settled in Pittsburgh. I assure her this was definitely worth the effort and angst.

I made this cake in honor of Jamnesty and the refugees of the Sudan who have landed in the fast-spinning and not-so-new world of America in the twenty-first century.

Jamnesty Torte

Both Lizzie and I love cakes with jam in the middle. This cake is a modification of another cake from the *Book of Great Chocolate Desserts* by Maida Heatter. According to Heatter, this cake was served on the Orient Express during its heyday, when it was renowned for luxurious food and service. This is a flourless, not-too-sweet sponge cake with a smooth, rich chocolate buttercream icing. I added Oregon blackberry jam in between the layers, instead of icing, and covered the entire cake with a generous layer of the frosting. We took it to a farewell dinner party for my friend Steve, who is leaving for a sabbatical and not likely to return to my university. The evening's food and fellowship will long be remembered and, though we didn't ride the Orient Express, it did feel as though we had taken a long and sweet journey.

Preheat oven to 300° F.
Butter a 9" round cake pan, line the bottom of the pan with wax paper cut to fit, butter the paper and dust all over with fine, dry bread crumbs. Invert to shake out excess, and set pan aside.

Torte

3 ounces (3 squares) unsweetened chocolate
1 ½ cups ground unblanched almonds
5 eggs, separated, plus 2 egg yolks (bring egg whites to room temperature)
¾ cup granulated sugar
pinch of salt

1. Finely grind chocolate and almonds together in a food processor and set aside.

2. Place the 7 egg yolks in the small bowl of an electric mixer. Add the sugar and beat until the yolks are pale lemon in color, but stop before they become thick.

3. Add the ground chocolate and almond mix and beat until well mixed. Transfer to a larger mixing bowl.

4. Add the salt to the room temperature egg whites and beat (with clean beaters) until they hold a definite shape but not until they are stiff or dry.

5. Add the beaten egg whites to the chocolate mixture and fold together only until incorporated.

6. Turn into the prepared pan and rotate it a bit briskly, first in one direction, then the other, to level the batter.

7. Bake for about 65 minutes until the top barely springs back when lightly pressed with a fingertip.

8. Remove from the oven and immediately, with a small, sharp knife, cut around the sides to release. Let the cake cool in the pan for 10–15 minutes.

9. Cover with a rack and invert cake pan and rack, remove the pan, peel off the paper slowly and carefully, cover with another rack and invert again, leaving the cake right side up to cool on the rack.

10. The cake will be cut to make two layers. (It is a delicate and fragile cake, so if you freeze it first it will be easier to cut and safer to handle.)

11. Meanwhile, prepare the buttercream.

Chocolate Buttercream

6 tablespoons (¾ stick) room-temperature unsalted butter
½ teaspoon vanilla
½ cup sugar
2 eggs
3 ounces (3 squares) unsweetened chocolate

1. Place chocolate in the top of a double boiler over medium heat and cover it until the chocolate is partially melted. Uncover and stir until completely melted; set aside.

2. In a small bowl cream the butter with the vanilla. Add the sugar and beat for 3–4 minutes. Add the eggs and beat at high speed for a few minutes.

3. Add the melted chocolate to the buttercream and beat again for several minutes.

4. Place the bowl of buttercream, with the beaters, in the refrigerator, and leave until the mixture is quite firm.

5. Remove buttercream from the refrigerator and beat again for several minutes. It should be beaten until it is soft enough to spread easily, light in color, and as smooth as honey. Don't be afraid of overbeating at this point.

Cake Assembly

1. Prepare a cake plate, or stand, by placing four strips of wax paper around the outer edges.

2. Using a serrated knife, cut the cake horizontally to make two even layers.

3. Place the bottom layer of the cake, cut side up, on the plate, checking to see that the wax paper touches the cake all around.

4. Spread the jam and about one-third of the buttercream over the bottom layer, cover with the top layer, placing it cut side down, and spread the remaining buttercream smoothly over the sides and top.

5. Remove the wax paper strips by pulling each one out toward a narrow end.

6. Serve at room temperature

Pining for Childhood

"Wherever they go, and whatever happens to them on the way, in that enchanted place on the top of the forest, a little boy and his Bear will always be playing."
—Winnie the Pooh

'Twas the week before Thanksgiving and all through the house not a pre-teen was stirring—not even by noon.

Kat is about to turn twelve. As my mother used to say, "Nobody ever liked being twelve." She even had an essay clipped from the *Detroit Free Press* that hung on our refrigerator for years. I have searched the Internet for the essay but can't find it. While annoyed, I must admit that I do like that some things have never made it to the Internet. Is it possible that mystery still exists somewhere in the world? The gist of the essay was that when you are twelve and no longer a child or a teen, you are a tween. A tween has neither the unsullied joys of childhood nor the rights and privileges of teenagerdom.

I do remember the summer I was twelve, mostly because my mother pointed to the newspaper clipping on the refrigerator and said, "Read this." The essay was supposed to abate my tween angst, but after reading it I only felt less understood. Perhaps other tweens made peace with their lack of status in the world through reading the essay, but I was not one of them. I bridled at questions about where I was going when I left the house and when I would return. I wanted two things: to be left alone by my family and to never be left out by my peers. Too much to ask? I think not.

As if on cue, Kat announced this week that she is tired of keeping everything in her pockets and needs a purse. Just yesterday I could find stones, sticks, and detritus-of-the-day in those pockets (Wayne and I knew to check Kat's pockets before washing her clothes). I realized that before she entered the halls of the junior high school in August, I would have to buy her a purse. Junior high school, that cruel and self-conscious era replete with rumors, complicated dress codes, and a popularity-driven hierarchy, is the age when the material girl in each of us rises up and demands to be obeyed. The tracings of junior high treasons are painfully tattooed on my own heart.

Soon enough Saturday morning cartoons will be replaced by Saturday morning texting and Saturday afternoon trips to the mall. I vowed to spend this last pre-teen birthday doing something a material girl would not do. The four of us piled into the van and headed to a pine forest near a gorge and glen less than an hour from our house. I had never been to this pine forest before but both of my daughters had, and they sigh with reverence whenever it is mentioned. Lizzie and Kat had discovered it searately during a four-day camping expedition that is part of the fifth grade curriculum in our town.

We set off in search of the mythical patch of pines. The girls couldn't recall exactly how to get there, so we meandered through our very own version of the hundred-acre woods. Suddenly the pines appeared as if by magic and the girls took off running. Wayne and I followed and what we found was a cathedral of sorts, a cathedral of conifers with a teeter-totter fashioned from two of the fallen. After taking turns on the teeter-totter, we all lay down on the downy bed of needles, as Kat said they had done on their night hike. Soon the only sound we heard was the wind whispering in the pines.

I have always loved trees. I love to climb them, to hang suspended between them in a hammock, and to lie beneath them. As I listened to the pines I remembered the legend of the candy tree, a myth we always perpetuated for our daughters' birthdays. A candy tree drops its candy only on a birthday. On our daughters' birthdays, Wayne or I would sneak out early in the morning and scatter candy around a tree in our backyard. Later that day, during the party, we told the assembled kids the story of the tree that blooms only two days every year. The kids would rush outside to gather up the candy. It has been a long time since the candy tree has "bloomed" in our yard. Today rather than focusing on candy trees, we focused on our reverence for nature.

My thoughts began to drift like clouds, settling on no one thing until I felt as if my body had melded with the needles and I was in an ancient forest. Finally we stirred one by one and headed out, back to our twenty-first century combustion-engine-driven vehicle. Our ride home was a quiet one.

Tower of Coconut Cake

My mother always made a big deal out of our birthdays—making us whatever we wanted for dinner and hosting parties for our friends. However, she was cake-impaired and never made a birthday cake. For this reason, I suppose, I have always made my daughters a birthday cake. For Kat's birthday this week I attempted to find a cake that would wow her still wowable pre-teen heart. Kat is a fan of the fruit from the Coco nucifera palm tree, a taste she acquired on a trip to Hawaii where coconut is as common as snow in the arctic. She devoured toasted coconut on the road to Hana, coconut shaved ice on Kaui, and coconut ice cream on Oahu. She is nuts about coconut. So I decided to make her this cake for her birthday.

I made this cake for the first time for the departmental Christmas party a few years back. I frosted it before the cake was completely cooled—something I often do—and then went off to shower and prepare myself for the festivities. When we were about to leave, I noticed the frosting had melted into the cake, giving an odd appearance to the stranded coconut flakes. They looked like the detritus left after a high tide.

Everyone assured me it tasted great (which meant it looked truly awful). I did not make that mistake this time and my coconut cake was the white and fluffy tower of my dreams. Kat loved it!

This recipe is a combination—a coconut chimera—of several recipes I've used over the years.

Preheat oven to 350° F.
Butter and flour three 9" cake pans.

Cake

½ pound (2 sticks) room-temperature unsalted butter
½ cup solid vegetable shortening (like Crisco)
2 cups sugar
5 eggs
2 teaspoon vanilla extract
1 cup milk
3 cups all-purpose flour
2 teaspoons baking powder

1. In the large bowl of an electric mixer, cream the butter, shortening, and sugar until light and fluffy—about 5 minutes.

2. Add the eggs, one at a time, beating until thick and pale yellow. Add the vanilla and then gradually add the milk.

3. Sift together flour and baking powder and fold into the egg mixture, mixing just until combined.

4. Pour the batter evenly into the prepared cake pans and bake for 35 to 40 minutes or until a toothpick or cake tester inserted into the center of the cake comes out clean.

5. Cool the cakes in the pans for 10 minutes and then invert them onto wire racks to cool completely.*

Frosting

(This is a marshmallow-type frosting that is worth the extra beating and chilling. Or so my daughter tells me.)

½ cup shredded unsweetened coconut
1 cup water
3 cups sugar
3 egg whites
1 teaspoon vanilla extract

1. Spread coconut on a baking sheet and bake in the preheated oven, shaking the sheet from time to time, just until coconut is golden brown. Set aside to cool.

2. In a small saucepan combine water and sugar and stir over medium heat until all the sugar is dissolved (be sure not to boil or brown the syrup as this will discolor the icing). When the liquid has become a syrup, remove pan from heat.

3. In the bowl of an electric mixer, beat the egg whites on high speed until fluffy. Continue beating while slowly pouring the warm syrup into the egg whites.

4. Add the vanilla, reduce speed to medium, and continue beating the mixture until it is smooth and very thick in consistency. This could take as long as 10 minutes or more. Once it is smooth and thick, but not thick enough to stand up on its own, you can put it in the refrigerator to thicken further.

Cake Assembly

To assemble the cake, place one layer on a serving plate or cake stand. Cover with icing. Repeat for all three layers and then frost the sides and top. Sprinkle the sides and top with the toasted coconut, pressing gently into the frosting.

Keep the cake in a cool, dark place, covered, until ready to serve. If you refrigerate the cake, cover it loosely with plastic wrap. The cake is better the day after it is made.

What's So Funny About Fruitcake?

"The worst gift is a fruitcake. There is only one fruitcake in the entire world, and people keep sending it to each other." —Johnny Carson

Johnny, Johnny, Johnny, Ima gonna prove you wrong. I've been told that the Canadian Air Transport Security Authority has banned fruitcake from carry-on luggage because it is so dense that X-rays cannot penetrate it. I haven't made one myself in twenty-eight years, but I'm predicting that fruitcake will be making a come-back any millennium now. For the record, I have always loved fruitcake, although I admit I was the kid who picked out the cherries (and fed the rest of the cake to the dog). What is prompting me to make this much-maligned cake? When I tell Wayne about my plan, he hands me a Ziggy cartoon that shows Ziggy standing in front of a large garbage truck lettered with the phrase "Fruitcake Disposal Unit." I explain that at our Thanksgiving feast I'd asked my sister-in-law Marty if her family had any cake traditions. My brother-in-law gave me a look that telegraphed "Hoo-boy, did ya have to ask that question?" I waited for the story to unfold and it was a sad one. Turns out that Marty's mother made a fantastic fruitcake but the recipe had been stolen. Her mother's caretaker in her final years had stolen the cookbook with the fruitcake and many other precious family recipes. (Marty grew up in Baltimore where her father owned and ran a restaurant.) The caretaker even admitted to taking the recipe book but wouldn't give it back—even after they offered her money. Marty said she could picture the page in the book with the fruitcake recipe and see her mother's scribbled changes and her running tally in the margin of how many she made each year. I knew I had inadvertently upset Marty terribly. This sad fruitcake saga speaks of the power of food and family.

Today Marty and other fruitcake aficionados buy their cakes from Trappist Monks who derive much of their income from making and selling them. The Monks of Holy Cross Abbey in Virginia offer an unconditional guarantee that their fruitcake is "the best you'll ever eat or we will cheerfully refund your money." Their cakes weigh more than two pounds. Marty says they are close to her mother's but not the same. And the Monks' fruitcake doesn't include a book with personal notations in her mother's handwriting.

My plan is to arrive at Christmas with this fruitcake in tow for Marty, hoping it will recapture the spirit of her mother's cake.

The Best Fruitcake (really, there is such a thing)

This cake was made, with love, for my sister-in-law Marty. The recipe comes from *The New McCall's Cookbook*, by Mary Eckley.

This recipe is quite long and the mind reels at the list of ingredients. But if you have a friend or relative who is a fruitcake lover—not just a fruitcake—it is more than worth the look on their face when you give it to them. It is one impressive (and heavy) cake.

This cake is best if let to cure, soaking in spirits, for a few weeks before serving.

Makes a 5-pound fruitcake

Read the directions carefully before starting because you will need to soak the fruit overnight before making the cake. Do not turn on the oven until the directions tell you to!

Cake

1 pound golden raisins
½ pound seeded raisins
¼ pound currants
½ cup dark rum or brandy
1 pound candied pineapple
½ pound candied red cherries
¼ pound candied citron
⅛ pound candied lemon peel
⅛ pound candied orange peel
2 cups all-purpose flour
½ teaspoon mace
½ teaspoon cinnamon
½ teaspoon baking soda
¼ pound almonds, blanched and coarsely chopped
¼ pound walnuts or pecans, coarsely chopped
½ cup room-temperature unsalted butter
1 cup granulated sugar
1 cup brown sugar, packed
5 eggs, slightly beaten
1 tablespoon milk
1 teaspoon almond extract
Rum or brandy
A roll or can of almond paste

1. In a large bowl, combine raisins and currents. Add ½ cup rum and toss to combine. Cover and let stand overnight.

2. The next day: Draw an 18" circle on a piece of heavy brown paper (a paper bag will do) and cut it out. Place a 10" tube pan in the center of the circle and draw around the base of the pan with a pencil. With pencil lines on the outside, fold the paper into eighths; snip off the tip. Unfold circle and make one cut from the outer edge to the center. Butter both the tube pan and the paper well. Fit paper, greased side up, into pan.

3. Butter both the tube pan and the unpenciled side of the paper well. Fit paper, greased side up, into pan.

4. Prepare fruits: With a sharp knife cut pineapple into thin wedges; cut ½ pound of cherries into halves; cut citron and lemon and orange peels into very thin strips. Add to raisins and currants and mix well.

5. On sheet of waxed paper sift 1½ cups flour with spices and baking soda; set aside.

6. Preheat oven to 275° F.

7. Combine remaining ½ cup of flour with nuts and fruits and toss lightly.

8. In the large bowl of an electric mixer, at medium speed, cream butter until light. Gradually beat in granulated sugar, then brown sugar, beating until very light and fluffy.

9. Beat in eggs, milk, and almond extract until thoroughly combined.

10. At low speed, beat in flour mixture, mixing just until combined.

11. Turn batter into fruit and nuts mixture and mix well, using your hands.

12. Turn batter into the prepared pan, pressing batter down evenly all around.

13. Bake 3 hours and 15 minutes, or until a toothpick (or cake tester) inserted near the center comes out clean and dry.

14. Let cake stand in pan on wire rack for 30 minutes to cool completely.

15. To store: Wrap cake in cheesecloth soaked in run or brandy. Place cake in a tin with a tight fitting lid (or wrap tightly in double layer of foil). Store in a cool place for several weeks (until Christmas). Check on the cake every week and resoak the cheesecloth if it has dried.

16. To decorate: Roll almond paste between two sheets of waxed paper into an 8" circle. Remove top piece of wax paper and invert paste onto cake; remove paper. With a sharp knife, trim edges of the paste, then press paste to cake. Spread paste with frosting glaze, letting it run down side of cake. Decorate with cherries cut in half.

Frosting Glaze

1½ cups confectioners' sugar
2 tablespoons light cream
¼ teaspoon almond extract

In small mixing bowl, combine all the ingredients and beat until the mixture is smooth.

California Dreamin'

"Oh, but California I'm coming home."
—Joni Mitchell

I started out for northern California this week anticipating eagerly my first visit to wine country. I felt certain it would capture my fancy but I was wrong. The highlight of my trip was the produce I found at the farmers' market in Davis, over an hour's drive from Napa. It was the first week of December and in my part of the world ice was beginning to form. But in Davis, California, the weather was sunny and warm. I felt like I was coming home to a place I'd never been before.

The stalls of the market were filled with herbs, nuts, tomatoes, lemons, limes, raspberries and persimmons. To an Ohioan, persimmons looked like small suns. Elementary school children wearing short sleeves and Santa hats were playing Christmas music. Christmas California-style seemed like heaven on earth. I thought of Lizzie, who would love all the fabulous foods, and I wished she had come with me.

I was on a mission that day to prepare a special dinner for my PhD advisor and his wife who were hosting me for my week of research and grant writing. I found the Meyer lemons called for in the cake recipe I had chosen, along with fresh salmon and chili peppers for the main dish. I also purchased a sampler of dried fruits for Lizzie in honor of her birthday, which she was celebrating today thousands of miles away from me. Nineteen years ago when she permanently left the warm embrace of my womb, I could never have imagined we would ever be apart on her birthday.

I spent a happy afternoon in my hosts' kitchen juicing and grating lemons for the cake until the whole house was filled with their atomized sunshine. The next day we took the long route to the Napa Valley, winding up and over the hills through olive and lemon groves. The vineyards looked like intricate quilts laid out across the land. The first winery was pocket-size, tucked inside an olive grove. It was a small place, with big wines and a charming history. I tasted and listened to the stories in the humble barn of a tasting room, but I didn't buy any of their wine.

I was holding out for the wines of a particular cult-like cellar, which I had never tasted; part of their allure is their expensive price tags. By the time we arrived at the cellar of my wine-soaked dreams, my mouth was ready to be amazed. I purchased tickets for the three of us and we were handed fancy wine glasses with the name of the winery etched on the side. As we moved to the steel-and-tile fermentation galleries, among us was a wine critic from the *San Francisco Chronicle*. The presence of an august wine person only added to my pleasure as I sipped the chardonnay. I sniffed, I swigged, I swished—it was liquid *awful*. Could this be? I glanced around the room to check the reactions of the others. To my surprise, everyone was smiling and praising the wine: "A good nose, velvety mouth feel, and redolent of raspberries." Every wine was worse than the last one. Still the group gushed. I began to feel a bit nuts and I leave Napa vowing to never again be fooled by expensive price tags or shiny fermentation tanks (as a microbiologist shiny fermentation tanks are my idea of excitement).

The last night of my visit made up for the disappointing trip to the winery. We drove to Berkeley to have dinner at *Chez Panisse*. For over twenty years, ever since my sister and brother-in-law gave us Alice Water's first cookbook, *Chez Panisse Menu Cookbook*, I had dreamed of visiting the epicenter of the real-food cooking quake that continues to rock this country. I recognized the front of the restaurant, on a narrow street, from the cover of my cookbook. Inside we were seated in a lovely Arts & Crafts dining room. A waiter approached and told us that the turkey they were serving this night was the same one Prince Charles and his Camilla had ordered the week before. He corrected himself, saying, "The same as that served," allaying any fears I had about eating week-old turkey. Dinner was long, with lively conversation and a variety of Zinfandel wines. The cost per person was reasonable, especially if I amortized it over the twenty years I'd spent yearning to eat there.

On the flight home I decided to make this an annual pilgrimage. I will migrate to northern California in the waning sunlight of late fall to talk science, wander the Davis farmers' market, and learn the language of the grape.

Lemon Polenta Pound Cake

This week, far from home and my own humble (but familiar) kitchen, I decided to make a cake for my hosts. I found this recipe in one of their many cookbooks, *The San Francisco Chronicle Cookbook*, by Michael Bauer and Fran Irwin.

This pound cake was created to serve at a dinner honoring some of San Francisco's top chefs. For this event I paired it with lemon curd, softly whipped cream, and blueberries.

My friends thought it perfect all by itself. It keeps very well.

Preheat oven to 350° F.
Line loaf pan with parchment paper or waxed paper (or butter and flour).

Cake

½ cup yellow cornmeal
1 cup all-purpose flour
½ teaspoon baking soda
½ teaspoon salt
3 room-temperature eggs, separated
½ cup (1 stick) room-temperature unsalted butter
1 tablespoon finely grated lemon zest
1 ¼ cups sugar
6 tablespoons lemon juice (from Meyer lemons if possible)
2 tablespoons evaporated milk (or substitute yogurt)

1. Combine cornmeal, flour, baking soda, and salt; set aside.

2. Beat the egg whites until stiff; set aside.

3. Cream butter, lemon zest, and sugar until fluffy, and then add egg yolks and mix well.

4. Add lemon juice and milk, alternating with flour mixture.

5. Blend just until dry ingredients are moistened.

6. Carefully fold into the beaten egg whites. Spoon batter into prepared pan and bake 60–75 minutes or until a cake tester comes out clean.

7. Let cake cool for 15 minutes in the pan before turning out onto a rack to cool.

8. Remove lining paper and serve.

Fancy Does It

"You don't have to cook fancy or complicated masterpieces—just good food from fresh ingredients."
—Julia Child

I am an introvert, a bona fide, verified, and certified introvert. I found this out for certain only last year, when I took the famed Meyers-Brigg personality test for the first time. But it was actually revealed to me when I was knee high to my mother, an exemplary example of an extrovert. As a child I observed my mother, because that is what introverts do. I observed that my mother was at ease in front of people, all people, from babies to Bob Hope. She once spotted Mr. Hope across a crowded New York City restaurant and made a beeline for him, dragging her friend Ginnie with her. What did my mother say when she reached him? She said, "Mr. Hope, I would like you to meet my friend Ginnie." I'm pretty sure she hadn't even thought about what she was going to say until it came out of her mouth.

I used to confuse being introverted with being shy, but I now know it has to do with where you get your energy. My mother lit up like neon when she was surrounded by people, and it is no surprise that she loved parties. She once entertained the crowd at a Pi Phi house party at the University of Wisconsin by sitting on the grand piano and smoking a cigar with her toes.

Lizzie is a sweet introvert whose serene countenance draws others to her. Wayne and Kat are extroverts. Kat is zany and jazzed by people in the way that my mother was. Kat was born screaming, which I am sure was her way of demanding a full social schedule. The teen years are going to be interesting with this one.

For me, parties are less a chance to perform than to observe. And when called on to perform, I immediately want to go straight back home and crawl into bed. So, when I wake up on the shortest day of the year and recall that we have a Christmas party to attend, I feel like pulling the covers back over my head and inviting Tula to join me. Then, I remember that it is Cake Day. The idea of taking a fancy and impressive cake to the party fires up my creative and competitive nature.

I throw back the covers and jump into the cold air of our bedroom. I am on one foot and it would be very easy to fall back into the warmth, but inspiration keeps me bolt upright. I will make a Yule log cake. I have always wanted to make one of these traditional French Christmas cakes, aka a Bûche de Noël. I suddenly recall how my sister and I watched Julia Child make one on our fifteen-inch black-and-white TV. Julia not only shaped it like a log, but she made it look like a *real* log—a log that had been on the forest floor far too long, a log that had been taken over by fungi and spiderwebs. Who would eat such a thing? My sister and I wanted to know. But we were transfixed by that voice and by the idea of spun sugar made to look like spiderwebs. It was brilliance, and we recognized it.

I spend the afternoon in the kitchen making the cake, the warmth of the oven a welcome companion on this frigid day. But as I whip the meringue for the mushrooms, the higher the egg whites rise in the bowl, the more deflated I feel. I am just not in the mood to party. So I call in sick and we eat the Yule log in the quiet of our own dining room, with a real log burning in the nearby fireplace. But this is truly a party cake. Word to the shy people of the world: bring this cake to a party and you will rule. And don't worry, this cake does not look like a log left too long on the forest floor.

La Bûche de Noël

Julia might be right that food does not always have to be fancy, but sometimes even Julia made things fancy, and when she did, fancy was fantastic. This is fancy enough for even the most fantastic of feasts.

This most famous and delicious of French pastries can be traced back to the ancient Celtic tradition of celebrating the winter solstice. On the shortest day of the year, the Celts would search for a large trunk of either oak, beech, elm, or cherry to burn. The burning log was a symbol of the rebirth of the sun as well as an offering of thanks to the sun for returning to the earth. The tradition of actually burning the log began to disappear with the arrival of small stoves. A big log was replaced by a smaller branch that was set in the middle of the table and surrounded by little sweets and delicacies. Eventually the branch gave rise to a cake that is essential to Christmas celebrations today.

I found this recipe in *The Martha Stewart Cookbook: Collected Recipes for Every Day*. It makes enough for one "log" and no extra branches. If you want branches, you can double the recipe.

Preheat oven to 350° F.

Butter a 13" x 11" jelly roll pan, line with parchment paper, leaving a 2" overhang on the short ends. Butter the parchment paper and the sides of the pan Lightly dust the pan with flour and tap out the excess.

Cake

¾ cup plus 1 tablespoon sifted cake flour
1 cup plus 1 tablespoon sugar
½ cup sifted unsweetened cocoa powder
1 ½ teaspoons baking powder
¾ teaspoon salt
3 whole eggs
5 egg whites
½ cup plus 1 tablespoon vegetable oil
1 tablespoon vanilla extract

Also needed: cocoa powder for dusting and sprigs of evergreens

1. In the medium bowl of an electric mixer combine flour, ¾ cup of the sugar, the cocoa, baking powder, and salt. Mix on low speed for 30 seconds.

2. In a large mixing bowl, whisk the whole eggs, oil, and vanilla until frothy. Stir in the flour mixture until well blended and thick.

3. In the small bowl of an electric mixer, beat the 5 egg whites for the cake until frothy. Increase the speed to medium-high and beat until soft peaks start to form. One tablespoon at a time, add the remaining sugar and continue beating until the whites are stiff but not dry.

4. Fold ⅓ of the beaten egg whites into the egg and flour mixture; gently fold in another ⅓ of the remaining whites and then the final ⅓. Do not overmix. Scrape the batter into the prepared pan and spread evenly.

5. Bake the cake for 12 – 15 minutes until it springs back when gently touched in the center. Run the tip of a knife around the edges of the pan.

6. Cover the cake with a large piece of plastic wrap, and then cover the plastic with a damp clean kitchen towel.

7. Invert the cake onto a baking rack.

8. When it is just cool enough to handle, start at a long side and roll the cake with the parchment paper, plastic wrap, and towel, into a cylinder.

9. Cool the rolled cake to room temperature.

Espresso Cream Filling

2 cups heavy cream
2 ½ ounces bittersweet chocolate, finely chopped
1 ½ tablespoons strong, brewed espresso, cooled
¼ cup confectioners' sugar

1. Heat ½ cup of the cream to scalding and pour it over the chopped chocolate and allow it to sit for 1 – 2 minutes until the chocolate melts.

2. Stir until smooth.

3. Add 1 tablespoon of the espresso and blend until it is incorporated. Set aside in a bowl to cool.

4. In the large bowl of an electric mixer, whip until thick the remaining 1 ½ cups of the cream with the confectioners' sugar.

5. Add the remaining espresso and continue beating at high speed.

6. Gradually add the chocolate mixture, and beat until light and fluffy; set aside.

Swiss Meringue Buttercream Icing

½ cup egg whites (3 – 4 eggs worth)
1 cup granulated sugar
1 ¼ cups (2 ½ sticks) room-temperature unsalted butter
¼ pound white chocolate, melted

1. Combine the egg whites and sugar in the large bowl of an electric mixer and place over simmering water (the bowl should not touch the water), whisking occasionally until the mixture is warm and the sugar has dissolved.

2. Remove from the heat.

3. Using an electric mixer, beat the mixture on high speed until stiff peaks form. Continue beating on medium speed until the meringue reaches room temperature.

4. Still on medium speed, add the butter, one piece at a time, until the butter is well blended. Scrape down the sides and bottom of the bowl from time to time.

5. Beat the buttercream at high speed for a minute or two. Add the melted white chocolate and continue beating at high speed until evenly blended, again scraping down the sides of the bowl from time to time.

6. Refrigerate until ready to use.

Cake Assembly

1. Unroll the cooled cake slowly, carefully removing the parchment paper, plastic wrap, and towel.

2. Spread the cake evenly with the espresso cream filling.

3. Starting from the other end, reroll the filled cake into a "log."

4. Chill the cake for at least 1 hour before proceeding.

5. Spread the cake log with the buttercream icing, using a small metal spatula.

6. Decorate the log with meringue mushrooms* and dust with cocoa powder.

Meringue Mushrooms (makes about 20 mushrooms)

Preheat the oven to 225° F.
Line 2 large baking sheets with aluminum foil.

3 egg whites (at room temperature)
Pinch of salt
⅛ teaspoon cream of tartar
1 teaspoon vanilla extract
¾ cup superfine sugar
Cocoa powder for dusting
3 ounces semi-sweet chocolate, melted

1. In the large bowl of an electric mixer, beat the egg whites until frothy. Add the salt, cream of tartar, and vanilla and continue beating until soft peaks form when the beaters are slowly withdrawn.

2. Add the sugar, 1 tablespoon at a time, beating for about 30 seconds between each addition.

3. When all the sugar has been added, beat for an additional 6 minutes. The egg whites should be very stiff, glossy, and extremely smooth, but not dry.

4. To make the mushrooms, spoon the mixture into 2 pastry bags, fitted with a ½" round tip for the stems and a ⅝" round tip for the caps.

5. Holding the ⅝" tip close to a baking sheet, press out round tops for the mushroom caps (any unwanted points can be smoothed with a finger dipped in cold water).

6. For the stems, use the smaller tip. Hold the pastry bag in one hand and a small sharp knife in the other. Press out the stem (about ¾" to 1" in height) and then cut off the meringue with the knife. The stem will have a flat end that will adhere more easily to the cap.

7. Lightly dust the caps and stems with cocoa powder.

8. Reduce the oven to 200° F and bake the caps and stems for 1½–2 hours, until they are dry to the touch and can be lifted from the foil.

9. Cool completely.

10. To assemble, with a small spatula spread a thick layer of melted chocolate on the underside of the cap.

11. Dip the flat tip of the stem into the chocolate and affix to the cap.

12. Turn upside down and dry.

Gingerbread Castles, and Cottages

"Run, run as fast as you can! You can't catch me, I'm the Gingerbread Man." —European fable

It's coming on Christmas and I am running as fast as I can. Unlike the Gingerbread Man, I am sure I will be caught—caught, that is, not ready for the holiday.

The holidays are about traditions—those we love and those we don't. As a child I dreamed of gingerbread houses, à la Hansel and Gretel, at Christmas time. My mother's magazines were full of them, colorful and fantastic and ready to grab and eat. I would dream about the sweet crunch of biting into a candy window pane; or chomping on the necco-wafer-shingled room. I wanted to do that more than anything, more than I wanted a Barbie Dream House on Christmas morning when I was nine. But, alas, my mother did not bake cakes, much less gingerbread houses. Mom's idea of dessert was Jello, which she convinced us took her all day to make.

So when Lizzie, whose birthday falls in early December, turned three I decided to start a gingerbread-house party tradition. Being a scientist, I researched how to make the gingerbread and construct the house and make icing (it is actually more like cement). This was pre-Internet, before its rich storehouse of recipes and remedies became available to all. It was even before the invention of gingerbread-house kits. I would spend days making the gingerbread, and on the night before the party, I would build the houses—one for each child coming. I'd buy bags and bags of candy: gumdrops for the pathways, red licorice for the gutters, and necco wafers, mini-shredded wheat pillows, and round peppermint swirls for the roofs. I bought nonpareils and M&Ms for me, and any other chocophiles in attendance.

I was desperate to see the children's eyes pop at the sight of all that candy. As a child there was nothing I wanted more than candy. At two I was found sitting on the table eating sugar right out of the bowl; at three I was found licking the glass of the candy display in the five-and-dime; at four my mother came upon me hanging with my feet off the ground while licking a sucker that was sticking out of a kitchen drawer. Yes, my gingerbread parties were going to be deeply satisfying personal experiences for me.

At that first party, the kids ranged from age three to seven. A brief forty-five minutes after the party started, the kitchen was in a shambles. (Fortunately, one of my friends had volunteered *her* kitchen for the event.) But the gingerbread houses were spectacular and the kids in a sugar stupor after consuming about the same amount of candy as they put on their houses. And like snowflakes (and children) each house was unique.

I've done this every Christmas season since, in spite of two moves over eighteen years. The second or third year gingerbread-house kits became available, and I happily gave up making the gingerbread. But I still got to make the cement icing, construct the house, and buy all that luscious candy. The always-humble houses never fail to bring out the child in me. If you want to experience extreme gingerbread enchantment vicariously, check out the National Gingerbread House Competition, held every year at the Grove Park Inn in Asheville, North Carolina.

I woke up today thinking this would be the last year for our gingerbread-cake tradition (at least until my children produce children of their own). Even Kat wasn't harboring the usual enthusiasm when I liberated the candy from the bags. Lizzie, presumably too old and sophisticated for gingerbread-house decorating, had planned a parallel event. She was going to host an art installation in her garret bedroom that involved a Jello fish.

I was enjoying every second of this year's festivities. The creative choices children make when candy is involved are fascinating. As with every previous year, all of the houses reflected the personality of their "architects." Lizzie and her friends even deigned to descend from their attic art-installation to ooh and aah and even help.

Just as the finishing touches were being added to the houses—and I was taking photos—the phone rang. Calling was the woman who recently bought the cottage where we have spent every summer vacation for the past twenty years. She wanted to tell me that they had decided to no longer rent out the place. She kept explaining and stumbling along, trying to make it sound not so bad, but I was no longer listening.

This was the end—*finito*—of a sacred family tradition. For twenty summers we had loaded up the sedan or the station wagon or the mini-van (the vehicle size increasing with the age of the children) with clothes, beach towels, toys, and water devices and driven the nine hours north to what I consider the best beach in the world, on the shores of Michigan's Grand Traverse Bay. For two weeks we turned our backs on the world and our faces to the sun. A steady stream of family and friends visited over the years, but mostly it was just us and our time to be a family. The days melted into one another as we repeated the strenuous task of stumbling the twenty yards from the cottage to the private beach.

Every morning we woke up later than the day before because we had stayed up later the night before playing games by firelight and lying on the beach staring at the stars. In northern Michigan the stars are made more brilliant by the absolute darkness of the big water and the pine forest that banks the beach. The day's entertainment included beach badminton and Frisbee, kayaking, sandcastle building, and beach walks. By the end of our annual two weeks, our skins were darker and our thoughts lighter.

Tonight I knew this was all in the past. One phone call and this gem of a cottage was no longer ours. While not exactly a tragedy, it was the end of my family's most revered tradition. What now?

I helped the kids wrap up their candy-studded dream houses to take home, feeling a bit less festive than I had a mere five minutes previously. I nodded my head when each one thanked me—again—for taking the time to do this *every* year. I didn't tell them that this was likely the last gingerbread-house party. I also didn't tell these kids, many of whom had been to visit us at the cottage, that we had just lost our favorite place, our touchstone on the beach. I was the only one aware that two of our sacred family traditions had been trashed in a single hour.

Months passed before I could ask, "What now?" I waited until after the holidays to tell my daughters. Kat cried and raged ("Why do they have the right to do this?") but Lizzie just sighed. I heard myself telling them we would find a new cottage—a better one. They knew, and I knew, this was impossible but we had to try, right?

And so I must echo Mother Theresa, who said, "What you spend years building, someone could destroy overnight. *Build anyway.*" While I doubt she was referring to gingerbread houses, the sentiment is an important one. When we started both of our family traditions, I had no idea how long they would last. But I kept them going one year at a time. All of the houses built of sand in July and the castles built of gingerbread in December may be gone, but they live on in my memories and those of my daughters. And, besides, we can always start new traditions to take the place of the old ones.

Gingery Good Ginger Cake

We don't eat the gingerbread houses we make. The secret truth is that gingerbread sturdy enough to make into houses is not very tasty. In the early years I'd notice that little pieces of the house trimmings disappeared as Christmas approached, and by Christmas Day the houses looked as if a tornado had hit them.

This year I made a gingerbread cake to eat the night before the party. I used what was left to make the gingerbread trifle that follows. Both the cake and the trifle were excellent and soon gobbled up. The trifle was consumed in the attic by Lizzie and her friends, who were home from college for the holidays.

This is Lynn Rossetto Kasper's recipe modified from the Splendid Table Web site.

Preheat oven to 350° F.
Butter and flour an 8" pan.

Cake

2 cups, less 2 tablespoons, unbleached all-purpose flour
1 teaspoon baking soda
½ teaspoon salt
1 tablespoon ground ginger
¾ teaspoon ground cinnamon
¼ teaspoon ground cloves
½ cup finely chopped crystallized ginger (optional)
⅛ teaspoon freshly ground black pepper
6 tablespoons melted butter
¾ cup dark molasses
¾ cup very hot water (190° F)
⅓ cup dark brown sugar
1 large egg

1. Combine flour, baking soda, salt, and spices in a bowl. Whisk to mix.

2. In a large mixing bowl combine the rest of the ingredients, minus the egg, and beat until frothy.

3. Add the egg and beat briefly, and then quickly add in the dry ingredients.

4. Stir in crystallized ginger and only until well blended.

5. Pour into pan. Bake 35–40 minutes, or until a tester inserted in center of cake comes out clean. Place on a rack and cool in the pan for a moist cake. For a drier consistency, cool 10 minutes, then turn out of pan.

6. Serve warm with fresh, real whipped cream that has been slightly sweetened with sugar and a splash of vanilla. Also great with ice cream.

This cake keeps 5–7 days, wrapped, at room temperature and freezes beautifully for up to 3 months.

Gingerbread Trifle

(A great way to use leftover gingerbread)

No baking is required if you have leftover gingerbread.

½ recipe of gingerbread (above)
1 package cook-and-serve vanilla pudding mix
2 cups milk (for the pudding)
A 30-ounce can pumpkin pie filling
½ cup packed brown sugar
⅓ teaspoon ground cardamom or cinnamon
1 pint whipped cream (or a 12-ounce container of frozen whipped topping)
½ cup crushed gingersnaps (optional)

1. Prepare and bake gingerbread cake (if you are not using leftovers).

2. Prepare the pudding according to directions on the package and set aside to cool.

3. Set beaters, small bowl of electric mixer, and whipping cream into the freezer for 10 minutes.

4. Whip cream until it holds soft peaks when you slowly lift beaters.

5. Stir pumpkin, sugar, and cardamom (or cinnamon) into the cooled pudding.

6. Crumble ½ of available gingerbread (approximately ¼ of the above full recipe) into the bottom of a large glass bowl (a punch bowl will work).

7. Pour ½ of the pudding mixture over the gingerbread and then a layer of whipped cream or whipped topping.

8. Repeat the layers until all ingredients are used, ending with whipped topping.

9. Sprinkle the top with crushed gingersnaps.

10. Refrigerate at least 2 hours or overnight.

Winter

Silent Night

"If there must be trouble, let it be in my day, that my child may have peace." —Thomas Paine

Cake Day falls on Christmas Eve this year. We will be up early that morning getting ready to make the trip north to my in-laws. Perhaps a coffee cake for breakfast? Or maybe a cake that travels well to munch on during the four-hour trip? Or a cake that signifies Christmas Eve? I have my fruitcake bundled in brandy-soaked cloth ready to share with all fruitcake lovers, but what to make for Christmas Eve?

In his excellent book *Silent Night: The Story of the World War I Christmas Truce*, Stanley Weintraub details the poignant cease fire that occurred during the Christmas season in 1914 on the battlefields of Flanders, France. The Germans had been in a fierce battle with the British and French, and both sides were dug-in and safe in muddy, man-made trenches six to eight feet deep that seemed to stretch forever.

Several days before Christmas, according to Weintraub, "Signboards arose up and down the trenches in a variety of shapes. They were usually in English or—from the Germans—in fractured English. Rightly, the Germans assumed that the other side could not read traditional gothic lettering and that few English understood spoken German. 'YOU NO FIGHT, WE NO F`IGHT' was the most frequently employed German message. Some British units improvised 'MERRY CHRISTMAS' banners and waited for a response. More placards on both sides popped up." Soldiers from a German regiment lobbed a carefully packaged chocolate cake across no-man's land into the British trenches. A message was attached asking whether holding a one-hour cease fire that evening might be possible, so that the troops could celebrate their captain's birthday.

What followed was a miracle of the Christmas kind: a spontaneous truce. Soldiers left their trenches, meeting in the middle to shake hands. The first order of business was to bury the dead, who had been unreachable. This was followed by Christmas carol contests and soccer games, the soldiers exchanging rifles for soccer balls on the same fields which only a few days before had displayed the carnage of war. Next they exchanged gifts: cognac, postcards, newspapers, tobacco, and the lobbed chocolate cake. The book is a reminder that hope and peace live in the hearts of all people, regardless of nationality. I am sure many discussions of peace have occurred over cake accompanied by tea or coffee.

It didn't last forever. In fact, some of the generals didn't like it at all and commanded their troops to resume shooting at each other. After all, it was wartime. Eventually soldiers did resume shooting at one other. But in many instances, war only resumed after a few days of wasting rounds of ammunition shooting at stars in the sky instead of at soldiers in the opposing army across the field. A small peace existed for a brief, precious time. Something about Christmas changes people. It happened over 2000 years ago in a little town called Bethlehem. It's been happening over and over again down through the years.

This week, Lord willing, it will happen again in the deserts of Iraq.

Old-Fashioned Chocolate Loaf Cake

We chose this for our Christmas Eve cake. I searched the Internet for any reference to the chocolate cake the German baker might have tossed across the trenches. I then asked Lizzie what kind of cake would make sense. She decided it had to have been a loaf cake. A loaf cake is dense, she said, and shaped somewhat like a football and therefore not likely to fall apart when lobbed across a field.

This recipe comes from *Maida Heatter's Book of Great Chocolate Desserts*. Later Kat pronounced this her "fave cake" of the year.

According to Heatter, "This is a plain, fine-grained cake similar to a pound cake. It slices beautifully, keeps well if wrapped airtight, and makes a great gift. Serve it with tea or coffee, with cold milk, or as a dessert with ice cream and hot fudge sauce. It is best to let it stand overnight before slicing." This is one cake that is much better the next day.

Preheat oven to 300° F and adjust rack one third up from the bottom of the oven. Butter an 8-cup loaf pan Dust with dry bread crumbs; invert and tap to shake out excess (or line the pan with buttered foil, butter side up).

Cake

2 cups sifted all-purpose flour
½ teaspoon baking powder
½ teaspoon salt
2 ounces (2 squares) unsweetened chocolate
4 ounces semisweet chocolate (chips will do)
½ pound (2 sticks) room-temperature unsalted butter
2 teaspoons vanilla
1 cup sugar and ¼ cup sugar
5 eggs, separated

1. In a medium mixing bowl, combine the dry ingredients and mix on low speed for 30 seconds; set aside.

2. Place both chocolates in the top of a small double boiler over hot water on medium heat. Stir occasionally until the chocolate is melted and smooth, and then remove the top of the double boiler and set aside to cool slightly.

3. Cream the butter in the large bowl of the mixer. Add the vanilla and 1 cup of the sugar and beat about 5 minutes. Add the egg yolks all at once and beat well, scraping the bowl with a spatula. Add the chocolate and beat until blended. On low speed, gradually add the sifted dry ingredients and beat, scraping down the bowl with a spatula, only until they are smoothly incorporated.

4. In the small bowl of the mixer (with clean beaters)

beat the egg whites on medium high speed until the whites hold a soft shape. Gradually add the reserved ¼ cup of sugar, and continue to beat until the whites hold a firm shape but are not dry.

5. With a wooden spoon or spatula, fold ⅓ of the egg whites into the chocolate mixture (make sure a bit of white shows); fold in another ⅓ in the same way; finally, add in the last ⅓, folding until no white remains.

6. Turn the mixture into the prepared pan and smooth the top.

7. Bake until a cake tester inserted into the center of the cake comes out clean (about 1 hour and 30 minutes).

8. Let the cake cool in the pan for about 15 minutes, and then very gently invert the cake onto a rack and remove the pan. With your hands, carefully turn the cake right-side up and let it cool on the rack. Cover with a clean towel to make the top soft.

9. Wrap the cake in plastic wrap, and let it stand at room temperature (preferably overnight) before serving. Slice in thin slices with a long, sharp knife, using a sawing motion or keep it whole, and throw it to the troops.

Hidden Jewels

"A compromise is the art of dividing a cake in such a way that everyone believes he has the biggest piece."
—Ludwig Erhard, German politician

Christmas was full of family. Everyone got what their hearts desired and we were touched by the time we spent with every person in our small but close-knit family. We added 538 miles to the odometer of our new van on the same odyssey we've made annually for the past twenty years. We drive from our home in Dayton north to my in-laws' huge house on the bluffs of Lake Erie near Cleveland and then on to my sister's large house in the cornfields ninety miles to the west, and finally home again. A golden triangle.

Christmas night brought a rematch of last year's three-hour-long marathon Trivial Pursuit game. Just as last year, the "kids" (ages twelve to twenty-five) beat the "adults" (all over age forty) at the DVD version of Trivial Pursuit. After leading almost the entire time, the adults lost on the question, "Where does SpongeBob live?" We were sure it was "A starfish, no, a bucket, no, wait, wait, a TV?" The kids were beside themselves—how could we not know it was a "pineapple under the sea"? In our defense, we adults were playing the version of the game that covers only the last twenty years, the years we spent raising kids and working. We didn't have time to take an interest in a sponge (with square pants) that lives in a pineapple. Next year we will play the original version that has questions about history and books rather than questions about sponges and "The Simpsons."

And I am pleased to report that the fruitcake made all but the last 140 miles of the trip. My sister-in-law Marty pronounced it fabulous and said it was the closest anyone had come to her mother's recipe. A stunning success for me—I would have taken a victory lap if I hadn't been too full to move. I then wrapped the remainder of the cake and took it to my sister's house, where it joined an already crowded field of cookies and was subjected to some curious pokings and questions. When my sister offered it to one of my niece's friends, she said, "Fruitcake? Wow, what a cliché." After two days of neglect (unless you count me tearing off bits of nuts and citron), I threw the remaining quarter of the cake into the trash. And so it will end up in a landfill where most jokes about fruitcake claim it belongs. Still, everyone who loves fruitcake did pronounce it excellent (I shamelessly shopped it at work and at our gingerbread-house party in search of compliments, under the guise of research).

As I write this, the house is a mess and a new year is about to descend. It is time to get our house in order, both literally and figuratively. I take the coming of the new year quite seriously. I don't make a lot of resolutions—except to resolve to not make silly ones—but I do pause to reflect on the previous year and give thanks for all the bounty we have received. I also look ahead to the new year and give thanks in advance, rededicating myself to living fully and with gratitude. To hedge my bets, I also make sure everyone has a bite of sauerkraut for good luck. I toyed with the idea of making a sauerkraut cake but that sounded worse than eating it straight.

I believe that how someone spends New Year's Day is a predictor of the year to come. If you spend the day squandering money, then the year will be one in which money will flow away from you. If you spend the day passively watching football, you will spend the year observing the action instead of taking part in the game. As for me, I wish for peace and quiet and time to dream in the upcoming year. In that spirit, today I set aside time to take a nap. I had been about to start this week's cake, when Wayne decided to install his new under-the-counter radio/CD player, a Christmas present from me. We had to remove everything from the counters of our very small kitchen, rendering cake-making impossible. Hence, my nap. (I also believe that all bickering should be avoided on the first day of the new year and the nap rescued me from violating this belief.)

Since we do not have a tradition of eating cake on New Year's Day, I decided to check out what other cultures do on this day. Many, I discovered, do have a special New Year's Day cake tradition. The Jewish New Year, Rosh Hashanah, includes honey cake, with the honey signifying a wish for a sweet new year. The Irish and Scottish New Year's celebration also involves cake, but my favorite is the Greek tradition. In Greece, January 1 is both the first day of the new year and St. Basil's Day. St. Basil, one of the forefathers of the Greek Orthodox Church, was thought to have died on this date. He was known for his kindness and generosity to the poor.

According to one legend, St. Basil tried to return money to people who began arguing about who was owed what. He solved the problem by asking a woman to bake a large cake and place the coins inside of it. When he sliced the cake, the money found its way back to its rightful owners. St. Basil is also purported to have visited children on New Year's night, leaving gifts in their shoes. On St. Basil's Day the Greek people visit their friends and relatives to exchange gifts and celebrate with music and a feast of food and drink. Many special dishes are prepared for the New Year's feast but the most important is a cake called Vassilopitta, or St. Basil's Cake, which contains a silver or gold coin that has been baked inside of it. The person who finds the coin in their piece of cake will be lucky throughout the next year.

In my extended family, coins and trinkets found their way into birthday cakes. For every family member's birthday, my German grandmother would bake an angel food cake and insert a variety of trinkets before frosting it with chocolate icing. The trinkets included a quarter, a penny, a thimble, and a ring. The lucky person who got the quarter could expect to attract wealth in the following year and the person who got the penny was going to have to count their pennies that year. My grandmother, a 1919 graduate of the School of Commerce at the University of Chicago, was always trying to teach us the value of money. The thimble meant a year of hard work to follow (she was also an alumnus of the Great Depression and believed in hard work as the path to salvation—and wealth). The person who got the ring could expect to marry in the next year. By some miracle the ring usually went to my aunt, who my grandmother was always hoping would marry. My aunt, despite her repeated success at unearthing the ring, remains unmarried at age eighty-five. I did notice a few spry gentlemen eyeing her at her retirement home when I took her back after Christmas.

I made this cake in tribute to St. Basil's dedication to the poor and in honor of New Year's, when we should all count our blessings. By some minor miracle both of my daughters got the quarter. It was actually in Kat's piece, which was bigger than Lizzie's, who took notice immediately and reached over to cut off a slice from her sister's and found the quarter. An argument ensued until I reminded them that arguing on New Year's Day meant a year ahead of arguing. To my surprise, they changed their tune and agreed to share in the good fortune.

Vasilopita (St. Basil's New Year's Cake)

This is a traditional Greek New Year's cake that celebrates the life of St. Basil. Quick and delicious any time of the year, this cake comes in many, many versions. All involved almonds and citrus (either lemon or oranges), or both. I picked this version because I had only lemons and I wasn't about to go shopping on New Year's Day. I was later told by one of Kat's friends that this cake was very similar to her Greek grandmother's cake.

Preheat oven to 350° F and butter a 10" round cake pan.

Cake

1 cup room-temperature unsalted butter
2 cups sugar (plus 2 tablespoons for sprinkling on the top after baking)
3 cups flour
6 eggs
2 teaspoons baking powder
1 cup warm milk
½ teaspoon baking soda
1 tablespoon brandy
1 tablespoon lemon zest
1 teaspoon orange extract (or 1 tablespoon orange zest)
¼ cup blanched slivered almonds

Clean silver or gold coin wrapped in aluminum foil (a quarter works well)

1. In the medium bowl of an electric mixer, on medium speed, cream butter and 2 cups of sugar until light in color and fluffy—at least 5 minutes.

2. Stir in the flour and mix on low speed until the batter resembles coarse breadcrumbs.

3. Add the eggs, one at a time, mixing well after each one. Then beat in flavourings (lemon zest, orange and brandy).

4. In a small bowl, combine the baking powder and milk, and then add to the cake batter and mix well.

5. Pour the cake batter into the prepared pan, and insert the foil-wrapped coin.

6. Bake for 20 minutes.

7. Remove the cake from the oven, sprinkle the nuts and 2 tablespoons of sugar over the cake, and then return it to the oven and bake for another 20 to 30 minutes until the cake springs back to the touch.

8. Allow cake to cool on a rack for 10 minutes, invert onto a plate, and then invert again so that the nuts and sugar topping are right-side up.

9. Ideally the cake should be served warm. Each person gets a slice of the cake, starting with the most senior person.

Epiphany

Epiph-a-ny *n* **1** *cap*: January 6 observed as a church festival in commemoration of the coming of the Magi as the first manifestation of Christ to the Gentiles or in the Eastern Church in commemoration of baptism of Christ **2**: an appearance or manifestation esp. of a divine being. **3a** (1): an usu. sudden manifestation or perception of the essential nature or meaning of something (2): an intuitive grasp of reality through something (as an event) usu. simple and striking **b**: a literary representation of an epiphany.

—*Webster's New Collegiate Dictionary*, 1980

My epiphany this week was to ignore the post-holiday blues (and mess) and simply bake a cake. In a week when nothing much is happening, or you are trying to avoid what is happening, a cake is a great and comforting diversion. Clinging to culinary diversions is one of the ways I make it through Ohio winters.

This cake, which is really more of a pastry, beat out lots of contenders in my hunt for an epiphany cake. The reason is simple—all the others had raisins in them, while this one had rum and almonds. But there is not enough rum to result in a sudden manifestation of a divine being as spelled out in definition number two above. Pity.

Galette des Rois (King's Epiphany Cake)

In France Epiphany cake is sold in the bakeries for all twelve days of Christmas, and it is the traditional dessert for Epiphany. It is typically topped with a golden paper crown, and little charms, a Jesus figurine or a bean, are baked into the cake. The person who gets the piece of cake with the bean gets to wear the crown and is named King for the Day. Kat got the crown (it was rigged).

Preheat oven to 375° F.
Butter a 10" springform pan.

Cake

14 ounces frozen puff pastry (Dufour Classic Puff Pastry is spectacular and can be found in the freezer section of the better-stocked grocery stores; will need 3–4 hours to defrost).

½ cup (1 stick) room-temperature unsalted butter softened to room temperature

½ cup plus 2 tablespoons sugar
3 eggs
3 tablespoons rum or amaretto
½ cup freshly ground almonds

1. Thaw frozen puff pastry (3–4 hours in the refrigerator).

2. Divide thawed pastry in half. Roll each half into a round about 11 inches in diameter. Let rest while you make the filling.

Note: The pastry must be at room temperature before filling.

3. In the large bowl of an electric mixer, cream butter and sugar on medium-high speed, until light in color and fluffy (at least 5 minutes).

4. Beat in 2 of the eggs, the rum or amaretto, and the ground almonds.

5. Work until smooth.

6. Place one of the pastry rounds into the bottom of the buttered springform pan.

7. Spoon the paste onto the pastry, leaving a 2-inch margin.

8. Hide the baby Jesus figurine or bean in the filling.

9. Beat the remaining egg with a little water and paint the pastry margin.

10. Place the second pastry round on top and gently press edges together.

11. Use a sharp knife to make a lattice or star-shaped pattern on the pastry surface, but do not cut all the way through.

12. Pinch the edges prettily together.

13. Paint the top with the egg wash.

14. Bake for 30–40 minutes, until the pastry is crisp and brown. Transfer to a rack to cool.

15. Decorate by placing a golden paper crown on top.

16. Whoever gets the bean or figurine is the King or Queen of the feast and gets to wear the gold crown.

Wolf Moons and Mink Coats

"The timber wolves will be our friends. We'll stay up late and howl at the moon, till nighttime ends, before going on the prowl."
—Hobbes the Tiger, from *Calvin and Hobbes*, by Bill Watterson

Tonight I feel like howling at the moon, which hangs full and bright in the winter sky. The holidays are gone, gone, gone. Lizzie is back to her studies at Pitt, Kat to the waning days of elementary school, and me to the grind of the winter semester with no vacation in sight. I am feeling heavy with pounds and heavy with envy of those who live in a warmer clime or don't work for a living. It feels like there is a wolf at the door, or maybe a wolf within.

But snow, that white powder of hope, is covering the frozen ground, and few things are prettier than fresh snow under a full moon. January's full moon is known as the *Wolf Moon*, according to the *Farmer's Almanac*. Amid the cold and deep snows of midwinter, the wolf packs howled hungrily outside Indian villages. It is sometimes referred to as the *Old Moon*, or the *Moon After Yule*, and some called it the *Full Snow Moon*. I'm going with the *Wolf Moon*. It is said that wolves howl at the moon, but it is a myth. Wolves are simply more active at night and more visible in the light of a full moon. Wolves howl for many reasons: to claim their territory, to summon their pack for a hunt, to draw a mate, or to announce a birth. Or maybe because they have the post-holiday blues?

I think I know how my foremothers survived the *Wolf Moon* and long winters of the north country. Like my grandmother, they wore mink. As she swept into our house with the cold snowy air and picked me up in her arms, I'd press my face against the soft mink fur. The smell of leather and her lilies-of-the-valley perfume melded until it became my grandmother's smell. I'd beg to wear the coat and she would always indulge me, a girl who loved luxury from the get-go. I'd parade around, sweeping the coat past the adults, swiveling as I imagined mink-draped models would do in some exotic place like New York City. The lining was heavy and silky and felt so good against my skin. My mother, who had worked at Detroit's J. L. Hudson Company, bought my grandmother the coat as a sixtieth birthday gift. Daughters, are you listening?

A childhood friend's grandfather was a retired furrier who continued to make and repair fur coats. On a table in my friend's basement recreation room, where we played while her grandfather worked, pelts were laid out and pinned in various stages of becoming a coat. The mystery of how animal pelts became clothing to adorn our furless fragile human bodies was revealed to me in that basement. My friend's grandfather never spoke while sewing the skins together. As his sausagelike fingers felt and stitched the pelts, I'd wonder if he meditated on the lives of the animals that gave up their skins for human vanity. Was he curious about where they had roamed and what conditions gave rise to their thick and lustrous coats? Did he think about their deaths? Did he wonder about the person who had skinned and tanned their pelts? Had he ever made a coat for a woman he loved or lusted for, taking more care than usual or perhaps stitching in a secret message? Or perhaps he performed his craft while meditating on the stitching and not on the woman who would find comfort in the warmth of the coat. I wish I knew.

Coming of age in the 1970s, I eschewed fur of all kinds, even telling my grandmother, "Hey, Grandma, you really shouldn't be wearing mink—don't you know it's cruel?" My grandmother kept wearing her mink coat defiantly; now it was not only a shield against the cold winters but her granddaughter's frigid judgment. Today my own daughters are against wearing fur. But my grandmother belonged to the generation that survived the Great Depression and Hitler. Having dealt with such terrors, perhaps the politics of wearing fur seemed trivial to her.

When I visited the Pasteur Institute in Paris in 2003 I learned that Pasteur, the patron saint of microbiology, was his generation's version of a rock star. This man not only had proven that microbes cause disease but he saved minks in Russia from rabies. A stuffed mink in a glass box sat in his living room, a gift of gratitude from the Russian government. Pasteur saved humans from rabies as well, but I wonder if the Russian government valued that as much as his efforts on behalf of their mink population.

I don't know what happened to my grandmother's coat, but I sure wish I had it now. The cold winds of middle age have suddenly sparked in me the desire to wear fur. I want the protection it provides against the cold, against the ravages of time. I want its beauty next to my aging skin. I wouldn't save it for parties and holidays like my grandmother did. I'd wear it to the grocery store and out to walk my dog (who might even be envious, although her coat is more stunning). I would turn the thermostat down low and wear it around the house, invite my husband inside, and fall asleep under its warm weight. I would travel to my favorite beach—where I only go in summer—to feel the winds of winter and defy them with my coat, my shield. And each time I slipped my arms into the satiny sleeves I would give thanks to the animals that made the coat, their immortalized skins forever young and beautiful.

I check eBay, where I find mega bays of mink coats. One, listed as vintage, reminds me of my grandmother's. No one has bid on it yet and three days and twenty-four minutes are left on the clock. Dare I buy it and risk the judgment of my darling daughters? It is snowy and cold today and the dog needs to be walked. Well, I have time to decide.

Postscript: I posted this on my blog and several weeks later received a mink cape in the mail. No lie. A child-

hood friend who follows my blog relayed it to her 75 year-young neighbor, Nancy, who graciously gave me her mink. A mink arriving in the mail is not an everyday occurrence and cause for great celebration. It was a snowy day so I donned the cape and set out in the snow with my dog for a walk in the moonlight.

Mink Coat Chocolate Cake

I make this cake in honor of my grandmother, a member of the mink-without-guilt generation; when a tyrant like Hitler is on the loose, wearing the pelts of small animals pales by comparison.

As soon as I had spread the word about my cake book, everyone started offering up family favorites. This is from my masseuse Lauren's family and, of course, there is a story. Her great-grandmother always made this cake for Lauren's grandfather, who loved it. When his mother died, he offered a mink coat to any woman who could make it as well as she had. He had many takers but no mink coats were given out, which sounded like a cake racket to me. I asked Lauren if she thought this might be true. She told me that her grandfather was definitely one to run a cake scam.

Preheat oven to 350° F.
Butter and flour a 9" round cake pan.

Cake

1 cup sugar
1 ½ cups all-purpose white flour
½ cup sour whole milk (you can make this by adding 1 teaspoon of vinegar to the milk)
½ cup hot water
½ cup oil
1 egg
Pinch of salt
1 teaspoon vanilla
1 teaspoon soda
3 tablespoons cocoa

1. Mix all ingredients in order listed.

2. Spread into the prepared pan and bake for 30 minutes or until a toothpick inserted in the center comes out clean.

3. Leave to cool in the pan on a wire rack.

4. When cool, frost with caramel icing.

Caramel Icing

½ cup (1 stick) unsalted butter
1 cup brown sugar
¼ cup warm milk
3 to 3 ½ cups sifted confectioners' sugar

1. Melt butter in a small saucepan on medium-low heat.

2. Add the brown sugar. Increase heat to medium-high and bring to a boil, stirring for 1 minute until slightly thickened.

3. Remove from stove.

4. Cool slightly and then add milk and beat until smooth.

5. Add 3 cups of sifted confectioners' sugar and beat again until smooth.

6. Cool completely before spreading on cake.

Steel Magnolias

"Time marches on, and sooner or later you realize it is marchin' across your face." —Truvy (in the movie *Steel Magnolias*)

This week my hair stylist, Jill, died suddenly from a massive heart attack. Jill was forty-eight, only six years older than she admitted to. In any case, she was way too young to die.

When we moved to this city twelve years ago, some of my friends moaned in horror—you will have to find all new doctors. To which I replied, "Even worse, I've got to find a new stylist." Every one of them shuddered. I don't know a woman past college age who does not stress about her tresses and fear losing her stylist. The relationship between a woman and her stylist is special—something mystical happens when we put our "crowning glory" into the hands of a stylist. We typically let our hair down, in both the literal and the virtual senses. It is a relief to shed the split odds and ends of our hair and our lives. A friend of mine recalls asking her stylist if women canceled their appointments on 9/11 and the day after. The stylist assured her that the salon was completely full, so strong is that bond, so necessary, apparently, for our well-being.

The three-way relationship between a woman, her hair, and her stylist is best described in *Steel Magnolias*. The story revolves around Truvy's Beauty Parlor in the Chiquapin Parish of modern-day Louisiana and a close-knit circle of women dealing with family issues, death, and bad-hair days. Their lives are revealed during their weekly appointments at Truvy's. In fact, in the stage version *all* the action takes place at Truvy's. The play celebrates strength and grace in the face of tragedy and what it means to be a strong but gentle woman, a Steel Magnolia.

Jill was a Steel Magnolia. Her life was always on the brink of disaster, yet she consistently managed to laugh and find something true to believe in. I attend the memorial service with a colleague from work who had introduced me to Jill. Her daughters and her grandson, the lights of her life, looked sad in that "too deep for tears" way. I don't know how they will cope without Jill, the person who managed to take care of them all.

This week's cake is in honor of Jill. Oatmeal is touted as being good for the heart, but I think it is just as good for the soul. It cannot be shaped into an armadillo like the cake made famous in the film version of

Steel Magnolias, but it sure is satisfying. Eating it will make you forget time is marchin' across your face.

Martha's Oatmeal Cake

When my father died of a heart attack at age sixty-six, I didn't eat butter or meat for months. Oatmeal and fruit dominated my diet during that time. So, when Jill died suddenly this week of a massive heart attack, I felt the need to eat oatmeal. Comfort in a cake.

This recipe comes from my sister-in-law, Marty, who first introduced it to us on a hot September day in Washington, D.C. This cake is wonderful served warm with vanilla ice cream and for breakfast with a cup of steaming hot tea, and it is much better to eat it in deep winter than on a sweltering September day.

Preheat oven to 350° F.
Butter an 8" square pan.

Cake

½ cup (1 stick) room-temperature unsalted butter
1 ½ cups boiling water
1 cup oatmeal (not instant)

Mix butter, boiling water, and oatmeal and set aside for 20 minutes.

Add:
1 cup granulated sugar
1 cup brown sugar
2 eggs, 1 at a time, beating well after each addition

Add:
1 ⅓ cups flour
1 teaspoon each cinnamon, baking soda, and vanilla

Pour into greased pan and bake for 35–40 minutes.

Prepare topping while the cake is baking:

Topping

6 tablespoons butter
½ cup brown sugar
1 cup chopped pecans
¼ cup coconut
½ teaspoon vanilla

Combine all ingredients and heat to boiling in small saucepan. Spread on slightly cooled cake. Brown under broiler, watching constantly.*

*I was busy talking to my guests while I was doing this and almost burned the top beyond recognition—but I was able to scrape off the burned parts and everyone agreed it was the perfect comfort cake for a midwinter's night.

A Midwinter Night's Dream

"We grow great by dreams. All big men are dreamers. They see things in the soft haze of a spring day or in the red fire of a long winter's evening. Some of us let these great dreams die, but others nourish and protect them."
—Woodrow Wilson

Midwinter lacks the romance of midsummer. Proof of this is that Shakespeare did not write a play called *A Midwinter Night's Dream*. But it is definitely a time for dreaming: of summer and long days, warm nights, and tomatoes. Still, we have friends who are putting romance into this midwinter by getting married. The wedding—her second, his first—started out life as a big country-club affair. But the couple quickly decided they were too middle-aged and tired for all that hoopla and cleverly switched to one of those location weddings that is all the rage (sorry I missed out on that trend myself). So following a simple ceremony at city hall, they are headed to Cabos San Lucas for another ceremony on the beach with any family and friends who wish to join them. Since we are unable to make the beach ceremony, we invited them for a pre-wedding dinner party complete with cake. Kat attended the ceremony at city hall but we did not.

Dinner was festive and fueled by wine and conversation. Our friends waxed poetic about Cabos, love, and the new family they were creating. Chris, the groom-to-be, had presented his bride-to-be Maureen's two daughters with rings when he popped the question. Chris, with no children of his own, was about to become the father of two pre-teen girls. I thought, "God bless him and pass the Advil."

They were touched by the small but credible wedding cake I had concocted in my small but credible kitchen. The younger daughter politely refused a piece of cake: "Too full," she said. But her mother reminded her that "When someone offers you a homemade sweet, it is bad luck to not take at least one bite." A good rule. Why offend someone who has spent the day in the kitchen?

The weather was cold and snowy, and they walked out into the night a family in the making, with sweet dreams in their heads. I felt light and filled with hope, believing that as long as people choose to create new families, where others have fallen, we will survive as a society.

Princess Daisy Cake

I selected this as the wedding cake because I liked its name and the cookbook where I found it. *Hollyhocks and Radishes* by Bonnie Stewart Mickelson, touts it as a good cake for weddings and christenings. It is as light and elegant as the author claimed and since we were celebrating our friends' upcoming nuptials, it was the perfect choice.

Preheat oven to 350° F. Depending on how thick you want your layers to be, butter two or three 8" cake pans, line the bottoms with wax paper cut to fit and butter the wax paper.

Cake

1½ cups sugar
½ cup (1 stick) room-temperature unsalted butter
1 teaspoon vanilla
¼ teaspoon lemon extract
2 ½ cups sifted cake flour
2 ½ teaspoons baking powder
1 cup whole milk
4 egg whites (reserve 2 yolks for the filling)
¾ teaspoon salt

1. In the large bowl of an electric mixer, cream together sugar and butter until light in color and fluffy (at least 5 minutes).

2. Beat in vanilla and lemon extract.

3. In the small bowl of an electric mixer, combine sifted flour and baking powder. Mix on low for 30 seconds.

4. Add ⅓ of the flour mixture to the butter and sugar, and mix on low just until blended. Next add half of the milk, again mixing just until blended. Repeat, ending with the flour (it is important to blend thoroughly but to not over beat).

5. In a clean mixing bowl, using clean beaters, beat the egg whites with salt until stiff but not dry.

6. Gently fold egg whites into the batter.

7. Pour batter into prepared pans.

8. Bake 20 to 25 minutes, or just until cakes begin to loosen from the edges of the pans.

9. Cool completely on racks.

Lemon Filling (makes enough for 2 or 3 layers)
¾ cup sugar
2 tablespoons cornstarch
⅛ teaspoon salt
¾ cup water
2 egg yolks, slightly beaten
3 to 4 tablespoons fresh lemon juice
1 tablespoon butter
1 teaspoon grated lemon rind

1. In a small saucepan, combine sugar, cornstarch and salt.

2. With a whisk, stir in water, egg yolks, and lemon juice until smooth.

3. Cook over medium heat until thickened, stirring constantly.

4. Remove from heat, and stir in butter and lemon rind.

5. Refrigerate until cool (about 30 minutes).

Note: Double the recipe for a 4-tiered cake.

Fluffy White Icing (makes enough for 2 or 3 layers)

This type of frosting is referred to as "Italian meringue" (pronounced mair-en-goo by Kat when she was learning to read). It is soft and easy to swirl into any pattern you like—and it doesn't wilt like whipped cream. This frosting is very versatile and is suitable for many different types of cakes.

1 cup sugar
⅓ teaspoon cream of tartar
⅓ cup water
1 tablespoon lemon juice
2 large egg whites
1 teaspoon vanilla
¼ teaspoon lemon extract (optional)

1. In a saucepan, combine sugar, cream of tartar, water, and lemon juice.

2. Bring to a boil, without stirring, and cook until it reaches the thread stage (242° F). Experts on Italian Meringue insist reaching this exact temperature is the key to this icing.

3. Meanwhile, beat the egg whites until stiff but not dry. When the syrup is ready, pour steadily, in a thin stream, into egg whites, beating constantly. Add vanilla and lemon extract, and continue beating until mixture reaches spreading consistency.

Cake Assembly

1. Place a cake layer on cake plate or stand.

2. Spread ⅓ of the lemon filling on top of the layer, repeat for the remaining layers.

3. Ice the entire cake with the Fluffy White Icing.

My Momma Said, "Listen to the Groundhog"

"If a groundhog sees its shadow it means there will be six more weeks of winter, but if a groundhog rolls around on the ground, it means you don't bake me nearly as many cakes as you should; and if a groundhog takes three steps forward, it means you're a non-cake-baking jerk." —C. Monks, from his blog "utter wonder the ideal thoughts of C. Monks"

Today is Groundhog Day. My mother's roommate at the University of Wisconsin, Boomer T. Blumberg, was crazy about this holiday. Boomer and my mother exchanged cards every year on February 2. I don't know why, but my mother thought it was a vastly underrated holiday. Groundhog Day was a big deal at my house—my mother made Jello. One year she even tried to make it in the shape of a groundhog. (My brilliant mother convinced us Jello took all day to make.) I've come to understand that while there was not nearly enough cake in my childhood, there was plenty of whimsy.

This week the Super Bowl is in Detroit and when the groundhog emerged from his den, he did an end-zone dance and dived right back in. I was twelve, the same age as my daughter Kat, the year of the first Super Bowl. I sense some weighty symmetry in this but I cannot quite put my finger on it. Our local paper had a big spread on all things Detroit, including this cake, in honor of the most important game in America (I suspect they were trying to fill up space). Unfortunately, the "home" team was nowhere close to being in the running. The Super Bowl is all about gathering together friends and sharing food. And cake is highly appreciated when serious sports are in play, particularly if your team loses.

I was born in Detroit's Henry Ford Hospital. I think my newborn self was imprinted, somehow, with the stamp of Detroit. Perhaps that is why I lust to own a 1954 blue Ford pick-up truck, even though I am a city dweller and only mildly interested in Country and Western music. My family later moved on to Long Island, then to Kalamazoo, Michigan and we finally ended up in Ohio.

But I remain enamored of Detroit.

My Detroit memories are vivid: baseball games at Tiger Stadium, Motown music, and fireworks over the Detroit River viewed from the roof of a thirty-two-story unfinished building. My civil engineer father was overseeing the construction of this building and I am pretty sure we weren't supposed to be on that roof. But the fireworks were spectacular, appearing close enough to touch.

And I remember the Sanders Chocolate store in downtown Detroit. My mother and my mother's mother lived and worked in downtown Detroit. Sanders was it for them. My grandmother always had a private stash of Sanders' toffee candies in her nightstand drawer at the family's summer home. There were times in the middle of the day in the middle of the summer, when there was nothing happening, that I couldn't keep myself from sneaking into her room and ever so carefully prying open that drawer. I never took more than one at a time, but I am sure she knew what I was doing. After all, I was the kid who at age two was caught shoveling sugar out of the sugar bowl directly into my mouth, while sitting on top of the dining room table.

To most people Detroit is synonymous with the automobile. For me it is synonymous with chocolate cake, Sanders chocolate cake. This was the one cake my mother loved. It had a rich chocolate glaze over raised furrows of delectable buttercream. My mother requested this cake every year on her birthday. Just looking at it made me drool.

Detroit has traveled a bumpy road since I left it behind—violence and corruption have plagued this once proud and productive city. When I tell people I was born in Detroit, the response is predictably negative. That continues to sting, even though I am decades removed and living three hours south in Ohio.

So I made this cake in honor of the city of Detroit: to its past, which is a part of me, and to its future, which I hope is a lot less bumpy. I also make this cake in loving memory of my mother, who would be happy to know that I do take Groundhog Day seriously.

Detroit's Bumpy Road Chocolate Cake

You will find this cake on the Sanders Web site (www.sanderscandy.com) under "Bumpy Cake." It is described this way: "This classic takes its name from the ridges of sweet buttercream hiding under a decadent layer of candymakers fudge frosting." The buttercream ridges are reminiscent of speed bumps—only sweeter. It was not called Bumpy Cake back in the day when my mother was in love with it. I recall it as "marshmallow chocolate layer cake." This cake has been made by Sanders for more than ninety years. On their Web site it is a single-layer cake, but when I was a kid it was made and sold as a double-layer cake. Sanders only sold it by the half cake so customers could see the bumps in cross section. Check out the Web site for a photo.

This recipe appeared in our local paper and is a knock-off attributed to Detroit radio personality Bob Allison.

Preheat oven to 375° F.
Butter a 9" x 13" pan.

Cake

½ cup hot black coffee (or water)

½ cup cocoa powder
½ cup vegetable oil
1 cup buttermilk
1 ½ teaspoons baking soda
½ teaspoon salt
2 teaspoons vanilla extract
2 eggs
2 cups sugar
2 cups all-purpose flour

1. In the large bowl of an electric mixer, combine coffee and cocoa and beat on medium speed for 30 seconds.

2. Add oil, buttermilk, baking soda, salt, vanilla, eggs, and sugar, beating for 30 seconds after each addition.

3. Add flour and beat for 5 minutes; batter will be very bubbly.

4. Pour batter into the prepared pan and bake for 35 to 40 minutes.

5. When cake is cool, place in freezer for at least 30 minutes before assembling it as described below.

Sander's Buttercream Frosting

2 cups (4 sticks) room-temperature unsalted butter
3 cups sifted confectioners' sugar, divided
⅔ cup sweetened condensed milk
2 large egg whites
½ teaspoon salt
½ teaspoon vanilla extract

Pastry bag and tip (or use a clean plastic bag and cut off the tip)

1. Using a very clean bowl and beaters, whip egg whites until stiff, while slowly adding ½ cup of confectioners' sugar; set aside.

2. Using the same beaters, but the large bowl of an electric mixer, cream butter and then add 2 cups of the confectioners' sugar, mixing at low speed to obtain a smooth paste.

3. Turn mixer to medium speed, adding milk slowly, and mix until light and fluffy.

4. Mix egg whites slowly into the butter mixture.

5. Add vanilla and remaining ½ cup of confectioners' sugar (make it a cup of sugar, if a stiffer icing is desired).

Pourable Fudge Frosting

½ cup buttermilk
1 cup sugar
⅓ cup dark corn syrup
⅓ cup cocoa powder
Dash of salt
½ pound (2 sticks) unsalted butter, divided
2 ½ cups confectioners' sugar
1 teaspoon vanilla extract

1. Over medium high heat, combine buttermilk, sugar, corn syrup, cocoa, salt, and half the butter.

2. Bring mixture to a boil; when it reaches the soft-ball state, remove from the heat.

3. Add remaining butter, confectioners' sugar, and vanilla. The frosting will have a "pouring" consistency.

4. Let cool at room temperature.

Cake Assembly

1. Remove cake from the freezer.

2. Shape buttercream into (1 inch) rolls and place on frozen cake, 1 inch apart, across the top of the cake. Alternate method: Fill pastry bag that has a ½" tip with buttercream frosting (or use a clean plastic bag with the corner cut off). Pipe cylinders of icing, at 1" intervals, across the width of the top of the cake.

3. Return to the freezer for at least 15 minutes.

4. Apply cooled fudge frosting to top of cake, covering buttercream rolls completely. Return to freezer for several minutes or more.

5. Return cake to the freezer for at least 15 more minutes.

Nutritional Analysis: Don't ask.

Love Is Nearsighted

"If love is blind, why is lingerie so popular?" —anonymous

Valentine's Day. How many marriage proposals launched, how many foundering love affairs shipwrecked on this day? How many red velvet undies bought by husbands greeted with blank stares and hands reaching for the gift receipt? (Fine chocolates encased in a red velvet box perhaps the better idea?) No one keeps these sorts of statistics, which is probably for the best.

So who was this guy, Saint Valentine? What do we know about the man who launched this lovely or lonely (depending on your point of view) holiday and the multibillion-dollar flower-and-gift industry that now bears his name? One legend contends that Valentine was a priest in third-century Rome. When Emperor Claudius II decided that single men made better soldiers than those with wives and families, he outlawed marriage for young men. Realizing the injustice of the decree, Valentine defied Claudius and continued to secretly perform marriages for young lovers. When Valentine's actions were exposed, Claudius condemned him to death.

Other stories suggest that Valentine may have been killed for attempting to help Christians escape harsh Roman prisons, where they were often beaten and tortured. According to one legend, Valentine actually sent the first valentine greeting himself. The story goes that while he was in prison Valentine fell in love with a young girl, his jailer's daughter, who visited him regularly. Before his death, he wrote her a letter, signing it "From your Valentine." Although the truth behind these legends remains murky, the stories have in common a sympathetic and romantic hero. It's no surprise that by the Middle Ages Valentine was one of the most popular saints in England and France.

For me this holiday is about the cards. I have always loved making Valentine's Day cards. As a kid I was a wizard with paper doilies and red velvet. One of my fondest grade-school memories was decorating the box into which my classmates would secretly place their cards. In third grade I couldn't wait to see the card Alan Kowalski would place in my stunningly decorated box, which that year was created as a lair to snag his card. Alan's desk was directly across the room from mine and all year he had been staring at me. I knew he was in love with me and my nine-year-old heart belonged to him. I couldn't wait to get to school every day to bask in his gaze.

To my horror, I was discovered that year to be terribly nearsighted. Glasses with frosted blue metal frames (to match my eyes) and sparkles in the corners soon adorned my face. I worried that Alan would find my new bespectacled self unappealing and stop looking at me. I was terrified the first time I wore my new glasses to school. All morning I stared down at my desk, afraid to even glance across the room at Alan. After lunch I slowly gathered my courage, raised my head, and looked in his direction. Alan was no longer staring at me! My heart sank as my worst fear was confirmed. I heard buzzing in my ears, which felt like they were on fire.

Suddenly, the budding scientist in me kicked in and a hypothesis materialized: What if Alan Kowalski hadn't been looking at me in the first place? What if my nearsightedness, which was only slightly this side of legally blind, had only made it seem that he was staring at me with love in his eyes? Slowly I lowered my glasses. Sure enough, the love stare was there. But when I raised them again to my eyes, Alan was clearly looking at the teacher and not me. I performed this experiment the requisite three or four more times and obtained the exact same result. This was the end of my first love affair. Fortunately, it was also the birth of my scientific self. I have since learned that true love at times does require nearsightedness. And true science requires one to not be afraid of the truth.

Wayne has always presented his daughters with something heart-shaped on Valentine's Day: lockets, earrings, even flashlights. This year he gave both Lizzie and Kat a necklace with a silver free-form heart. A percentage of the proceeds from the sale of these necklaces is going to women in Third World countries for training and microcredit loans. This will appeal to the budding social worker Lizzie's caring heart. I do not know yet what my Valentine has in store for me; it may not be heart-shaped, but I am sure it will be heartfelt.

Valentine's Day Red Velvet Cake

This particular cake is a favorite at our house and perfect for Valentine's Day. Lizzie launched her baking career with this cake. Our dog once ate twelve red-velvet cupcakes. Tula's feat was revealed to me when I took her out for her daily constitutional. What emerged was riveting in both color and form.

A favorite in the American south, a red velvet cake, when shaped like an armadillo, makes a great groom's cake, as anyone who has seen the play or movie *Steel Magnolias* can attest. The legend of the red velvet cake is that it debuted during the Civil War, when southern wives baked them to keep their husbands home. All sorts of fancy and fancifully named Valentine's Day cakes (for example, the Husband-Catcher Cake) are out there, but with its deep red color, rich chocolate taste, and white icing this one wins my heart.

This recipe is traced to an old New Orleans family recipe. I read through dozens and all that claimed to be the real deal called for a full two ounces of red food coloring. Sounds crazy, but that's my story and I'm sticking to it.

Preheat oven to 350° F, and grease and flour two 8" or 9" round cake pans.

Cake

1½ cups room-temperature unsalted butter

1 ½ cups sugar
2 eggs
2 ounces red food coloring
2 tablespoons cocoa
1 cup buttermilk
1 teaspoon salt
1 teaspoon baking soda
1 teaspoon distilled white vinegar
1 teaspoon vanilla extract
2 ½ cups all-purpose flour

1. Mix dry ingredients; set aside.

2. Cream butter and sugar until fluffy (5 minutes); add eggs and beat well. Make a paste out of the cocoa and food coloring and a few drops of water (if necessary), and add this to the butter and sugar mix.

3. Mix together buttermilk, vinegar, and vanilla.

4. Add buttermilk and dry ingredients until well mixed. Divide batter between the two prepared pans.

5. Bake thirty minutes or until a cake tester comes out clean, but not dry. Remove from the oven and cool 15 minutes before inverting onto racks.

6. Cool completely before frosting

Frosting (also excellent with cream cheese frosting)

1 cup whole milk or half-and-half
3 tablespoons flour
1 cup room-temperature unsalted butter
1 cup granulated sugar
1 teaspoon vanilla extract

1. Whisk flour and milk in saucepan over low heat until thick; set aside to cool.

2. Cream butter, sugar, and vanilla until fluffy (5 to 10 minutes). Add cooled milk mixture and beat until it is the consistency of whipped cream.

Cake Assembly

Put cake layer on a serving plate and cover with a layer of icing; top with the second layer and cover sides and top with frosting.

Why I Am Obsessed with Cake

"It's better to criticize after the cake's risen; not, if one's wise, when it's on the rise." —John G. Young, M.D., from his Web site "Adventures in Creativity"

This week marks the anniversary of my mother's death. And so I am thinking about her in all of her complexity. I've already mentioned that my mother's lack of a sweet tooth cramped my childhood and left us dessert-ed. Nowadays this would be classified as a form of child abuse. This is the story of an actual cake that my mother baked. Let me say now that I did not criticize the cake while it was on the rise.

My mother typically could not bake a cake to save her life, or mine. The year I was in third grade and my brother in fifth, we both served on the student council. This led to an invitation to the annual spring student council luncheon. Each mother was assigned a side dish to contribute. Our mother's assignment was to bake a cake. Because I had never known my mother to bake a cake, I was quite nervous about it. I bugged her incessantly: What kind of cake? How tall would it be? How beautiful? She assured me it would be spectacular and that all of the other kids would be envious. I drove her nuts the entire day before. By the time I was sent to bed that night, she still hadn't begun to make the spectacular spectacle of a cake that she had assured me was going to dazzle my friends.

I awoke early the next morning and snuck into the kitchen with all the anticipation of Christmas morning. On the counter I saw a plate with a cake on it. The cake was spectacular all right, hideously spectacular. An angel food cake, it was lopsided, rising several inches high on one side and barely an inch on the other. It was riddled with cavities in odd places and, worst of all, it was not frosted. The year was 1963 and rocks had yet to be brought back from the moon, but in my memory the cake bears an uncanny resemblance to moon rocks. I didn't want to hurt my mother's feelings, but how could I take this to school?

I don't remember how we got it to school. I must have refused to carry it, leaving the task to my brother. We had been told to drop off our contribution in the cafeteria in the basement—the cafeteria ladies would put out all the dishes for the lunch, sorted by type. All morning I was a wreck. I had barely recovered from the realization that Alan Kowalski did not love me. How much more suffering could I be expected to bear?

I stoically endured lunch, but when the other kids started lining up at the dessert table my terror level rose. My brother was in line ahead of me, blocking my view. I heard him ask one of the serving ladies for a slice of cake. He took it and moved on. Now I could see our mother's cake, which was missing only one slice, the one my brother had asked for. A girl standing in line next to me asked me which cake my mother had made. Without a moment's hesitation, I pointed to the most luscious and beautiful cake on the table and claimed it for mine, speaking loudly so that all could hear. I can still picture that cake and only now realize it was obviously store-bought from a bakery. Some mothers have a lot of nerve. The cafeteria lady cut me a slice of that cake and I headed back to my seat.

All these years later I am ashamed to admit that I didn't choke on that other mom's cake, or ever confess my lie. As I left the room I noticed that our mother's cake was still only missing a sliver, while all the other cakes had been devoured. Back in Mrs. Sagy's third grade classroom, it occurred to me that I would have to retrieve the cake plate from the cafeteria. Everyone would see the actual cake my mother had made. I suffered all afternoon, hatching a plot to skip out without picking up the plate after school, although I knew I would have to face my mother's questions back home. I will be forever grateful to the lunch ladies at Northwood Elementary school in Royal Oak, Michigan, for dumping the remains of the cake and cleaning the plate for me. My mother never learned the fate of her cake.

My feelings for my brother changed a bit that day. He was a better person than I. I thought about this all this week and then called to ask him what he remembered about that day. He had no real memory of it and was surprised to learn, and then recall, that he had been on student council. I shared with him my recollection of the student council luncheon and he laughed and agreed that it was like me to pick the prettiest cake and call it my own. But now that I know that he doesn't remember, I can go back to thinking that maybe he really isn't a better person than I.

My brother's daughter, Monica, and her significant other were our guests this weekend and so our guests for Cake Day. Monica was here to give a reading of her poetry at my university. At twenty-six she has her MFA and is an accomplished horsewoman and poet. I cannot wait to see what she has accomplished by age forty. She stayed in Lizzie's third-floor garret, mentioning several times that she would be a better writer if she had spent her teen years in such a room. I decided this was a compliment but I did wonder if she meant that it was a great room for the nurturing of suffering and angst.

My mother is long gone and long missed. Making my cake this week brought back an oddly cherished memory—one my own children know by heart. It is a memory of a woman who could not make a cake to save her daughter's third-grade life. But it is a memory, also, of a woman who taught me to never take myself too seriously. And, most important, to never trust, or heaven forbid marry, someone who doesn't have a sense of humor. I am happy to report that I did learn that lesson. I married a man with a spectacular sense of humor, and both of my children are more like my mother and brother than they are like me. In fact, when I announced to my mother that I was going to marry Wayne, she said, "Oh, he has a great sense of humor—if the marriage succeeds, it will be because of him." It is nice to have your mom on your side.

Life, like cake, should never be taken too seriously. Suffering is best left to poets in third floor garret rooms and to the cakeless.

Absolutely Angelic Angel Food Cake

Thinking about my mother's disastrous angel food cake demanded that I try to make my own. This recipe comes from my friend Gretchen and it is the best angel food cake I've ever had. Gretchen got the recipe from her mother-in-law, who says the best recipes come from the newspaper. Amen. This cake is tall, perfectly shaped, snowy white, and has a delicate crumb. As with all angel food cakes, it is best to make it on days that are not humid, for example, on a winter day. I can't help but wonder how my mother's 1963 cake would have turned out if she had used this recipe.

Because I knew that my guests love chocolate, I prepared a recipe of the pourable fudge frosting from the Bumpy Cake on page 116 to serve on top of the angel food cake. Also great with orange glaze (page 153).

Bring egg whites to room temperature first and then preheat oven to 375° F. Cake requires an ungreased 10" tube pan.

Cake

1 ¾ cups egg whites (12 to 14 eggs, depending on their size)
1 ¼ cups sifted cake flour (measure after sifting)
1 ¾ cups granulated sugar
½ teaspoon salt
1 ½ teaspoons cream of tartar
1 teaspoon vanilla extract
½ teaspoon almond extract (I think this is crucial)

1. Separate eggs while still cold from the refrigerator. Measure and pour into the large bowl of an electric mixer. Allow to come to room temperature; it should take about an hour.

2. Resift already sifted and measured flour with ¾ cups sugar three times.

3. Preheat oven.

4. At medium speed, beat whites with salt and cream of tartar just until soft peaks form when the beaters are slowly raised; do not over beat. (Bowl, beaters, whisk, and rubber scraper must be clean and free of any grease as it retards beating of egg whites.)

5. With mixer now at high speed, gradually add 1 cup of sugar, ¼ cup at a time, beating well after each addition. Continue until stiff peaks form when beater is slowly raised. With wire whisk or rubber spatula, gently fold vanilla and almond extracts into whites.

6. Sprinkle ¼ of flour mixture over whites. With wire whisk, using an under-and-over motion, gently fold flour mixture into the whites (about 15 strokes), rotating the bowl a quarter turn after each stroke, folding just until flour mixture disappears.

7. Continue folding in the flour mixture, ¼ at a time, as in step 6. With a rubber scraper, gently push the batter into an ungreased 10" tube pan. Cut through the batter twice with a sharp knife to remove any large air bubbles. Spread evenly and smooth the top.

8. Bake on the lowest rack for 30 to 35 minutes, or

until the top springs back when gently pressed with a finger.

9. Invert pan over neck of a bottle to cool completely (about 2 hours). Loosen cake from sides of the pan with a knife and turn out on a serving plate. Turn the cake right-side up.

10. Cut cake with a knife with a serrated edge, using a slight sawing motion to avoid squashing the cake.

If you are baking the cake a day ahead, leave it in the pan and remove it just before serving.

Science Is Not a Cake Walk

"Results! Why, man, I have gotten a lot of results. I know several thousand things that won't work."
—Thomas Edison

I did not want to make a cake this week that would leave every bowl and pan dirty. Here it is Saturday and I'm arriving home from work at 4 PM. I fix myself a cup of tea and sit down to read the issue of *Food and Wine* that I have just snatched from the mailbox. I find the answer to my cake dilemma on page 78: Chocolate-Pecan Cake. It promises to be easy. It promises to taste like a praline!

It has been a long week. As I've gotten older I've concluded that days and weeks seem to go on forever, while months and years whiz by at lightning speed. A trick of the aging mind, no doubt. I read recently that this acceleration of time happens because in the blur of our daily duties we rarely notice that the sun rises and sets. Without nature's punctuation marks of sunrise and sunset, one day becomes the same as the next and time appears to speed up.

The week had started out cold and with many mountains to climb: papers to submit and a seminar to create. I am headed to Dartmouth in five days to give a talk. This will not be a cake walk, and I really need to impress this particular audience. Science in the twenty-first century is a costly and competitive endeavor, requiring numerous connections and collaborations. I am going to Dartmouth to work on the latter. And I am doing it without all of the results I had hoped for. Thomas Edison would understand.

Apparently Wayne has had a terrible week as well. Soon after I arrive home today, he leaves in a hurry muttering something about buying a punching bag. I decide to serve the cake before he comes back, although I sense that his mood might benefit from a slice of something sweet. I've learned that when Wayne has that look on his face, it is time for running-errands therapy. He heads for the hardware store, the office supply store, and the sporting goods store.

So I serve this cake still warm from the oven to Kat and her friends. When they are finished, not a crumb remains. One of the girls emerges from the dining room to tell me, "I really didn't like it, can't you tell?" as she holds up a plate that had clearly been licked clean.

I grab my own plate and start licking, closing my eyes with satisfaction. When I open them, the setting sun is peering over the rim of the plate. Time has slowed. It is now a rich caramel sauce pouring into my mouth and dripping down my chin.

Chocolate-Pecan Cake

From the February 2006 issue of *Food and Wine*.

This quick cake was inspired by New Orleans praline candies. It's more like a cookie than a cake, but it really fit the bill on a week that demanded a simple but satisfying cake.

Preheat oven to 375° F and butter an 8" round cake pan.

Cake

½ cup all-purpose flour
¼ teaspoon baking powder
¼ teaspoon salt
⅓ cup sugar
¼ cup salted, roasted pecans, *finely chopped
¼ cup semisweet or bittersweet chocolate chips
1 large egg, beaten
3 tablespoons heavy cream
3 tablespoons melted butter

1. In a medium bowl, whisk the flour with the baking powder and salt. Stir in sugar, pecans, and the chocolate chips.

2. In another bowl, beat the egg with the heavy cream and melted butter.

3. Whisk in the dry ingredients until combined. Pour into the cake pan and bake for about 22 minutes, or until the cake is springy to the touch.

4. Cool cake on a wire rack for 5 minutes before inverting onto a plate and cutting into wedges.

5. Drizzle the praline caramel sauce over the cake wedges and serve.

Praline Caramel Sauce

⅔ cup sugar
4 tablespoons water
2 tablespoons butter
6 tablespoons heavy cream

1. Mix sugar and water together and cook over medium-high heat, stirring with a wooden spoon until the sugar is dissolved; wash down the sides of the pan with a moistened pastry brush. Cook the sugar until it becomes a medium-amber color (about 4 minutes).

2. Remove from the heat and add butter and heavy cream. Stir until smooth.

Note: The cake can be wrapped in plastic and refrigerated overnight; bring to room temperature before serving. The caramel sauce can be kept at room temperature overnight.

*If you can't find salted and roasted pecans, do it yourself by putting pecans on a cookie sheet in a 375° F oven for 10 minutes. Chop and add a pinch of salt.

Ladies Who Lunch

"Nine-tenths of the people were created so you would want to be with the other tenth." —Horace Walpole, eighteenth-century English writer

I was lunching with my dearest and oldest friend, Valori Treloar, at the Simon Pearce restaurant in Quechee, Vermont. Crafted out of an old mill cantilevered out over the Ottaquechee River, the restaurant's sign advertised "Waterfalls, Pottery, Glassblowing, and Hydropower." I met Val, a highly regarded Boston dermatologist, in junior high school. She is securely part of the 10 percent of those I want to be with.

The seminar at Dartmouth now behind me, I was ready to let down my hair and eat until I had to unbutton my jeans. It was too early to tell if I had won the hearts and minds of the colleagues I hope to collaborate with at Dartmouth, but I had conducted my seminar as well as could be expected at nine in the morning after a harrowing inbound flight the night before. (I am not a morning person, or a late night person for that matter—I am a late-mid-morning person.)

My flight had been on a Beechcraft 1900D nineteen-seater from New York's La Guardia Airport. I had no idea that I would be boarding such a tiny plane and so had failed to either visit the ladies room or purchase a bottle of water. I was therefore not thrilled to discover that the plane had no bathroom or beverage service. As I was adjusting to this news, a fellow passenger, who said she took this flight regularly, announced that we were going to have "some ride" since they "usually cancel flights when it is this windy." No bathroom, no beverages, and no way out. We left forty-five minutes late and as we were taxiing to the runway, I heard one pilot say to the other, "Did you bring the GPU?" (geographic positioning unit).

The flight reminded me of my recent awful trip to a theme park where I convinced Kat to go on rides that looked like a whole lot of fun to me, but had caused her to utter the words, "Mom, I will never speak to you again." At this moment I wanted my own mom and I wanted to tell someone on that plane that if it took off, I was never going to speak to them again.

But this lunch made the whole trip worth it. Val had called to announce she was going to drive up from Boston to see me. We pondered many possibilities before deciding to be ladies who lunch. While glancing out at the spectacular frozen waterfalls, devouring excellent lamb burgers, and sipping delicious wine served in expensive wine glasses blown on the premises, we discussed topics ranging from science to skin to glassblowing to child rearing (the latter two, we agreed, are much harder than one might anticipate).

After lunch we wandered through the rest of the stunning building, taking in the pottery and the glassblowing studio. Valori charmed the resident glassblower into giving us a tour. Our last stop was the in-house shop, where we each bought the same small, lovely pottery pitcher. I bought it to hold the maple syrup I had purchased down the road to serve with Wayne's never-fail buttermilk pancakes. As the sales clerk was wrapping them for travel, we agreed that we liked the idea of both having the same objet d'art in our far-apart homes.

On the drive back to the tiny Lebanon, New Hampshire, airport Val and I never stopped talking and more than once spoke the same words simultaneously.

At lunch I had told Val all about my cake book and she offered up the apple cake recipe below. I decided on the flight home (uneventful, thank heavens) to make it for Cake Day this week.

I arrived home on a Friday, which was coming-home night for Lizzie, whose college spring break was beginning. She had dictated that dinner must be spinach lasagna. I added a nice salad of greens and mushrooms, a French baguette, and cake, of course. Ironically the lasagna that Lizzie has loved since she was a tiny girl is a recipe from Valori's mother, Donna, my seventh-grade English teacher. Every time I drag out the stained twenty-seven-year-old handwritten recipe card, I conjure up Donna and her seventh-grade classroom.

Wayne had left me a voice message on his way out of town to pick up Lizzie, telling me that he had bought everything to make the lasagna. Still, I made four trips to my favorite market. First, for the cake ingredients; second, for Parmesan cheese; third, for spaghetti sauce; and finally, for the greens to make the salad. Between trips I made the cake and set the table. The cake, and the lasagna, came out of the oven minutes before Lizzie and her friend Elaina from school burst through the door at 8:45 PM. Wayne had driven ten hours to retrieve them. I was so happy to have everyone's feet under the same table that night. Kat also had a friend over and dinner sparkled with conversation and love (and champagne). Elaina admiringly described the cake as "like apple pie all the way through." A great and accurate endorsement for the easiest cake I've ever made. I floated off to bed dizzy with the pleasure of good company and champagne.

Val's Boston Apple Cake

Valori gave me this explanation for how this cake came into her life: "Cut from *Boston Globe* over twenty years ago as I procrastinated while working at the check-in desk at the medical school library. Taped to a blue library file card. Easy and good."

Note: This is the only recipe for which I am including nutritional information. This is because I think cake should be exempt from such scrutiny. But Valori, who has a special licensure in Nutritional Medicine, is keen on dispensing such information.

Preheat oven to 350° F. Grease and flour a 9" by 9" pan or an 8" round cake pan or a pie plate.

Cake

1½ cups diced apples (Granny Smith are spectacular in this and available throughout the winter)
1 cup sugar
1 egg
½ cup oil (safflower or olive)
1½ cups all-purpose flour
½ teaspoon baking soda
1 teaspoon cinnamon
½ teaspoon salt
½ cup nuts or raisins or both!

1. Add sugar to diced apples and let stand 10 minutes (Valori insists this is key).

2. Add egg and oil.

3. Sift dry ingredients together and add to the apple/egg/oil mixture.

4. Transfer to baking dish and sprinkle with powdered or turbinado sugar.

5. Bake for 40 minutes to an hour.

Note: Approximate nutrition information per slice (recipe makes 9 slices): 310 calories, 3 g protein, 9 g fat, 50 g carbohydrates, 250 mg sodium. (This is the only recipe for which I am including nutritional information. I believe cakes should be exempt from such scrutiny. But Valori has a special licensure in nutritional medicine and is very keen on such information.)

Spring Break, Take 1: How Sweet It Is

"The world's largest roach (which lives in South America) is six inches long with a one-foot wingspan." — Yucky Discovery

Spring break: does anything sound better than a break, in spring, after the long, cold, lonely winter? My spring break starts today.

Lizzie returned yesterday from her college spring break, which she spent in Asheville, North Carolina. She drove the seven hours alone, and I did not relax until I got the call on my cell phone that she had arrived in one piece.

Gone are the days when I headed to the Florida Panhandle with Lizzie and Kat. We would set out with a caravan of vehicles filled with my sister and brother, nieces and nephews, and various friends. A week of sun and sand and shuffleboard on the beaches of the Gulf Coast was worth the fourteen-hour drive through the middle of the night with, inevitably, some huge traffic jam, somewhere. Even the Florida roaches, revealed when I pulled the covers back on my bed, and just shy of the size of the South American record holders, have, in retrospect, acquired a sheen of charm.

Sometimes we went north on spring break. My kids have vivid memories of the year we headed to Buffalo to visit friends. The photos from that spring break show us at Niagara Falls with the swirling snow so heavy we looked like any family who had gotten lost in the Arctic on their way to spring break. Several years after that, we drove exactly two thousand miles to the East Coast and back on a tour of colleges. On that trip, not one mile of driving wasn't accompanied by precipitation of some sort: snow, sleet, hail, or rain. And something I dubbed "sneethain," which is a combination of all of the above. When we finally pulled into our driveway on the last night of spring break, it was nearly midnight and raining. Lizzie and Kat were asleep, so Wayne and I decided to sit in the driveway for just a few minutes before waking them up and dragging everything into the house. But the peace was broken by the wail of a tornado siren. It was a perfectly awful trip, but at least there were no roaches in the beds.

The tradition of us all heading somewhere together for spring break seems to have expired. Lizzie has started her own tradition of going to the mountains of North Carolina, but Kat still bugs us to take her someplace, preferably to the south. I complain, but I love being bugged to hit the road in search of memories. I wouldn't trade any of those overly long and less-than-post-card-perfect trips for anything.

This week's cake was really a welcome-back-from-spring-break cake for Lizzie. A few other folks stopped by, since it is now general knowledge that cake is served at 7 PM every Saturday.

After we eat cake and after our guests depart, we play two rounds of Chutes and Ladders and then spend several hours looking through old photographs. Times change and traditions fade, but we can always start new ones.

Sacher Torte

Sacher Torte just seems to be the cake version of spring break—a sweet and rich escape from the daily grind. The Original Sacher Torte is the world's most famous chocolate cake, its recipe a well-kept secret since 1832. The story of this legendary chocolate cake filled with apricot jam began in 1832. Eduard Sacher was a sixteen-year-old apprentice at the court of Prince Metternich, Imperial Chancellor of Austria, when he was asked to create an especially delicious desert for special guests. The guests loved it, and it became known as the Sacher Torte. Sacher later built the Hotel Sacher, which became Vienna's most distinguished hotel, and the Sacher Torte became world famous.

The cake consists of two layers of dense, not overly sweet chocolate with a thin layer of apricot jam in the middle and dark chocolate icing on the top and sides. It is traditionally eaten with whipped cream, as most Viennese consider the Sacher Torte too dry to be eaten without it.

Each year more than 270,000 original Sacher Tortes are produced. You can buy them on the Internet. Or you can make this recipe from *Maida Heatter's Book of Great Chocolate Desserts*. I modified the filling to include a full twelve ounces of jam, which is what the recipe I found on the Internet (that claims to be the original) calls for.

Preheat oven to 350° F.
Butter an 8" springform or layer-cake pan; line the bottom with wax paper cut to fit; butter the paper and dust with flour. Invert and tap lightly to shake out excess flour.

It is best to make the cake early in the day or a day ahead. If made the day before, wrap tightly in saran wrap.

Cake

6 ounces semi-sweet chocolate
1 ¼ cups (2 ½ sticks) room-temperature unsalted butter
⅓ cup sugar
5 large eggs, separated, plus 1 extra egg white
¾ cup sifted all-purpose flour
pinch of salt

1. Place chocolate in the top of a small double boiler over hot water on medium heat. Cover until partially melted, then uncover and stir until completely melted and smooth. Set aside, uncovered, to cool slightly.

2. Add the salt to the egg whites in the small bowl of an electric mixer and beat with clean beaters until the whites hold a definite shape, but not until they are stiff or dry; set aside.

3. Cream the butter and sugar in the large bowl of an

electric mixer (you can use the same beaters used for the egg whites), until well mixed and creamy. Pour in all the egg yolks and beat well, scraping the sides with a rubber spatula. On low speed beat in the melted chocolate. Then add the flour and beat only until mixed.

4. Add half the egg-white mixture, two large spoonfuls at a time, into the chocolate batter, mixing to lighten, but not until all egg whites are thoroughly mixed. Now add the remaining half of the egg whites and mix just until no egg whites show.

5. Turn the mixture into the prepared pan and rotate the pan swiftly clockwise, then counterclockwise, to level the top. (In an 8" layer pan the batter will be only ¼ inch from the top, and that is OK.)

6. Bake for 40–45 minutes until the top feels firm and springs back lightly when pressed with a finger tip or a toothpick inserted into the middle comes out clean and dry.

7. Let the cake stand in the pan for 10 minutes, then cover the cake with a rack and invert to release. Remove paper and invert, using a second rack so that the cake is right-side up. It will be 1½ inches tall.

8. Let stand for several hours, or overnight (it can also be frozen).

9. When it is time to fill and glaze, slice the cake into two equal layers. Place the bottom layer on a cake plate or stand which has four strips of waxed paper placed around the outer edge.

Filling

12 ounces apricot jam
1 tablespoon water
1 tablespoon rum (optional)

Add all ingredients to small saucepan and bring to a boil. Remove from the stove and let cool slightly. Spoon over the bottom half of the cake, allowing it to soak in. Cover with the top half of the cake.

Chocolate Glaze

This will have an incredible mirror-like sheen, but it does not form the hard shell that the original has.

8 ounces semi-sweet chocolate
¼ cup light corn syrup
3 tablespoons water
2 tablespoons butter

Coarsely chop the chocolate if it is in 1-ounce squares. Place the syrup and water into a small pan. Place over medium heat and bring to a boil, stirring occasionally. Remove from heat, immediately add the chocolate, and stir until it has melted. With a wire whisk, beat briskly until completely smooth. Set aside, stirring occasionally, until the glaze reaches room temperature and begins to thicken slightly.

Pour the glaze carefully onto the middle of the cake. It will spread out and run to the edges and down the sides. With a long, narrow metal spatula spread across the top to make a smooth layer and cover the sides with the glaze and smooth it out.] Do not remove the wax paper strips until the glaze has stopped running.

Whipped Cream

Serve with whipped cream. Sacher Torte is always served with a generous helping of whipped cream—it is an important part of the dessert.

2 cups heavy cream
¼ cup sifted confectioners' sugar
½ teaspoon vanilla

Make sure cream is cold and that you have chilled the bowl and beaters in the freezer. Whip ingredients on high until the cream holds a soft shape, but not until it is stiff.

Spring Break, Take 2: Appalachian Spring

"O Appalachian Spring!
I gained the ledge;
Steep, inaccessible smile
that eastward bends
And northward reaches
in that violet wedge
Of Adirondacks!"
—from the poem "The Bridge," by Hart Crane

Spring break went too swiftly, perhaps because I spent it working. My university's spring break has never coincided with those of my daughters'. I have always worked like crazy on my spring break so that I can be off for theirs.

I confess that I like working on spring break because it is so quiet in the absence of the undergraduate students. And so it is a time I get to do my real work. I once heard a career columnist say, "One's job is what one does in order to buy little bits of time to do one's work." My job consists of all the committee work and administrative stuff I do, my work is my research. During spring break I spend as much time in the lab as possible, much to the discomfort of my graduate students. I try not to get in their way, but I am sure I do. While they are nice about it, I am pretty sure I can hear them sigh with relief when classes start up again and I go back to my office. I am crazy about all my students, so I love being in their way and catching up on what's going on with their research and their lives.

The end of the week brought visitors that induced me to leave the lab. Jackie and J.P. are here to attend a conference on Appalachia. Jackie, a student at a college in Appalachia, is working toward a major in global studies and a minor in Appalachian studies. What a great combination. I think that what we stand to lose in the whole globalization process are the very types of deep and rich cultures that Appalachia represents. Owls and moths are not the only things that suffer extinction—cultures and languages are being lost every day. J.P. is an environmental studies major, and he descends from people who populated the deepest pockets of Appalachia. He wants very much to understand his roots and perhaps learn how to preserve them.

Our visitors are both vegans, and so we trot out our best vegan recipes and are none the worse for the healthy fare. The dinner conversations center on their hopes and dreams and what they are learning from the conference. By the end of the week, we feel as if we've known them a very long time, and this turns out to be ironic. They came here under the guise of being friends of Lizzie's friend Erin. We didn't know until after they were gone that Erin barely knew them herself. She had overheard Jackie in the college cafeteria saying she was trying to find a place to stay in Dayton so she could afford to go to the Appalachia conference. Erin jumped in, telling Jackie that if she was going to Dayton, she simply must stay with the Andersons. Jackie was worried about whether we would accept her and J.P.'s tattoos and piercings. Erin must have done a great job selling us, or Jackie really was broke and willing to take a chance on some old people that a girl she didn't know had recommended.

We are sorry to see them go, although we quickly discover they haven't entirely left. Jackie has left all of her credit cards behind. We send a care package along with the cards, and I find myself wishing I could deliver it in person in order to see an Appalachian spring of my own.

Postscript: Years later Jackie played angel to Lizzie by taking her in when she moved to Asheville, North Carolina, after college.

Toffee Nutmeg Cake

We happily stuck to a vegan diet along with our visitors. But after they left, I made this decidedly non-vegan cake. It is unforgettable, especially if served with butter pecan ice cream, or so the trailer for this cake claims. If you love crumb toppings, you will love this. I had toyed with making it ever since I got a nutmeg grater for Christmas a few years ago. New kitchen toys always send me looking for new recipes, and I love nutmeg (eggnog for me is an excuse to consume nutmeg). This is another cake from the excellent cookbook, and all-around good read, *Hollyhocks and Radishes*.

Preheat oven to 350° F.
Butter and lightly flour a 9" tube pan with a removable bottom.

Mixture 1

3 cups sifted flour
1 pound light brown sugar
1 teaspoon baking powder
½ teaspoon salt
¾ cup (1½ sticks) room-temperature unsalted butter

Mixture 2

3 cups of Mixture 1
½ cup finely chopped pecans (not ground)

Mixture 3

The rest of Mixture 1 (what wasn't used in Mixture 2)

1 egg, lightly beaten
2–3 teaspoons freshly ground nutmeg
1½ teaspoons vanilla
1½ cups sour cream
1½ teaspoons baking soda
¾ cup coarsely chopped pecans

1. Create Mixture 1 by combining with a pastry blender the flour, brown sugar, baking powder, and salt in a large bowl. Blend in the butter until the mixture is crumbly.

2. Create Mixture 2 by combining 3 cups of Mixture 1 with the ½ cup finely chopped pecans. Place in the bottom of the tube pan, but do not pack down.

3. Create Mixture 3 by stirring egg, nutmeg, and vanilla into what remains from Mixture 1. Combine sour cream and baking soda and add to the mixture along with the coarsely chopped nuts. Pour into the tube pan.

4. Bake 1 hour or until cake tester comes out clean.

5. Cool on wire rack for 15 minutes. Remove sides of the pan and cool completely. Invert onto serving dish. Serve with butter pecan ice cream or whipped cream.

Spring

Happy Birthday to Me

"The journey is the reward."
—Taoist proverb

Where do I go to get permission to rewrite this proverb? The journey in this instance is four years of research written up, submitted, and then rejected for publication. The student who toiled for four years is named Paul and he probably wouldn't agree with this proverb either, since his PhD degree hangs on his work being published. When I asked how he was doing, he told me that he had asked his wife to hide the guns. I am not sure if his plan was to shoot himself, or me, or both of us (PhD advisers have been shot over less). But Paul is a man of strong faith and this setback is not enough to break him. We developed a strategy together, after the excruciating exercise of reading through the reviewers' comments, and climbed back on the horse. We are hoping for a higher score, one that will result in publication and Paul's PhD. This is how my week started.

The curse of modernity is that our lives are too often reduced to numbers, starting with our APGAR score at birth and going on to our SAT, MCAT, LSAT, and GRE scores. We continue well into old age with the often ominous numbers that signify our HDL, LDL, FSH, LH, PSA, blood pressure, age, and weight. On Friday I called to find out the results of some recent blood tests and e-mailed the numbers to my doc friend Valori, in Boston. She e-mailed back: "Welcome to menopause." My response was Aaawwwcckk! I decide Val was just being sarcastic. In any case, I didn't have time to dwell on it, so I went about my day with a new and annoying sensation—not unlike heartburn—that my life's numbers are starting to change and it isn't going to be good.

I will turn fifty-two this weekend—the average age for the onset of menopause. I hate being average and so I suspect it is a bit of a cosmic joke that on the literal eve of my fifty-second birthday I've discovered I'm entering the great pause. Not to boast, but I have braved each era of womanhood—puberty, sex and birth control, pregnancy and childbirth, and motherhood—with pragmatism and the discernment that comes from reading everything possible before making important decisions.

Before I became pregnant with Lizzie, I had read everything out there about how to have a healthy pregnancy and child. While pregnant, I gained the recommended twenty-five to thirty pounds, religiously took my prenatal vitamins, mostly abstained from caffeine, totally abstained from alcohol, and ate only healthy foods during the entire nine months. Unfortunately, the day after I delivered Lizzie I discovered that I had neglected to read about baby care. I had missed the whole point: the actual baby I would have to take care of. I immediately sent Wayne to the library to fetch a stack of child care books. I caught up quickly and I've stayed on top of the situation for twenty years.

This menopause thing seems different. I'm worried that it may be about coming to the end of being a woman. Here's the strangest part: I have less than zero desire to read up on it. I came home early and shared my misgivings with Wayne. He gave me a hug and then asked me to read a chapter in the book he is writing. We were sparring over the fine points of his presentation when Kat burst through the door. Returning from the school playground, she had cooked up the idea of going to a movie with friends. Dismayed to learn that one of us would have to accompany them, Kat began to wail, "Mom, you are ruining everything. You always ruin everything!"

And so I am about to experience the one thing I had hoped to avoid in life: going through menopause simultaneously with a daughter going through puberty. Life is about to get very interesting. Wayne ended up as the chaperone while I stayed home and felt sorry for myself. I went to bed early, still in the dumps and wondering if all the good stuff in life had already happened.

In the morning, I forced myself to go to the killer early yoga class and when I returned home the day's mail had arrived full of birthday cards. I saved Lizzie's package for last. It contained an Irish green T-shirt made in Los Angeles without the horror of sweatshop labor and a Red Fire chocolate bar by Vosges, a *haut chocolat* that contains Mexican *ancho y chipotle* chili peppers, Ceylon cinnamon, and dark chocolate. Lizzie's package also included a letter typed on a 1970s vintage typewriter that was decorated by hand with a few drawings. The letter really got to me.

Lizzie reflected, as directed by her Free Will horoscope, on reconnecting with her childhood memories, "Like the time you and Dad and I went on that bike ride up in Omena and I was on dad's bike and it started to rain so hard and we rode back to the cottage and we [she and I] took a bath in the big bathroom and played that waitress game. At the time, those minutes, it didn't seem like there was anything else more important than escaping the rain and just being together."

I had forgotten all about the waitress game we played at bath time. I invented it to distract her while I rinsed her hair. I'd let her order whatever drink she wanted, fill a cup with bath water, and deliver her order by "accidentally" spilling it on her head. "Oh, I'm so sorry," the waitress would always say. Lizzie went on describing other golden moments from her childhood, concluding: "These exact moments will never happen again."

Lizzie is right. What with age, and change, and the selling of cabins to people who no longer want to rent to nice families with happy memories and new hopes, these moments will never happen again. This knowledge, along with the stresses of everyday life–homework, petri dishes, family tiffs, misbehaving dogs, and the degradation of the environment—make it seem sometimes as if the simple and wonderful are stationed on another planet. It is sad.

But where there is cake there is hope, and as both Lizzie and I know, there is always cake (at least on Saturdays). Lizzie ended her letter by writing, "When families care about other people's children and their children's friends, it is something good. Sweatshop-free clothing, spinach lasagna, and fireflies offer hope."

Lizzie signed her birthday letter to me with the line I have spoken to each of my lovely and amazing daughters almost every day of their lives: "I love you heaps and heaps, today and for keeps."

And so I got my life sense back. I have always tried to teach my kids to notice and appreciate the simple things, the everyday wonders, and my daughter was telling me that I had taught her to do this. Now she is teaching me the same thing. I had been trying to control the journey this week and became worried that all the good parts of the journey were behind me. I can only hope that I never get too old to learn this lesson anew.

A few days later Val wrote back: "I probably should have said 'welcome to *peri*menopause'—a process that starts as early as the late thirties and may go on for ten years before menopause." I wasn't average after all. Anyway, I had already decided that menopause would have to wait. I am too busy living my life.

Japanese Green Tea Cake with Ginger Sauce

The date says spring, but winter still has a grip on my part of the world. My daffodils are braving the cold and just might escape the dangers of frost. Even though the forecast said "snow possible" I headed to my indie garden store for pansies, as is my custom. I spent the afternoon clearing out the beds (with Wayne's much-appreciated help) and planting pansies, the baby face kind. They are actually violas but some marketing person decided that the words "baby face" would sell them better than the word "viola." Later I went to work for an hour to confer with my students and prepare my lecture for the following day.

When I returned from my office, Kat and friends were making this cake. I love all things related to tea, but Kat was not making this just for me. She had received the assignment to make a cake for a Japanese Tea Ceremony and this was the recipe she had found. She and her friends made two, one for the class and one for me. I had previewed the recipe, which they had found on the Spice House Web site, and noticed that it recommended the ginger dessert sauce. Since it was my birthday, I requested it.

The trailer on the Web site announced, "If you like green tea you will love this cake." A neighbor stopped by shortly after the cake came out of the oven and I cut us both a piece. We loved it.

Preheat oven to 350° F; butter a 9" x 11" pan, line with parchment paper, butter and lightly flour the paper.

Cake

4 whole eggs
6 egg yolks
4 room-temperature egg whites
1 cup plus ¼ cup sugar
⅔ cup plus 2 tablespoons cake flour
½ cup cornstarch
¼ cup matcha (green tea powder)
½ teaspoon cream of tartar

Sifted confectioners' sugar for dusting top of cake

1. Sift dry ingredients together: flour, cornstarch, and green tea; set aside.

2. In a mixer whip egg whites with cream of tartar until they foam. Add the ¼ cup sugar and continue to beat until stiff peaks form (not until they are dry).

3. Using the same beaters, but a fresh bowl, beat whole eggs, egg yolks, and the 1 cup of sugar until tripled in volume (about 5 minutes). Carefully fold in the flour mixture in three portions. Do not overmix.

4. Gently fold the egg whites into the cake batter in thirds, using a whisk or a rubber scraper with an under-over motion. Do not overmix.

5. Carefully spread the batter into the prepared pans, taking care not to deflate the air whipped into the eggs.

6. Bake 20 minutes or until brown on the edges and the center of the cake springs back when tapped. Let cool in the pan for 10 minutes, then run a knife around the edge and invert onto a clean towel on the counter. Invert onto a serving platter and dust with powdered sugar. Serve warm or cold, alone or with ginger sauce.

Ginger Dessert Sauce

Yields 2 cups.

1 cup heavy whipping cream
1½ tablespoons minced fresh ginger
¼ teaspoon grated lemon peel
⅛ teaspoon crushed coriander seeds
6 tablespoons lightly beaten whole eggs
3 tablespoons sugar
½ teaspoon vanilla

1. Mix the cream, ginger, lemon peel, and coriander in a small saucepan. Bring up to boiling point on the stove; cover and remove from heat. Let stand 15 minutes to infuse flavors (this also allows the mixture to cool sufficiently so the eggs added in step 3 will not cook).

2. In a mixer, beat the yolks and sugar until thick and pale (2 to 3 minutes).

3. Add the eggs to the warm cream mixture, and slowly whisk together.

Spring Break, Take 3: Forget the Alamo

"Worry kills more people than work because more people worry than work." —from a sign hanging in Floore Country Store, San Antonio, Texas

Kat and I are headed to San Antonio tomorrow to visit transplanted friends. Their son, Will, was Kat's dearest friend until he moved away this past year. We are traveling with two other moms and their sons (also Will's friends). Kat is miffed that we are only staying for three days, but I must be back to work in time to host an international icon who is visiting my university. I remind Kat of Ben Franklin's warning that visitors and fish alike stink after three days; we don't want to stink, do we? This is one of those facts of life a parent should teach their offspring.

We arrive to the heat of the southwest and are assigned to out host's pool cabana, which is really a small and charming house. The kids don their suits and spend the next few hours in the lovely backyard pool, which is surrounded by thirty live oaks. For kids coming from the end of a long Ohio winter, this is heaven. They dive and swim like a pod of dolphins that have been reunited after a long separation.

The next morning our hosts treat us to made-to-order breakfast in their spectacular kitchen that opens to a deck by the fabulous pool; they also provide us with individualized itinerary packets. In two days we will visit Sea World and the River Walk and tour the Alamo and the Missions.

My friend Lauralee and I set off for Sea World with Kat, Will, and her son, Christopher. We survive the day and are rewarded with margaritas by the pool and a trip to Rudy's Bar-B-Q. Rudy's is known far and wide for its true Texas barbecue. The menu promised meat, meat, and more meat: brisket, turkey breast, pork loin, chopped beef, pork spare ribs, and baby back ribs, all barbecued, all by the pound. The only carbs in the place are served on the side in the form of corn and coleslaw. I am a recovering vegetarian, and eating at Rudy's assured that I would not be slipping back into my old ways.

After Rudy's we head deeper into Texas Hill country to the John T. Floore Country Store, Dance Hall, and Café. Visiting Floore's, you feel like you really are in the old Texas, rather than in the sixth largest city in the U.S. Genuine cowboy boots hang from the ceiling, and by genuine I mean worn and scruffy. They appear to have been pulled off the cowboy's feet against his will. I didn't get close enough to smell them, but the overall olfactory ambiance of the place suggests the boots play a role. The rafters are festooned with Christmas lights and signs, with sayings you won't find on either coast: "Home cookin' is where a man thinks his wife is" and "$100 fine for fighting." Floore's has made the National Register of Historic Places for its sixty years of music and good ol' Texas food. It has also hosted the greats: Willie Nelson, Johnny Cash, Elvis, Hank Williams, Patsy Cline, Merle Haggard, and Bob Dylan. On this night the entertainment is being provided by the Jimmy Crib Band.

While it is clear that this is a night for boot skootin', I am content to sit while others in our group dance. I get myself all settled, cold beer in hand, and begin skootin' in my mind. I suddenly sense someone approaching my table and look up to see a man at least twenty-five years my senior. He stands there smiling, leaning on his cane, and says, "young lady, would you care to dance?" I am a sitting duck, but my introvert self is skilled at ducking such offers. "Uh, I don't think so, I am really quite tired" (OK, maybe not so skilled). The gentleman looks disappointed, and I immediately I feel guilty. "Gee, that's too bad, because I am recovering from double hip-replacement surgery, and my doctor tells me the best rehabilitation for me is dancing." How can I refuse to be part of his rehabilitation? We dance to "Just Close your Eyes" and "Old Time Rock 'N' Roll," while Kat captures it on camera and calls her father to let him know what I am up to. YouTube is still off in the ether of the future, otherwise my dance would have been immortalized. Then a miracle occurs: Jimmy Crib quits for the night. My dance partner tells me he hopes I'll be back on Wednesday night because that is the best night for dancing. I tell him I'll be back in Ohio by then, and he makes me promise to look him up the next time I am in San Antonio. I promise and am surprised to realize I mean it.

I hadn't even learned my dance partner's name, but dancing with him has reminded me of how much I really do love to dance. When I was nineteen, I lied about my age to get a gig as a dancing cocktail waitress because they pulled in the big bucks (I needed the money). During three shows a night, I and my fellow waitresses danced and sang to cabaret hits, including some from the musical of the same name. Yes, we wore fishnet stockings, but everything else was pretty well covered. During the same period, I also worked at the classy steakhouse down the street, where Wayne was a fellow employee (we met there). He would come watch my cabaret act after the restaurant closed for the night. It would be absolutely spot on for Simon Cowell to say I sang like a cabaret singer. But I danced like an idol. Somehow I never danced or sang much after that. I guess I was too busy winding my way toward a PhD Ultimately, the world of science snatched me away from a life in show business. It took a visit to Floore's and a gentleman recovering from double hip-replacement surgery to make me nostalgic for two of the passions of my youth.

The next day we head to the Alamo, where I am stunned by the peaceful beauty of a place known for being the site of a historic battle. One of the greatest things about having kids is that you finally learn what you should have learned in school.

I truly would not tell anyone to forget the Alamo. And if you are visiting San Antonio, definitely go to Floore's.

When you get there, dance with anyone who asks, particularly if they are sporting a cane. Floore's is the kind of place where you leave your worries at the door and proceed directly to the Texas two-step.

Wayne's Failproof Featherlight Buttermilk Pancakes

Leaving on Saturday morning for Kat's spring break trip to San Antonio put Cake Day in jeopardy. Wayne came to the rescue, making us these "cakes" as a going-away breakfast. Pancakes hold a special place in my culinary heart.

My mother was not ever big on formality of any type. She was the kind of mother who would get down on the sidewalk to watch ants with us, when she might have better spent her time tidying the house and planning something more than a casual dinner. At the end of such a day she would inevitably call out, "Hey kids, how 'bout pancakes for supper?" We loved this and bragged about her to other kids whose mothers would never have let them eat pancakes for supper. (This was the 1950s and mothers were still smothered under a heavy layer of food guilt.) It took us years to figure out that pancakes were easy and cheap to make, and that our mother wasn't just serving them for dinner because it was fun.

Wayne cut this recipe out of our local newspaper many years ago and has prepared them on countless weekend mornings for guests or for "just us." All of the girls' friends love them, and I sometimes think the only reason they want to spend the night at our house is just to eat Wayne's pancakes in the morning. The key is the buttermilk—it must be fresh and whole (do not use low-fat buttermilk). These pancakes are light and fluffy and really soak up the butter and syrup.

Preheat griddle to medium hot.

Cake

¾ cup whole buttermilk (pancakes will not be as fluffy if whole buttermilk is not used)
¼ cup milk
2 tablespoons melted unsalted butter or vegetable oil
1 egg
1 cup all-purpose flour
1 teaspoon sugar
½ teaspoon salt
½ teaspoon baking soda
extra oil or butter for the griddle or pan

1. Combine ingredients and mix with whisk just until blended (it is fine for there to be small lumps, but do not overmix).

2. Let sit for 5 minutes to allow the baking soda and acid of the buttermilk to react.

3. Heat 2 tablespoons of oil in a skillet over medium-high heat. When hot, wipe away excess oil, leaving a thin film.

4. Add ¼ cup pancake batter per pancake, and cook until bubbles appear at the edges.

5. Turn with a spatula and cook the other side (do not flatten with spatula).

6. Keep making them, adding more oil or butter as needed.

Reason for Hope: Driving Dame Goodall

"One real reason for hope is that the people of the world are uniting everywhere to speak out strongly, but for the most part peacefully, against war." —Jane Goodall

My job this week is to host Dr. Jane Goodall—Dame Jane Goodall (the honorific "Dame" is the equivalent of a knighthood in Britain). She is coming to Dayton to give the keynote speech for my university's annual undergraduate symposium.

When I learned Goodall would be joining us the day after her birthday I itched to be the one to bake a cake for her. I was thrilled when the event planner asked if I would do the honors. But how would I manage this feat when I would be in San Antonio until hours before her arrival? Simple, I would do what those who bake cakes for a living do—freeze the cake and frost it when I returned. So I made the cake and stuck it in the deep freeze, but while in San Antonio I received this e-mail from my bosses' boss:

Jayne: Go ahead and buy the cake from Dorothy Lane Market. I will pay for it.

I am pretty sure she envisioned the kind of cake my mother made (page 122) or, worse, that Goodall would end up with food poisoning. My friends in San Antonio advised me to ignore the message but lacking confidence in the presence of an icon I asked Wayne to pick up a carrot cake at the market. We deposit the cake in Goodall's hotel room before picking her up at the airport.

We make it to the airport on time, but it is close to midnight before her plane lands. I've had plenty of time to think about what to say to the great lady. Soon the passengers are straggling off the plane, and I feel genuine awe when I quickly spot a simply dressed and rather tired looking traveler carrying a stuffed chimpanzee. She could easily be anyone's grandmother visiting her grandchildren instead of one of the world's most well-known and best-loved scientists. Goodall catches sight of the sign I am holding up and moves toward me, looking, well, relieved. We embrace, and she says, "I am terribly sorry to have kept you up so late." It is true that we are tired—Kat and I had returned only hours earlier from a spring-break trip to San Antonio. But the lateness of the hour becomes irrelevant once I find myself in the presence of this icon and legend who is putting me at ease with her gratitude and humility.

We manage to get her to the family minivan without anyone recognizing her and without any international incidents. I climb in beside Wayne while Kat helps Dr. Jane, as she prefers children to call her, into the backseat. Kat starts to pull the sliding door shut and I hear a squawk, reminiscent of the sound a chimpanzee makes, as the door barely avoids dissecting Goodall's arm. Before I can turn around to look, I hear the loveliest laugh (can a laugh sound British?). Kat starts to stammer an apology, but Dr. Jane is having none of it.

The next morning I pick up Goodall and her assistant, Mary, who had arrived ahead of her boss, and escort them to the lecture hall. On the short ride to the university Mary fills Goodall in on her messages, informing her in the most casual of tones that "Kofi" has called. It seems safe to assume that this is secretary general of the United Nations Kofi Annan. I'm dying to find out what Kofi was calling her about, but we've arrived at our destination. I'm the one now who wants to issue a chimp squawk. Dr. Jane goes off to prepare for her talk, and I take my reserved seat in the front row next to the president of my university.

Goodall walks out on the stage and heads toward the podium, issuing the morning call of a chimpanzee. The audience explodes in laughter. I suppose we all understood, without really knowing, that this is what she would do. Her message is one of hope and persistence. She shares with us her certainty that hope emanates from the wonders of the human brain, the marvels of modern technology, the resilience of nature, and the indomitableness of the human spirit. She first spoke of these beliefs, she tells us, on the day after 9/11. Dr. Jane travels over three hundred days a year spreading her message of hope and raising funds for her beloved Gombe National Park in Tanzania.

It is my deep belief that it is the job of parents and all adults to offer children hope in this crazy world and to help them understand that what they do matters. Jane Goodall is the best ambassador of hope imaginable, and this is embodied in her Roots and Shoots program for young people. Roots creep everywhere underground, she explains, and they establish a firm foundation. Shoots, by contrast, seem very weak. But when shoots reach toward the light, she says, they can break through brick walls. Imagine that the brick walls are all the problems we have inflicted on our planet. Hundreds and thousands of roots and shoots, hundreds and thousands of young people around the world, can break through these walls. "You can change the world" is Dr. Jane's message.

After her talk, Goodall happily signs books for hours. When she is done, I take her to tea in the president's dining room with a select group of students. I notice that Mary, Goodall's assistant, brought the carrot cake I delivered the night before and that it has not been touched. The students are enthralled to be in her presence and she, in turn, is equally enthralled with them. I sit quietly, watching in wonderment as she engages with these young people. Dr. Jane seems both young and ageless. Had I not known that she had celebrated her seventy-second birthday only the day before, I would have put her age at least a decade younger. This was most evident after the tea, when I observed her literally skipping on her way back to my car.

On the trip back to the airport the subject of cake comes up. I tell them how I had made a cake for the occasion, as part of my year of cake, but had been scared off. Goodall makes it crystal clear she would have preferred the homemade cake. Then the two women tell me about the cakes their mothers and grandmothers baked during World War II, when the wolf was at the door and butter and sugar in short supply. Goodall recalls how her dear grandmother Danny once made a cake during those years using every ingredient she had on hand, including glass (discovered when an uncle bit into the cake).

I learn that ginger cake is Dr. Jane's favorite. Had I known this, I would have made Goodall the ginger cake in this book. She tells me that ginger was at one time an important crop in Tanzania and how she has, through her Jane Goodall Institute, gotten Tanzanians to once again grow ginger and coffee. Today Tanzanians are exporting their coffee and ginger around the world. Through the sales of these two crops, Goodall hopes to save the habitat of her beloved chimpanzees and give the Tanzanian people a living wage. The lesson is that although hope can be purchased; homemade cakes are preferred.

Daffodil Cake with Orange Glaze

I chose this cake for Cake Day this week because, when we arrived home from San Antonio, where it is always summer, the daffodils I had planted with such high hopes in November were in full bloom. This inspired me to find a cake as inspiring as the flowers themselves. The recipe comes from the cookbook I received as a wedding present, *The New McCall's Cookbook*, by Mary Eckley (1973 edition). My well-used copy has pages falling out and spots on it from all manner of food and drink (especially tea and butter stains). This is like an angel food cake, with a bit more flavor and color than is typical.

Preheat oven to 375° F.
You will need an ungreased 10" tube pan.

Note: This cake takes about twenty minutes to prepare, thirty-five minutes to bake, and two hours to cool. This does not count letting the egg whites come to room temperature, which takes about an hour. I suggest starting to make this cake about three hours before you are planning to serve it.

White Batter

1¾ cups egg whites (12–14 eggs) at room temperature
1¼ cups sifted cake flour (sift before measuring)
1¾ cups sugar
½ teaspoon salt
1½ teaspoons cream of tartar
1½ teaspoons vanilla extract

Yellow Batter

5 egg yolks
2 tablespoons cake flour
2 tablespoons sugar
1 tablespoon grated orange peel

1. Separate twelve eggs, putting the whites into a large bowl and bringing them to room temperature (if twelve eggs don't result in 1¾ cups, you can separate another egg or two).

2. Make the white batter by sifting the flour with ¾ cup of the sugar; resift three times and set aside.

3. Beat the egg whites, on high speed, with salt and cream of tartar, until soft peaks form.

4. Gradually beat in remaining cup of sugar, ¼ cup at a time, beating well after each addition, until stiff peaks form when the beater is slowly raised (do not beat until dry).

5. With a rubber scraper, or wire whisk, gently fold vanilla into egg whites until well combined.

6. Sift one-fourth of the flour mixture over the egg whites; using a wire whisk or rubber scraper, gently fold the flour in with fifteen strokes, using an over-and-under motion and rotating the bowl a quarter of a turn after each addition. Repeat with each one-fourth portion of flour.

Note: These are the type of detailed instructions I would have ignored as a young cook, but they really make a difference.

7. Now fold the flour in with an additional ten strokes—the flour mixture should be completely blended into the egg whites. Put one-third of this batter into a medium-size bowl.

8. Make the yellow-cake batter: In a small bowl, combine egg yolks with cake flour and sugar. With an electric mixer (using the same beaters you used to make the white-cake batter), beat on high speed until thick and lemon-colored. Stir in the orange peel.

9. With a rubber scraper or wire whisk, using an under-and-over motion, gently fold, with fifteen strokes, the yellow-cake batter into the one-third of the white-cake batter you set aside in the bowl from Step 7 above.

10. For a marbled effect, spoon the batters alternately into the ungreased ten-inch tube pan, ending with the white batter on top. With a spatula or knife, cut through the batter twice.

11. With a rubber scraper, gently spread batter in the pan until it is smooth on top and touches the sides of the pan.

12. Bake on lower rack of the oven for thirty to forty minutes, or until the cake springs back when gently pressed with a fingertip.

13. Invert pan over the neck of a bottle (a beer or wine bottle works well); let the cake cool completely (about two hours).

14. With a dull knife, or spatula, carefully loosen the cake from the sides of the pan; remove and place right-side-up on a cake plate or stand. Spoon glaze over the cake and serve.

Orange Glaze

1 cup confectioners' sugar
½ teaspoon grated lemon peel
1 teaspoon orange juice
2 tablespoons milk (approximate amount)
1 drop yellow food color

Mix all ingredients until smooth. Spoon over the cooled cake that you have placed on a cake plate or stand.

Bob, the Easter Bunny, and the Apache Helicopter

"There are two ways to live your life—one is as though nothing is a miracle, the other is as though everything is a miracle."
—Albert Einstein

The parking lot was as empty…as empty as a Catholic university parking lot on Good Friday. When I decided to work on this particular Friday, I knew I would get a lot done because no one else would be there. Also, my e-mail system was down, so I had no choice but to do some real work. I dug in like the Energizer Bunny and caught up in two hours instead of the four I had estimated.

Leaving work, I headed to the market to pick up the ingredients for our Easter feast. I was stunned into silence by the Easter cakes on parade, all pastel missionaries of the holiday. I struggled to not buy one because I had decided to give my mother-in-law a break from cooking and make Easter dove breads for Easter morning breakfast. Bread, a close and darling cousin of cake, seems more appropriate for Easter, as Christ himself blessed many a loaf of bread.

What is the difference between bread and cake? Not much. Mostly it is that bread uses yeast for leavening, which results in dough instead of batter (dough is drier and you can't pour it). While technically not cake, this bread is sweet and light and sure to satisfy both bread and cake lovers.

After the "cake" was consumed on Easter morning and Easter bunnies put to bed in their baskets, I lingered at the breakfast table talking to my father-in-law, Bob. Bob, at eighty-six, is razor sharp. An electrical engineer, he was once the top expert in the country on rotating machinery. Bob worked for the navy during World War II and then for NASA, Lear Corporation, and Otis (of elevator fame). He designed the alternator that is in your car today. Back in the 1970s he developed an electric car for NASA.

But Bob's greatest accomplishment came after he retired. I asked him to tell me, once again, the story of how at the spry age of seventy-one he saved the Apache helicopters in the first Iraq war. The story goes like this: In 1991 Desert Storm was in full force. Retired and sitting around his house on Lake Erie, Bob took a call from the folks who made the fuel pumps for Apache helicopters. They explained to Bob that 300 helicopters were grounded in the desert with sand and grit embedded in their rotating parts. Bob is one of only two or three people in the United States who understands this motor because he helped design it. He asked for the relevant specs and promised to call back the next day.

Getting to work, Bob uncovered his slide rule. As planned, within twenty-four hours he called the company back, explaining that the rotor was the problem. "It needed to be skewed out to the third harmonic," he tells me. Say what? Bob is drawing this out for me, putting all manner of details on paper while keeping up a steady lecture. "I didn't know I still knew that," he said at one point. The final solution: "Trim 7/1000 of an inch off of the ¾" rotor and they will get lift off," Bob tells the company representative, who is skeptical. The two men argue, and finally Bob says, "Just try it." Bob's calculations are passed along to the people babysitting the grounded helicopters. They shave 7/1000 of an inch off of one rotor on one helicopter. The helicopter rises into the sky.

Easter is about hope and miracles. Surely saving the Apache helicopters from the desert sand qualifies as a modern-day minor miracle. What was the price of this miracle? Bob charged the company $485. He saved soldiers' lives and the company $10 to $20 million. And he did it with a slide rule.

Bob revealed another miracle on this Easter morn. A life-long conservative, he announced that there is something terribly wrong with George W. Bush. No one goaded him into this epiphany. It would have required an apache helicopter motor to pick me up off the floor.

Italian Easter Dove Cake

Note: Much easier than it sounds—and also fabulous!

Anyone with little kids knows what I mean when I say that making something the day before to serve on Easter morning is a sure route to sanity. This recipe results in two loaves of a fragrant dove-shaped bread. Make one and give one away. We gave our extra Easter dove to Mr. Gerber, who lives across the street. Mr. Gerber (no one calls him by his first name, Charlie) has lived in his house since the day he was born and he is now well into his nineties.

"Golden with egg yolks and butter, this sweet bread resembles pound cake," says the trailer for this recipe from the *Bread Baking* cookbook, a Nitty Gritty book published in 1975. This is another example of a cookbook in my collection that has been used and loved until it is falling apart. Lizzie learned to bake bread with me using this book.

Italians celebrate holidays with specialty flavored breads baked in unique shapes. This rich and tender loaf, molded into a dove, graces Italian tables at Easter as a symbol of hope and peace.

Preheat oven to 325° F.

Cake

1 package active dry yeast
¼ cup warm water
½ cup room-temperature unsalted butter
½ cup sugar
6 egg yolks (save 2 whites for topping)
½ teaspoon salt
2 tablespoons sugar
¾ cup warm whole milk

1 teaspoon grated lemon peel
2 teaspoons vanilla
4 ¼ cups flour

1. Sprinkle yeast over warm water; let stand until dissolved.

2. Beat butter and sugar until creamy, and then beat in egg yolks and salt.

3. Stir in warm milk, lemon peel, vanilla, and dissolved yeast.

4. Blend in 2 cups of flour on low speed, beating for 5 minutes.

5. Gradually add in the rest of the flour with a heavy duty mixer (using dough hook) or by hand, using a wooden spoon.

6. Turn out onto a lightly floured board or countertop and knead until smooth (about 5 minutes).

7. Place in a greased bowl and butter top of dough lightly. Cover with a towel and let rise until doubled in size (about 1 ½ to 2 hours).

8. Turn dough out onto floured surface and knead lightly.

9. Divide into four equal pieces and roll pieces into balls.

10. Roll two of the balls of dough into ovals, about 4-inches x 9-inches.

11. Transfer the dough ovals to baking sheets (1 per sheet)—these are the doves' wings.

12. Roll the other two balls into triangles, about 4-inches wide at the base and 9-inches long.

13. Place a triangle, like a cross, over the wings.

14. Holding the triangle at the center, twist it over once and press the base down for the tail. Twist the point of the triangle the opposite way and then with your fingers pull out the point of the triangle to make a beak.

15. Score the tail with a sharp knife to resemble feathers.

16. Spread each of the wings and the tail of each dove with ½ of the almond paste topping.

17. Cover and let rise in a warm place until doubled in size.

18. Brush egg white over entire surface of each dove.

19. Sprinkle wings and tail with sugar and almonds.

20. Insert a single raisin to make the eye of the dove.

21. Bake for 45 to 50 minutes, or until browned.

Almond Paste Topping

⅓ cup almond paste
1 egg white
2 ½ cups sliced almonds
1 egg white lightly beaten

The Smallest Shall Become the Greatest

"To raise new questions, new possibilities, to regard old problems from a new angle, requires creative imagination and marks real advance in science." —Albert Einstein

So sayeth the scientist. Sitting in the dark auditorium on the edge of my seat—because I had dropped my only tissue and my nose was dripping down my sleeve—I gazed at photographs of heart plaque and tumors ratted out with nanoparticles. For those of you who don't know, nanoparticles are particles roughly one billionth of a meter in diameter. (Saying "roughly" here is really just being sarcastic, because nothing is rough when one is at a nanoscale.) Nano is the new micro and nanoparticles are being used to do everything from detect tumors to deposit sunscreen on our skin. Sometime during the lecture, delivered by a prominent cardiologist who had agreed to be the keynote speaker at this symposium I had spent a year of my life planning, I flashed back to 1966. In that year, I recalled, I also sat in a darkened theater to watch the film *The Fantastic Voyage*. In the movie a medical team is shrunk small enough to be injected into a scientist's brain in order to save his life. It was a fantastic but flawed adventure; and, of course, it was fiction. Still is. Nanoparticles are fantastic and flawed, but they are not fiction; they are just one more thing unleashed on the world before anyone really understood them.

The cardiologist finished his talk and I walked out into the diamond light of an April afternoon. The trees were covered with nanoparticles—I mean blooms. It is easy to get caught up in science-speak and view the entire world as various arrangements of atoms. I guess I mean easy to do if you are a scientist. I wonder, sometimes, how I would look at the world had I never studied how atoms move, genes sort, and flowers flower. I cannot help but see the world in all its astounding glory and not wonder at the brilliance that is created every day, all day long. I am told that many atheists are scientists and that biologists are the king of atheists.

An atheist, I am not. Having survived an agnostic childhood home, I chose science because of its objectivity and because it is something I thought I could control. I longed for the sterile laboratory, where I could design and execute perfect experiments with perfect controls and, thus, by the transitive property have a perfect life. The irony is that studying science made me a believer. I don't feel compelled to explain or defend my views. I prefer to quote a great chemist who said, "God is an awesome organic chemist."

A good friend and colleague of mine Albert was recently diagnosed with cancer of the prostate. While the prognosis is good, even better than ever before in history, I cannot help but worry. This is a man who helped shepherd me through the treacherous shoals of tenure and who led my family on an unforgettable trip to the Hawaiian Islands.

My hope, on this day, is that the promise of nanotechnology is not a fantasy and that we can live with any of the unintended consequences. Why? Because if we can use nanoparticles to detect cancer earlier, or treat it more effectively, then my friends' and family's lives may depend upon it.

Krumb Kuchen

I made this for Albert on the eve of his trip to Boston for prostate cancer surgery.

The recipe comes from his mother, Eva Greer Burky, by way of his great-grandmother Bessie Bauer Biel and his grandmother Mary (Mame) Biel Heitzmann. Eva made this Kuchen almost every Sunday for breakfast. Albert complains that his wife, Kathy (aka Saint Kathy), does not make it as often as he would like.

Preheat oven to 400° F and butter two 8" round cake pans (or one 9" x 13" pan).

Cake

3 cups all-purpose flour
2 cups brown sugar
1 teaspoon salt
1 teaspoon cinnamon
½ cup shortening (Crisco)
2 teaspoons baking powder
2 eggs, beaten
¾ cup milk

1. Mix together flour, brown sugar, salt, and cinnamon.

2. Cut in shortening until you have fine crumbs.

3. Reserve 1 cup of this mixture for topping.

4. After you've set aside 1 cup of the mixture, add baking powder, eggs, and milk and mix well.

5. Pour into prepared pans.

6. Top with reserved crumbs and bake 20 to 25 minutes.

Physics, Prayers, and Science Projects

"Science without religion is lame; religion without science is blind."
—Albert Einstein

The most astonishing thing about being a new mother is that you cannot find the time to take a shower. Today this was what I told a young woman I work with, who is about to pick up the son she is adopting: "Take a shower before you pick up your new son." She nodded as if she understood, but I knew she didn't. Every mother I know can attest to this maxim but none of us ever believed anything veteran moms told us when we were expecting.

I also found out today that being a mother of a twelve-year-old and a twenty-year-old still means that sometimes you can't find the time to take a shower. I woke up this morning at 6:25 to get Wayne out of bed. He was making the ten-hour round-trip to pick up Lizzie, who had just finished her second year at Pitt. I made Wayne a thermos of tea, waved good-bye, and began to plan how to spend the fourteen hours productively to minimize my anxiety.

Kat and a friend kept me busy putting together their sixth-grade science project poster. It was due, of course, the next day. I always do my best to promote physics, forbidding science projects that involve plants or rodents. Physics experiments are elegant and elemental. Einstein didn't do rats. Einstein only needed paper and pencil, and time, to do his work. Last year I managed to convince Kat to go the physics route. Feel free to steal the physics route idea (you will thank me). She compared the ability of thermoses of different materials (glass, plastic, or metal) to maintain the temperature of the liquid added. That was great fun. Chemistry experiments rank second. This year I had no control over the selection phase and was not excited about the project, which was to test whether sugar dissolved better in water, tea, or coke. I talked them into also testing for pH as well, since I knew their plan was a bit skimpy on scientific rigor.

I left the girls to set up the experiment and headed to my lab to fetch the pH paper. On the way back, my car pulled up unexpectedly at an open house. The house had the kitchen of my dreams and I stayed so long admiring it—imagining the cakes I could concoct in its environs—that the realtor began to cast odd looks in my direction. She caught me taking cookbooks down from the shelves. So what? I was only looking for cake recipes. As I was leaving, my cell phone rang and Kat's voice told me that she and her friend were ready for the pH paper. Could I please come home now? I understand the temporal demands of scientific experiments but I lingered a bit longer. I didn't want Kat to think that she determined the length of the chain I was on.

As I've already mentioned, biologists harbor the highest percentage of atheists among the sciences. But physicists are the scientists most likely to believe in a higher being. It is my opinion, though, that there are very few scientists of any stripe who don't whisper a prayer upon submission of a grant proposal. Same goes for kids presenting their science projects. I said thousands of prayers on this day for the safe return of Wayne and Lizzie. I also prayed that next year's science project, if there is one, has nothing to do with plants or rodents. God, are you listening? Einstein, are you?

Brownie Pudding Cake

The chemistry of cake is simple but not always "fail" proof. This great recipe is from *Yankee Magazine's Church Suppers and Potluck Dinners Cookbook* and it represents one chemistry experiment that is sure to please. I wanted an easy but good cake this week because Lizzie and her friends will be gathering to celebrate the upcoming summer. You won't have to pray that this comes out right. The cookbook has this to say: "Is it a pudding or a cake? As the dessert bakes, the cake rises to the top, leaving a fudgy layer of pudding below. An easy, excellent dessert that everyone loves." Serve warm, topped with whipped cream or ice cream.

Preheat oven to 350° F and butter a 9" x 13" baking pan.

Cake

3 cups all-purpose white flour
6 tablespoons unsweetened cocoa powder
2 tablespoons baking powder
2 ¼ cups white sugar
1 ½ teaspoons salt
1 ½ cups milk
6 tablespoons vegetable oil
1 tablespoon vanilla extract

Topping

2 ¼ cups brown sugar
¾ cup unsweetened cocoa powder
5 ¼ cups boiling water

1. In the large mixing bowl of an electric mixer, combine flour, 6 tablespoons cocoa, baking powder, sugar, and salt. Mix on low speed for 30 seconds.

2. Combine milk, oil, and vanilla and add to the dry ingredients, mixing on medium speed until smooth.

3. Pour into prepared pan.

4. For the topping, combine the three ingredients in a medium bowl and mix until smooth. Gently pour over the batter. Bake for 35 minutes. Serve warm.

The Calculus of Compassion

"Sooner or later we all discover that the important moments in life are not the advertised ones, not the birthdays, the graduations, the weddings, not the great goals achieved. The real milestones are less prepossessing. They come to the door of memory unannounced, stray dogs that amble in, sniff around a bit, and simply never leave. Our lives are measured by these." —Susan B. Anthony

Kat's last elementary school science fair is today. As a scientist, I wish I could say that I love science fairs and think they are effective at motivating kids to become scientists. But I cannot. I didn't like them when I was a kid, and I don't like them much better now. And I have serious doubts about their effectiveness. Watching men walk in space is what led that last great rush to science. What will fuel the next rush? We need it badly—the U.S. is falling, falling, falling behind in math and science. Why is this generation not enamored of the thrill of discovery, the desire to know the secret life of turtles or molecules? Perhaps it is because of too many science fairs that put too fine a point on the science, when all people really want to do is lie on the grass and stare at the sky? When I had nothing to do in the summer, my mother would tell me to do just that. It was delivered as an order and probably meant to buy her some peace and quiet, but it instilled in me a sense of wonder and curiosity that was not limited to finding out why the sky is blue.

So, Wayne, Lizzie, and I walk the two blocks to the school and enter a gym full of sweaty elementary school kids standing in front of their trifolds. We wander first as a threesome, then split up and continue our zig-zag trek. The titles are what draw you in, ranging from the scary: "Do You Know What Drinks Are Killing Your Teeth?" to the practical: "Absorbancy of Handy Towels." Somehow we converge at Kat's poster. We ask her a few penetrating questions—like "What is pH anyway?"—before heading back into the world of sunshine.

On the walk home, a dog runs right past us and into the street. I manage to grab it just in time to avoid a collision with a car. I examine the tag and discover her name is Penny, and we take her home and call the number on the tag. I leave a message. Our dog Tula has never met another dog she doesn't like, including Penny, and they settle quickly into amicable romping. We put Penny on the chain usually reserved for Tula, since Penny seems more attracted to moving vehicles. I return to the world of work-a-day science, leaving Lizzie on the porch with Tula and Penny; they appear a contented threesome.

When I return home later, I find out about the disaster that ensued in my absence. A neighbor girl had walked by with her dog, stopping to let it play with Penny and Tula. Soon a woman walking a Jack Russell Terrier wandered down our block. No one involved had ever noticed this particular woman and dog on our street before. The Jack Russell took one look at the three dogs, wriggled out of his collar, and set off down the block. Tula began to chase him, but she turned back when Lizzie called her. The Jack Russell kept going.

Our neighbor Gretchen witnessed this scene and offered to drive the Jack Russell's owner around to look for her dog. Unfortunately, he had tried to make it home by running across a busy street. Gretchen explained later that they had found the poor dog lying on the grass by the side of the road, looking more asleep than dead. The woman simply picked up the dog in her arms and Gretchen drove them both home.

A short while later, Gretchen, Wayne, and Lizzie visited the woman, taking her a single peony bloom, at Lizzie's insistence. The woman explained to them what a great companion the Jack Russell had been to her housebound husband, and how it had taken her two years to train the dog. Wayne and Lizzie promised to make a donation to the local Humane Society in her dog's memory.

I had returned to a broken-hearted Lizzie and this strange story. She was crying and blaming it all on Tula. Penny's owners finally arrived to retrieve their dog and seemed oddly unconcerned that she had been wandering the streets. Hadn't it ever occurred to them, we wondered, that their dog could be killed by a car?

Witnessing the cracking of my children's hearts is itself heart-cracking. Yet there is solace in knowing my children are compassionate beings. I cannot imagine having children without a conscience, or lacking in compassion, or unable to empathize. I read the book *The Bad Seed* when I was in junior high school, and it sent chills of fear up my spine. The pain a parent must feel discovering that their child is a psychopath is quite beyond the reach of my own soul.

When I was young my questions about what my future children would be like were based on the song *Que Sera Sera*: "Will they be pretty, will they be rich?" But I grew up, and I began to wonder more if they would be funny and sweet. What I've got for sure are funny, sweet girls. But back to that song: "the future's not ours to see."

We did not see the future when we stopped to save Penny. The Jack Russell would be alive today if we had not gone to the science fair, or if it had been a rainy day, or if we had tied up both dogs, or if the woman had crossed the street, or if the neighbor girl hadn't stopped by with her dog, or if the Jack Russell's collar hadn't been so loose, or if he wasn't given to escaping and running home.

And what if the dog that died wasn't such a great companion after all? People who know Jack Russell terriers all say the same thing: they are high energy, demanding, and not-very-companionable dogs. Maybe the woman was deluding herself about what a great companion her dog had been for her housebound husband. We will never know for sure, and I can only hope that they recovered from the loss of their dog and were able to find happiness with another one.

It is strange and unsettling that the saving of one dog led to the demise of another. What kind of calculus can describe these events? Once again I am reminded that math and science do have their limitations. Science fairs may teach the scientific method, and this is a great thing, but science cannot calculate compassion or loss.

Tres Leches (Three Milks) Cake

Cinco de Mayo is this week. In Los Angeles more than one million mostly Hispanic immigrants and their supporters skipped work and took to the streets, flexing their economic muscle in a nationwide boycott. The boycott succeeded in slowing or shutting many farms, factories, markets and restaurants in over 140 cities across the U.S. The purpose was to create a day without immigrants, to show what an integral role immigrants play in today's labor force. The signs they carried said, "*Today we march, tomorrow we vote.*" Sweeping immigration reform is the hope of millions.

On our spring break trip to San Antonio Kat ordered this cake at a restaurant on the River Walk and fell in love with it. It is traditionally served as part of a Cinco de Mayo feast. After witnessing the sad loss of a beloved dog this week, we really needed a great cake. I found this recipe in numerous places, including on the Internet.

Preheat oven to 350° F.
Butter a 7" x 11" pan.

Cake

1½ cups cake flour
1 teaspoon baking powder
1 cup plus 1 teaspoon sugar
½ cup (1 stick) room-temperature unsalted butter
5 large eggs
1 teaspoon vanilla extract
1 ⅓ cups of whole milk
1 cup sweetened condensed milk
1 cup evaporated milk
1 tablespoon light rum
1 cup heavy cream

1. In the small bowl of an electric mixer, combine the cake flour and baking powder.

Mix on low speed for 30 seconds; set aside.

1. In the large bowl of an electric mixer, cream butter and 1 cup sugar until light and fluffy (at least 5 minutes).

2. Add the eggs and ½ teaspoon vanilla extract, and beat until frothy.

3. With a rubber spatula, gently fold in the flour mixture in increments, alternating with increments of ⅓ cup of the whole milk, until the batter is smooth.

4. Pour cake batter into the prepared pan and bake for 30 minutes, or until a toothpick inserted in the center comes out clean and the top springs back when lightly pressed with a finger.

5. Allow cake to cool in the pan on a wire rack for 20 minutes, then invert onto a serving platter. Pierce the

cake with a fork in many places, and allow it to cool completely.

6. In a medium mixing bowl, whisk together the condensed milk, evaporated milk, 1 cup of the whole milk, and rum until well blended. Pour syrup evenly over the cake a little at a time, until it is saturated; you may not need the entire amount.

7. Refrigerate, covered in plastic wrap, for at least 3 hours.

Whipped Cream

In a large mixing bowl with an electric mixer, whisk the heavy cream until it begins to thicken. Add 1 teaspoon sugar and ½ teaspoon vanilla extract, and continue whisking until stiff peaks form. Using a spatula, spread the cream over the top and sides of the cake. Serve, cut into squares.

What Do Mothers Want?

"You were born in the morning... to take my place...whoever, wherever you are I'll love you."
—Carrie Newcomer, folksinger

"What Do Women Want?" That is the question Freud tried to answer. He might have asked an easier question: "What Do Mothers Want?"

I am twenty years into the life sentence aka motherhood and the answer to WDMW is simple and ironic: We want a day off. Even half a day off will do. We want silence and the chance to think. To think about things other than colic and science projects and the horrible things that might happen to our college-aged offspring on cross-country trips. We want to read uninterrupted, without having to Get Up and *Do Something*. We want a respite from having to make lunch or a sandcastle or from having to slather on sunscreen or play Frisbee. Getting up is what gets us down. There have been days when solitary confinement sounded better than a trip to a spa. As a girl child I watched the older sisters of friends join convents intent on becoming nuns. I sure as hell did not understand why *anyone* would choose such a life. Now, many days, I think it sounds pretty good. What could be better than a life in which you are regularly treated to silence and meals are provided.

Yet motherhood is the one thing I would not have missed in this messy thing called life. If you're getting the impression that motherhood induces schizophrenia, you would be correct. Children make you insane and keep you sane.

As a microbiologist, I sometimes envy the way single cells generate their offspring: the single chromosome is copied and the new copy is dragged into the new daughter cell that is forming. Then the cell splits into two cells, mother and daughter, as it were. All this happens in as little as ten minutes before the daughter cell is on her own. While I can visualize this form of reproduction, I have a hard time imagining it: hard and fast and without sentiment. These fleeting families of molecules bear little resemblance to what I've known and loved about being part of a family. The mother microbe has no pain, no attachment, and no reward. I have a very old T-shirt from some long-forgotten meeting of microbiologists with the following emblazoned on it: "Microbes do it and split." While this mode of reproduction has some appeal, it isn't really for me.

Today is Mother's Day and I awoke to the silence of a

house that no longer harbors children young enough to get up with the sun. There was no need to tip-toe past Kat's room, because at six months shy of age thirteen she sleeps the sleep of someone whose brain is being rewired. Because it is. And Lizzie is off visiting friends in the city of her birth and not due back until dinner. I made myself my morning cup of tea and walked with the dog through my gardens and then around a few blocks before heading back home for a second cup of tea and the morning paper.

I spent the afternoon of this Mother's Day working in the garden. Because it was both cold and rainy, I remained completely alone. I recommend gardening as bromide for motherhood–gardens are a lot like children, only silent.

When Lizzie's vintage Volvo, Penelope Rose, pulled into the driveway later that afternoon, the sun burst through the gray and lit the edges of the day. Lizzie emerged from the cocoon of her car, hugged me, and said, "Happy Mother's Day." I could see my gardens over her warm shoulders and I experienced the flow of life–that feeling of really being in your life.

Dinner was wonderful—I love any food someone else makes for me. Wayne made dinner, Lizzie made a cake, and Kat gave me a bundle of Mother's Day coupons proclaiming things like "This coupon is good for one nap, without me interrupting, but *only* one." After dinner and homework and Kat's bedtime, I started writing this. Lizzie came and showed me a drawing she had been working on, which I plan to add to the pop-up version of this book. No toddler's charm can trump this.

I think the only true reward for parenthood would be to have the chance, when your kids are grown and gone, to be able to go back in time to any day of their childhood and relive it. I can think of many with each of my daughters that I would love to relive. Perhaps this explains the great joy of grandchildren that everyone talks about. I hope I get the chance.

Caribbean Pineapple Corn Cake

Lizzie made this for me today to celebrate Mother's Day. This is a recipe that she brought into our lives, one she discovered in the crazy cooking days of her late adolescence. She was the hit of more than a few block parties with this recipe. Is it bread or cake? No one cares, they just want more. The recipe is adapted from *At Blanchard's Table: A Trip to the Beach Cookbook*. Lizzie owns a signed copy of this charming book and has graciously left it with us while she is away at college.

Preheat oven to 325° F, and butter and flour a 9" square glass dish. (You can use a metal pan, but glass works best for this cake.)

Cake

1 cup all-purpose flour
1 cup yellow cornmeal
2 tablespoons baking powder
1 teaspoons salt
½ pound (2 sticks) room-temperature unsalted butter
¾ cup sugar
4 eggs
1½ cups canned cream-style corn
½ cup canned crushed pineapple, drained
1 cup shredded Monterey Jack or mild white Cheddar cheese.

1. In the medium bowl of an electric mixer, cream butter and sugar on medium-high speed until fluffy (about 5 minutes).

2. In a medium bowl, whisk together the flour, cornmeal, baking powder, and salt; set aside.

3. Add eggs, one at a time, beating well after each addition.

4. Add the corn, pineapple, and cheese and mix to blend.

5. On low speed, add the dry ingredients and beat until well blended.

6. Pour the batter into the prepared pan and bake until golden brown around the edges and a toothpick stuck in the center comes out clean (about 1 hour).

Strawberries and Cream: A Return to the Sweet Life

"Cream doesn't rise to the top, it works its way up." —proverb

It is a perfect spring day. In my community we celebrate a holiday creatively titled "That Day in May." This local event takes place the week before Memorial Day, presumably to avoid eclipsing the sacred, somber, and personal nature of that holiday.

What happens on That Day in May is always the same: a parade, a carnival, an art show, a 5K race, a pancake breakfast, and a silent auction. Every year new people show up.

As the festivities wind down this year, we gather on our front porch to celebrate a hero. Ethan, thirteen, gets to eat cake again. He started having epileptic seizures when he was five. His parents, Gretchen and Kelly, began their journey down the tortuous tunnel of treatments for this horrifying disease. They tried many drugs, one after the other, but none eliminated the seizures.

Ethan began to lose ground at school and in every other part of his life. I met him when he was a toddler and his brain has always been one of my favorite ones on the planet. I treasure the way he thinks, and to see that brain under assault affected me, and all who love him, deeply. Finally, Gretchen and Kelly made the very difficult decision to try a stark and strict diet that puts the body into a ketogenic state that somehow rewires the brain. Patients can often be weaned off the diet and remain seizure-free for the rest of their lives.

Ethan was hospitalized, fasted and fed a diet of heavy cream and oil. His new regimen went on from there to a diet so restricted that on some days ten raspberries were the sum total of his carbohydrate intake. This sounded unimaginable to me, the person whose motto is "You can never have too much sugar."

Food is so important a part of our culture and celebrations that most of us can't imagine the holidays without sweets and special foods. For two years Ethan's family had to turn to something other than sweets to make Thanksgiving, Christmas, birthdays, and Halloween special. Ethan was eleven when his family started down this sugarless path. How many eleven-year-olds could endure this existence? How many parents? Gretchen, a gifted cook, took on the challenge and never looked back. Kelly, an accomplished engineer, developed a computer program that calculated the calories and ratio of fats, protein, and carbohydrates essential to the success of this diet.

One year, or halfway, into the diet Ethan's thinking was clear, his speech fluid and quickly catching up in school. The "old" Ethan was back! To celebrate, Kelly and Gretchen held a ketogenic dinner party. The menu consisted of only the foods Ethan was allowed to eat. As guests, we could select what we wanted, weigh it, and enter the information into Kelly's computer to learn if we were towing the ketogenic line. During the second year, the diet ever so gradually loosened a bit.

Woody Allen has claimed that "Ninety percent of life is showing up." I would amend that to say that ninety percent of life is about endurance. If you show up and endure the inevitable setbacks, trials, and tribulations, then you just might succeed. The difference between reality as shown on TV and actual reality is duration. Surviving thirty days in a paradise that has been deliberately made difficult is not the same as enduring two years (or five or twenty) of taking care of a loved one, especially a child who is ill and may never be well again.

There are people we would never entrust our children to for even a moment. More rare are those we feel privileged to send our children off with for a day or even a year. We conclude that our children will become better human beings for having spent time with these individuals. One of my most frequent prayers is to ask God to send such adults into my children's lives. Ethan's parents, Kelly and Gretchen, are people I would give my children to in a heartbeat. Cream does rise to the top and Gretchen and Kelly are the *crème de la crème.*

And so we gather on our porch on this day in May to celebrate the end of the ketogenic diet. And to honor Kelly and Gretchen's acts of faith, fortitude, and bravery. Ethan asks me, "Are you happier or better for eating cake every week?" "Yes," I tell him, "I believe we are." I have waited two years to make this cake for Ethan and it is sweet indeed.

Strawberries and Cream Shortcakes

This cake celebrates Ethan's return to the sweet life that includes a life with sweets. The local strawberries were not yet in, but in our part of the world spring begins with California strawberries.

This recipe comes from the *New York Times New Natural Foods Cookbook*, by Jean Hewitt.

Preheat oven to 450° F and beavily butter a 9" or 10" cake pan.

Cake

2 cups whole wheat flour (pastry flour, if you can find it)
1 teaspoon baking powder
2 tablespoon brown sugar
¼ teaspoon salt
6 tablespoons butter
2 eggs, lightly beaten
⅔ cup whole milk
1 quart strawberries, sliced
1 cup heavy cream, whipped with 2 teaspoons sugar and 1 teaspoon vanilla

1. Sift the flour with the baking powder; add brown sugar and salt.

2. Cut in 4 tablespoons of the butter until the mixture resembles course oatmeal.

3. Combine the eggs and milk and mix into the dry

ingredients with a fork just until mixed. **(If you overmix the shortcake, it will be heavy.)** The dough will be soft.

4. Transfer batter to the cake pan and bake for 20 minutes or until a knife comes out clean but not dry.

5. Remove from the pan, split horizontally, and butter the cut sides with remaining butter.

6. Cover the bottom half with sliced strawberries.

7. Cover with the top half and add remaining strawberries.

8. Top with the whipped cream.

Science Never Sleeps

"I am sitting here 93 million miles from the sun on a rounded rock which is spinning at the rate of 1000 miles an hour…and my head pointing down into space with nothing between me and infinity but something called gravity which I can't even understand, and which you can't even buy any place so as to have some stored away for a gravityless day."
—Russell Baker, journalist

I spent the week chasing science, which never sleeps, in a city where fun never takes a break. The weather in Orlando was warm and sunny outside and coldly competitive inside. Inside being a convention center where over 8,000 microbiologists from around the globe had gathered to strut their stuff—the stuff of science.

I had used the online schedule to make an itinerary that had me running all over the cavernous convention center. I sped from one dark room to another, taking notes and trying to read the minds of the presenters—trying to figure out what they were not telling us. You see, scientists only present the stuff they have already published or will be submitting electronically the day they return home from the conference (they might even send it out on the plane ride home).

What you really want to know is what is brewing in their labs right now. And this is the stuff that they are not going to tell you for fear they will be scooped. As I said, science never sleeps. When you leave your lab at the end of a typically long day, there are scientists in Japan (or Denmark or Australia) who are just arriving at work and they might be doing the same experiments you are (they might be doing them faster). It is unnerving when you think about it, and we all us scientists do. When I am sitting on my front porch holding a glass of iced tea or pinot, I try not to think about scientists in other time zones slaving over their benches and making notes in their lab books that look a lot like mine. The pace of science, like everything else, has accelerated to warp speed.

For five days in Orlando I woke up, grabbed a chai at the Starbucks in the lobby, walked past the gorgeous swimming pools where singles and families were lounging, walked past the buses headed for Disney

World, and disappeared into the convention center, emerging late in the day with reams of notes. At the end of the day, I repeated my walk past the pools, now empty, and through the luxurious lobby, taking the elevator to my room, where I crashed. I attended a few socials and had dinner with my students or my collaborators and colleagues. I even ate one evening with my PhD advisor and all of the fellow survivors of his lab. But this trip was work, plain and simple.

My PhD student, Amy, presented her work at a poster session that was mobbed four deep for three hours, leaving us elated and nervous because we weren't ready to submit the paper quite yet. Her findings were startling and significant and everyone wanted a copy of the work. I caught a few Japanese scientists trying to take photos, which is strictly forbidden, and had to ask them to stop.

Science is a high-stakes, high-stress arena where the egos are every bit as evident as in the fashion or film worlds. There are stars and wannabes and groupies—and failures. There are colleagues, collaborators, advocates, adversaries, and nemeses.

I have my very own nemesis, who was at the convention that week. This scientist is the undisputed leader in my area, royalty as it were. My "relationship" with him is the sum total of a few e-mails and a few reviews of my papers, all of which were negative. I have physically seen him only from the back or middle of a crowded lecture hall, where he is inevitably the keynote speaker. The feeling is not unlike watching a rock star from the upper deck, but I am not a groupie. I have tried to stay out of his way, even changing research areas, only to find myself swimming in the same pool again.

I am not implying that he is copying me or stealing my ideas. Typically, he remains totally unaware of my doings and his big lab includes so many pairs of hands that he often scoops me without even knowing it. It is as if he and I are both channeling the same muse but his muse is better connected than mine. Or we have the same muse, but I am the "B" client who never gets first dibs. So I am caught in this endless eddy of competition. He has garnered the usual praise and condemnation due someone of his stature. Some love him, some hate him, and most are wary. Since I don't travel in the same hallowed circles with this man, I may never have the opportunity to right his perception of me or to tell him off. I will just have to be content knowing that having a nemesis is something that not everyone can boast of—and that my nemesis is of a higher caliber than most.

I returned home a day early to have one day with Lizzie before she left on her long-planned grand summer journey to Canada, where she and her friends, Erin and Zoe, would be WWOOFing it (WWOOF stands for World Wide Opportunities on Organic Farms). A lot can be poured into a single day, when you've planned it. We woke up earlier than usual and made the rounds of my favorite garden stores. We stopped for a satisfying and leisurely lunch. After we returned home, I baked a cake for her to take on the first leg of her summer's journey.

Watching Lizzie back out of the driveway in her vintage Volvo vanished all thoughts of my nemeses. She was off to the wide open spaces of Canada and youthful searching. I still had Kat and science was far from my mind as she and I headed for the Lake Erie islands for the weekend.

Postscript: A few months later I finally met my nemesis face-to-face at a very small meeting of high-level scientists in Washington, D.C. My talk followed his and the colors on my slides got mixed up so that the audience could not see some of the text. I had to read to them. And then I fumbled a response to his rather loaded question. It was a disaster. And he treated me as he always does, with contempt. But now living fearlessly, I went up to him later and gave him the answer I should have given in the first place. To my surprise he shared an important piece of unpublished data with me. For a moment the sun shone. But the next day during the wrap-up session he made a few rather pointed swipes at me in front of everyone. I did not stop talking, which is what I would have done in the past. Others at the table responded positively to what I had to say. I left that room happy that I had not let this man, a soft-shelled animal the same as me, take away my voice. I had banished the bane of my existence. In the lobby, on my way out, the woman in charge of the workshop, and in charge of the money for her agency, quietly encouraged me to apply for a grant. Sometimes you win when you least expect it.

Garbanzo Cake (gluten-free)

I made this cake for Lizzie who was leaving, again.

I found this recipe for garbanzo cake in the *Mexican: Healthy Ways with a Favorite Cuisine* cookbook, by Jane Milton. This is a moist cake with a texture similar to Christmas pudding and it is flavored with orange and cinnamon. It contains no flour and so is a great choice for those on a gluten-free diet.

It smelled delicious, and so I stole a slice for myself before wrapping it for Lizzie to take on the first big road trip of her life. Her first stop was a visit with her boyfriend, where she would meet up with Erin, one of her childhood friends and fellow travelers. Lizzie and Erin then drove on to Toronto, via Niagara Falls, to pick up Zoe, before heading to their first assignment.

I learned later that Boyfriend loved the cake.

Preheat the oven to 350° F; and butter a loaf pan, line it with parchment paper and butter that as well.

Cake

2 10-ounce cans of chick peas, drained
4 eggs, beaten
1 cup sugar
1 teaspoon baking powder
2 teaspoons cinnamon
Juice and grated rind of 1 orange
Cinnamon sugar for sprinkling on top after baking (¼ cup sugar plus 1 teaspoon ground cinnamon)

1. Drain the chick peas in a colander, drain them completely and rub them between the palms of your hands to loosen and remove the skins.

2. Put the skinned chick peas into a food processor and process until smooth.

3. Spoon the puree into a bowl and stir in the eggs, sugar, baking powder, cinnamon, orange rind, and orange juice.

4. Pour the batter into the prepared loaf pan and level the surface.

5. Bake for about 1½ hours or until a cake tester inserted into the center comes out clean.

6. Remove the cake from the oven and let it stand in the pan for about 10 minutes.

7. Invert the pan to remove the cake onto a wire rack, right-side up.

8. Sprinkle with the cinnamon sugar.

9. Leave to cool completely.

10. Serve alone or with fresh pineapple slices.

D-Day

> "You will bring about the destruction of the German war machine, the elimination of Nazi tyranny over the oppressed peoples of Europe, and security for ourselves in a free world."
> —General Dwight Eisenhower

Eisenhower was talking to his troops before D-Day, June 6, 1944, the day when the invasion of Normandy began. Planned to liberate Europe from Nazi control, the invasion was the beginning of putting a decisive end to tyranny.

D-Day is a special day to me. My father landed at Normandy on June 7, Day 2 (called +1 by those who were in attendance) of the seventy-five day battle. Day +1 was not the longest day, but I imagine none of the soldiers thought it seemed short. My father would not talk about the war much and certainly never glorified it. But I think he was proud he was there when Europe was delivered from tyranny and those in Hitler's death camps were released.

The window for beginning the end of tyranny was just three days: June 5, 6, or 7, based on moonlight, tides, and military constraints. Ike didn't have to ask anyone for approval. Imagine that? (I have to ask for approval to launch a request to have the floors cleaned in my lab.) But he did have to deal with the weather. On June 4 the weather was menacing and reports were for more of the same. The soldiers were already at sea, sardines in metal boats, when Eisenhower gave the order for a twenty-four hour delay. It was another day of fear and seasickness for the soldiers and my stomach grows weak with the thought of the accumulation of odors on those ships. It was another day of worrying about whether the Germans would catch on to Eisenhower's grand plan. By now Ike was chain smoking Camels. Then a revised weather report indicated that a high pressure front would provide a few hours of clear weather on the morning of June 6. The decision was made, the order given.

I am always asking myself impossible questions. Today I wonder, "Would I have been able to give that order to send thousands to almost certain death?" I can't answer my question. I am certain, though, that giving that order made Eisenhower a better president, one who was reluctant to go to war because he knew the horrors and the true costs. It is my opinion that only those who have fought in wars should be allowed to start them, or to order good men and women into battle.

In 1953, eight years after the end of the war, Eisenhower delivered his famous "The Chance for Peace" speech. He spoke of the true cost of the Cold War and the arms race it had spawned. In his speech he concluded, "This is not a way of life at all, in any true sense. Under the cloud of threatening war, it is humanity hanging from a cross of iron." Eisenhower cautioned us to beware the military industrial complex. As I write this, my country has bought and paid for the military industrial complex to build an iron cross of huge dimensions and alarming cost, from which we all now hang. I can feel the cold metal under my skin and taste it in my mouth. Will we all flail on this cross of iron named terrorism or will an Eisenhower rise from this generation, lift us from the cross, and walk with us back down a road to peace? I can hope.

Lizzie brought me back a vial of sand from the beach at Normandy when she visited it on her high school trip to France. The way she tells it, the chaperone wasn't going to let her make the trek down to the beach until she told the woman that her grandfather had fought in that battle of battles. Lizzie described for me how far the beaches are from the cliffs and how fast she had to run to get there and back before the bus departed. It was sunny and peaceful on the day that Lizzie was there, nothing like June 6, 1944. I never visit battle sites, on purpose, because they lie. How is it that the beaches of Normandy can be peaceful with all the blood shed and lives ended on that sand? Still, Normandy is one place I would visit if given the chance. But to make it honest, I would have to make the trip over by ship on rough seas, without the seasickness medicine I need to keep from continuously wretching.

This D-Day we celebrated a friend's birthday. We found ourselves among Democrats and crates of champagne, my dream combination. As the bubbly flowed, so did the talk of how to end this most recent war and of whom to identify as the true tyrant. I wonder when D-Day will come in Iraq? Will we even know it when it happens? I am sure some folks thought it was the day Saddam Hussein was captured, but I don't agree. How many children and grandchildren of the fallen will visit those desert battle fields to take away a vial of sand?

Orange Marmalade Cake

This cake is so pretty and cheerful that it is hope itself. My father shared my love of marmalade and I sure wish he was still around now that I've discovered a cake made with this marvelous stuff. I picture us sitting at our old dining room table, with me asking him between forkfuls, and for the umpteenth time, to tell me about D-Day and all the rest of his travels on foot through Europe in that war. I have a dollar bill, safely behind glass, that he carried with him throughout the war. On the margins, written in his best penmanship, are the names of all the countries he trekked through: Luxembourg, Germany, Czechoslovakia, England, France, Belgium, and Holland. A lucky buck for sure.

The funny thing is that this cake started out as a fictitious one that became real, like the Velveteen Rabbit of storybook fame. Jan Karon, author of the wildly popular

Mitford books, all set in the same small town, decided to create a character known for baking great cakes. She invented Esther Bolick and then set about picking a cake that would be Bolick's specialty. It couldn't be chocolate, because it wasn't Karon's personal favorite. She decided on a cake she herself would love, one made with orange marmalade, and so the fictitious cake was born.

Readers wrote begging for the recipe. Karon would write back, explaining that the cake was fiction. Still the letters rolled in. Then, in 1997, she decided she needed to come up with a real recipe. Genius! So Edna Lewis and Scott Peacock, who wrote the fabulous *The Gift of Southern Cooking* cookbook together, gave birth to this recipe. It required almost every bowl I own, but it was so worth it.

Kat asked me, "Mom, do you think when you are all done with this cake thing you would know enough to invent your own cake?" Good question. My husband, who does not really like orange marmalade, pronounced this "The best cake so far."

Preheat oven to 350° F, and lightly butter three 9" round cake pans, line with parchment paper, lightly butter and flour the paper, shake out any excess.

Cake

1 cup room temperature unsalted butter
3 ¼ cups cake flour
1 tablespoon baking powder
1 teaspoon salt
5 large eggs, at room temperature
4 large egg yolks, at room temperature
⅔ cup vegetable oil
1 tablespoon grated orange zest
2 teaspoons vanilla extract
1 cup buttermilk, at room temperature

1. Sift the flour, baking soda, and salt into the large bowl of an electric mixer, and mix on low speed for 30 seconds.

2. In the medium-size bowl of an electric mixer beat the butter on medium speed until light in color (about 5 minutes).

3. Add the 2 ⅔ cups sugar in a steady stream while the mixer is going. Beat until fluffy and light (about 5 minutes).

4. Add the eggs and egg yolks, one at a time, beating well after each addition. Be sure to stop at least once and scrape down the sides of the bowl.

5. After all the eggs have been added, continue to beat on medium speed for 2 more minutes.

6. Switch to low speed, add oil, and beat for 1 minute.

7. In a small bowl combine orange zest, vanilla, and buttermilk.

8. Using a small rubber spatula, fold in half of the dry ingredients. Scrape down the sides of the bowl, and add half of the buttermilk mixture.

9. Fold in the remaining dry ingredients, scrape down the sides, and add the remaining buttermilk.

10. Pour the batter into the prepared pans, distributing evenly. Smooth the surface, rap each pan on the counter to expel any air pockets or bubbles, and place in the oven.

11. Bake for 30 to 35 minutes or until a toothpick inserted into the center comes out clean.

12. Let the cakes cool in the pans on racks for 20 minutes.

13. Prepare the orange syrup while the cakes are cooling.

Orange Syrup

1 cup freshly squeezed orange juice
¼ cup sugar

1. In a small bowl stir together the orange juice and ¼ cup sugar until the sugar is dissolved.

2. While the cakes are still in the cake pans, use a toothpick (or skewer) to poke holes at ½" intervals. Spoon the syrup over each layer, allowing the syrup to be completely absorbed before adding the remainder. Do not remove the cakes from the pans until they are completely cool.

Filling

A 12-ounce jar of orange marmalade

Heat the marmalade in a small saucepan over medium heat until just melted. Let cool for 5 minutes.

Frosting

1 cup heavy cream, chilled
4 tablespoons sugar
1 cup sour cream, chilled

In a chilled mixing bowl, using chilled beaters (put them in the freezer for 10 minutes minimum), whip the cream with 4 tablespoons sugar until stiff peaks form. Add the sour cream, a little at a time, and whisk until the mixture is a spreadable consistency.

Cake Assembly

1. Invert one of the cake layers onto a cake plate or stand and carefully peel off the parchment.

2. Spread one-third of the marmalade over the top, making an even layer.

3. Invert the second layer on top of the first, peel off the parchment, and spoon another third of the marmalade on top.

4. Place the third layer on top, remove the parchment, and spoon the remaining marmalade onto the center of it, leaving a 1¼" border around the edges.

5. Frost the sides and the top border with the frosting, leaving the marmalade on the top of the cake exposed. Or, if you prefer, frost the entire cake first, adding marmalade as a garnish on top.

6. Chill for at least 2 hours before serving.

Making Your Mark

"Make a mark and see where it takes you." —Peter Reynolds, from his children's book *The Dot*

Graduations have hit a crescendo this first week of June. In recent weeks the mail has brought announcements of the children of friends who are graduating from high school or college. Closest to home, Kat is about to "graduate" (they officially call it a promotion ceremony) from the sixth grade. Kat has the honor of being the youngest child of all the second generation of my own family and all of my friends. While I find the whole notion of a sixth grade graduation silly, I admit it is a lovely way to say good-bye to the enchanted years of elementary school.

This was the seventy-seventh sixth grade promotion ceremony at the Edwin D. Smith Elementary School in Oakwood, Ohio. The school is an impressive Tudor-style building that has been lovingly maintained and updated over the years, and it is full of the kind of nooks and crannies that delight children and adults alike. However, the gymnasium is just a gymnasium, typically hot and slightly sweaty smelling. Unfortunately, the ceremony was too long. Has there ever been a graduation ceremony that wasn't? I have always abhorred graduations and refused to attend any of my own. But when I was up for my PhD my family insisted, and so I went. There I was, a black dot in a sea of over 5,000 other black dots, on the hottest day of the summer in the famous Horseshoe Stadium (when it was still shaped like a horseshoe) of Ohio State University. A plane flying overhead provided the only shade. It was awful and it was wonderful. I recall coming to the realization that I was now expected to do something, to somehow make my mark on the world. Perhaps that is why I had always avoided these ceremonies. If I didn't show up, I could avoid the pressure of reviewing what I had achieved and what was still out there to achieve.

The day before Kat's graduation I had to make a trip to Atlanta and back to give a seminar. A university in that city wants to hire me and give me lots of money. My research seminar was going to be a performance so they could decide if they really wanted to pay me lots of money. They do. I just have to decide whether this is what I want and also what is best for my family. I haven't yet made my mark as a scientist and this would give me the funding to do that.

While I was in Atlanta, Wayne took Kat shopping for her graduation dress. I arrived home late to find Kat showing off the dress. I was overwhelmed by how beautiful and grown-up she looked. The dress was black with tiny white dots and it fit her perfectly. With a ruffle at the bottom and ribbon straps at the top, it was "elegant but simple," according to Kat, and she twirled while looking at herself in the mirror. I froze the moment in my mind.

In the gymnasium that night, the girls had curves and high heels and most could pass for sixteen; the boys looked, well, at least twelve. It doesn't make much sense in terms of evolution.

The ceremony had the obligatory slide show with baby photos of each of the eighty-three students side-by-side with a current photo. There were tributes to teachers and classmates all woven together with a theme that involved a book and a dot. None of the other parents I talked to understood the theme, because, like me, they were too busy admiring their kids while simultaneously pining to escape the heat of the gym.

The next day I asked Kat and her friends, "What was the point of the dot thing?" It was based on a picture book called *The Dot*, by Peter Reynolds. It is the story of a girl named Vashti, who does not think she is an artist and can only stare at a blank piece of paper. Finally her teacher tells her to make a mark and see where it takes her. Soon Vashti is off on a creative journey that teaches her something about surprises and self-discovery. Vashti had made her mark and Kat's principal was asking her students to do the same.

Postcript: I decided against taking the job at the university in Atlanta. The position was perfect, the location is not. Trading my present commute (1.9 miles downhill), lovely neighborhood, and good schools for an Atlanta commute made no sense. I am just not that ambitious.

The Great Flower Cake

Now that many people know I am writing a cake cookbook, I am asked, or feel obligated, to bring a cake to social functions. This is the cake I took to the graduation party.

It comes from Shirley O. Corriher's amazing book, *CookWise*, where her description of the cake is: " This is one of the most spectacular cakes imaginable. A spiral of dark nut roll and snow-white whipped cream is topped with thin slices of strawberries arranged like the petals of a big flower." Everyone raved and talked about how light it was. I decided to not apprise them of the fat content of the cake. Cake should not be a guilt trip.

Preheat oven to 350° F, and prepare an 11" x 17" x ½" jelly roll pan by lining it with foil, parchment paper, or a nonstick baking sheet liner; grease and dust well with flour. Shake to remove any excess flour; set aside.

Cake

¾ cup pecan pieces, roasted (see step #1 below)
6 large eggs, separated (put yolks in the large bowl and whites in the small bowl of an electric mixer)
1 cup superfine sugar
1 teaspoon baking powder
¼ teaspoon salt
1 teaspoon vanilla extract
¾ teaspoon cream of tartar (optional)
Confectioners' sugar

1. Roast pecans on a baking sheet for 10 to 12 min-

utes at 350° F. Remove from oven and sprinkle lightly with salt; let cool. Chop the pecans in a food processor with a steel knife, using quick on/off pulses until finely chopped.

2. Increase oven to 400° F.

3. Put cream of tartar in the bowl with the egg whites and beat until soft peaks form when the beaters are slowly lifted. Add 2 tablespoons of the sugar and beat well. Set egg whites aside and quickly move to step 4.

4. Add 1 tablespoon of water and the remaining sugar to the bowl with the egg yolks and beat on medium speed until well aerated and light in color. Stir in the chopped pecans, baking powder, salt, and vanilla.

5. Spoon about one fifth of the beaten egg whites into the yolk mixture with a large spatula; stir them in well to lighten the mixture. Add the rest of the whites to yolk mixture, and fold in gently.

6. Spread the batter evenly in the prepared jelly roll pan and bake until springy to the touch, 6 to 10 minutes.

7. Dust a clean dish towel heavily with confectioners' sugar, invert cake onto the towel, and carefully peel off the paper or foil or baking sheet liner.

8. Let cool completely.

9. While the cake is cooling, prepare whipped cream and fruit.

Whipped Cream and Fruit

2 cups heavy whipping cream
½ cup confectioners' sugar
2 tablespoons Grand Marnier liqueur
1 quart fresh strawberries cut lengthwise into thin slices
½ cup current jelly

1. Place clean beaters, small mixing bowl of an electric mixer, and whipping cream into the freezer for 10 minutes.

2. Whip cream to firm peaks. Stir in confectioners' sugar and 1 tablespoon Grand Marnier.

3. Spread the flavored whipped cream evenly in a thick layer on top of the cooled nut cake.

Cake Assembly

1. With a serrated knife, slice the cake lengthwise into eight equal strips, about 1½" x 17" long. The easiest way to do this—without measuring—is to slice the cake in half lengthwise, slice each half in half lengthwise, and then slice each piece in half again.

2. Take one strip of the cake and roll it up on the whipped cream side like a jelly roll. Now turn the spiral over on one side like a cinnamon roll and place it flat in the center of a serving platter.

3. Take another strip and carefully curl it around the first one to make a larger spiral.

4. Continue adding one strip at a time until all eight strips are used. The cake is now a spiral of dark cake and white whipped cream, about 1½" high and a little more than 10 inches in diameter. Starting at the outer edge, arrange strawberry slices with the tips of the berries pointing outward, overlapping all the way around the outside edge. Arrange another circle just inside the first so that the inner circle overlaps the first circle about halfway.

5. Continue with another overlapping circle inside the first two, and so on, until the entire cake is covered and looks like a great red flower blossom.

6. Warm the jelly just enough to melt and stir in the remaining 1 tablespoon of Grand Marnier to thin.

7. Glaze the entire top of cake with the thinned jelly.

8. Refrigerate and serve cold.

Note: This cake is worth the effort.

Flags of our Fathers, Flags of our Mothers

"There is hopeful symbolism in the fact that flags do not wave in a vacuum." —Arthur Clarke

Lately I've been flying the flag a lot. I have grown oh so weary of the debate over who owns it and who can dress themselves in it. To me the flag belongs to all of us and it is one-size-fits-all. I fly it, even though I oppose this unjust and stupid war, and I take it down every night at sundown, even though the trend is to leave it up around the clock. My momma taught me right.

My mother flew the flag every day of her adult life; she was proud to be an American, and proud to dissent when she thought it would make us a better country. Vietnam demanded dissent, in her view, and she would drag me to anti-war rallies and then home to make dinner. Such were the dichotomies of the 1970s. If my mother was alive today, she would have marched, waving the flag to protest the shameful atrocities of the current war.

My father, a World War II veteran, shared my mother's love of flag and country. During the Vietnam War my mother and father had a political split. Politics ceased to be fun and hopeful for my family; we were no longer the happy warriors as exemplified by Hubert Humphrey. My siblings and I were torn between our parents' opposite political views. My father embraced Nixon and Reagan as if they were messiahs, which drove my mother to despair. She considered my father's political defection the worst sort of infidelity. This is easy to understand, when you consider that their courtship began with a blind date on election night in 1948. They discovered on that night that they both had voted for Truman earlier that day. It was a marriage made in political heaven until 1970. After that, the only thing they could agree on was that flying the flag was a good and honorable thing to do.

My parents stayed together for the rest of their lives. I think near the end of his life my father started to see that the Republican Party was veering from the correct ideals, his ideals. Lately I find myself talking to my father, as if he were still here, telling him how badly things are turning out with this current Republican president, and I find he is agreeing with me more and more. Wayne and I are fortunate because our political views have stayed remarkably similar. There will be no broken home for our children.

So I fly the flag of my father, a flag that waves for veterans and the fallen from all of our wars. And I fly the flag of my mother, a flag that waves in the hope that there will be no more wars, no more fallen heroes.

Flag Day and Father's Day both fell during this week. This week's cake is dedicated to the father of my children. Wayne is a dad who carried his infant daughters gently, who pushed them carefully on swings when they were toddlers, and who picked them up anywhere, anytime, with no questions asked (until the next day), when they were adolescents. He deserves whatever cake he desires.

Wayne has also supported me in almost all of my endeavors. An English major in college, he won my heart with his ability to analyze literature, a skill that has been immensely helpful to Lizzie and Kat as well. When I took up writing as a hobby, I thought, "Great, I have my own built-in editor and reviewer." I'd ask him to read something I'd written and then wait, for what felt like a year. At the end of that year, he'd say, "Hmm, it's good." or "I liked it." or "Maybe it's a little too long." I could tell he wasn't being truthful, which led to some bad feelings. Then one day Wayne handed me a piece of paper. He had written to Garrison Keillor, who was hosting an online advice column on Salon called "Mr. Blue." Keillor announced that he was accepting queries from writers and the lovelorn. So Wayne wrote to Keillor and he wrote back. Here is Wayne's letter and Keillor's reply:

Dear Mr. Blue,

My wife is a wonderful, bright, beautiful woman with a need to write. Her problem is that she is too sensitive about my opinion of her work, and every hesitation, shrug, raised eyebrow, and suggestion creates deep insecurity, and now she no longer shows her work to me.

Keillor's reply:

Stop raising those big hairy eyebrows of yours mister. Shrugs and raised eyebrows suggest you don't care enough about writing to be critical, so you're merely sarcastic. You shrug, roll your eyes, you sigh, you push the work away and say, "Oh, I don't know. Maybe it's a little long." This beautiful woman deserves better than a shrug from you, and you don't have better to offer, so she's withdrawn her work from your dry gaze, and good for her, and boogers on you.

From then on all I had to say was "Boogers on you" if I thought Wayne wasn't being properly supportive of my writing. Keillor has no idea how much he has helped our marriage.

This week's flag flying is dedicated to something far less noble than Father's Day. Wayne has offered his unflagging support for my current obsession, which is flying the flag every day. My goal is to win the City Beautiful Award, which is the highest honor my city bestows upon its homeowners. When we moved here twelve years ago, I noticed hand-carved, hand-painted oval seals of public approval sprouting up in the spring on manicured lawns around town. I wanted one. I spent the next five years working on our landscaping. I've gotten lots of compliments, but an oval sign has yet to appear on our lawn. I started bugging Wayne to paint the trim and shutters, but to no avail. This year I am flying the flag and that should clinch it. Wayne informs me that he hinted to one of my friends that perhaps she could, you know, nominate me? Now that is support.

I am pretty sure, too, that my mother and father would be OK with me flying the flag for this purpose. After all, I still take it down at sunset (the contest judging takes place during daylight hours).

Hawaiian Wedding Cake

Wayne requested this for his Father's Day cake and proclaimed it, "Like carrot cake, only better." Several years back—the year Lizzie graduated from high school and I turned fifty—we took a trip to the Hawaiian Islands. We traveled with my friend and colleague Albert who has made more than sixty trips to the islands. This was no ordinary tourist trip for us. Wayne, a reluctant traveler, was hesitant to go. But he had the best time of any of us. He managed to get us safely around the island of Maui, including the tortuous drive to Hana.

Preheat oven to 350° F and butter a 9" x 13" baking pan.

Cake

2 cups all-purpose flour
1 ½ cup sugar
1 cup unsweetened coconut
2 teaspoons baking soda
1 20-ounce can crushed pineapple, with juice
2 eggs, beaten
1 cup chopped nuts (pecans or walnuts)

1. In the large bowl of an electric mixer combine flour and baking soda. Mix on low speed for 30 seconds (this serves the same function as sifting them together and is much easier).

2. Add the remaining ingredients and mix on low speed until blended.

3. Pour batter into the prepared pan.

4. Bake for 45 minutes or until a toothpick inserted into the center comes out clean.

5. Cool completely.

Frosting

½ cup (1 stick) room-temperature butter
1 8-ounce package room-temperature cream cheese
1 ½ cup confectioner's sugar
2 teaspoons vanilla

In the large bowl of an electric mixer, combine all the ingredients and beat until smooth.

Smooth over the completely cooled cake.

Summer Reprise

Gravity Lessons

"Gravity is working against me; and gravity wants to bring me down." —John Mayer, singer-songwriter

This week I am feeling heavy. Heavy with pounds gained in pursuit of the perfect cake recipe and heavy with anticipation of a new position in life. In less than a week I will become the chairperson of my department. I've spent six months making all of the dull and necessary arrangements and I've moved my office. Now I'm taking some time off to rest. After months of considering places I can get away to, I've settled on my own backyard, in a hammock suspended between two aging pines.

The hammock likes to flirt with me, swaying softly in the breeze and mocking me when I try to tame my backyard by weeding and pruning it. I succumb, more than I prefer to admit, to its gentle seduction. I love to dangle between two trees, barefoot, with the only blue screen a rectangle of sky above me, my only goal to become the envy of squirrels and birds. For a brief space of time, I have a reprieve from the gravity of middle age that pulls at my jaw and my soul. And since I live far from any sea, swaying in my hammock is the only time I can experience the sheer joy of floating.

When my children were small, they inevitably sensed my hammock-induced state of peacefulness and begged to join me. I would protest and then—always—let them in. We became the hammock beast—arms, legs, and toes mingling as we dangled dangerously above my untamed yard. Because children have no sense of the weight of their bodies, a hammock is not a place of rest to them. It is a place for them to test gravity, centrifugal force, and a parent's patience. They'd repeatedly push and spin until they fell to the ground, each time surprised by the outcome. This backyard lesson in gravity reminded me that not all things have to be taught. Many important things are simply and amazingly revealed to us.

I long ago accepted the reality of gravity. But I have yet to accept the gravity of mid-life. As I swing in my hammock, I find myself thinking of those places where we can find rest in this harried world. I intend to spend my week in the hammock thinking about this.

When Lizzie found out from her father that I had agreed to be chair of my department, she called and left me a message on my cell phone. One of her professors told her that there are no women chairing a science department at Pitt. I could tell that Lizzie was proud of me. I won't delete the message until I drop my phone in the sink, toilet, or lake, all of which I have been known to do. My daughter's pride in me might get me through the rough days. I have been told I exude a certain gravitas, which I take as a compliment. Will this job add to that or simply weigh me down?

I don't know yet what lessons I will learn from leading my department. Will my colleagues, who now seem charmingly eccentric, become annoyingly crazy when they have to answer to me? Other department chairs warned me about this. I imagine it could be true. But for the next ten days I will remain suspended between two trees learning the lessons that come from defying gravity.

Peach Upside-Down Cake

June is too soon for peaches in Ohio, but all the food magazines had peaches plastered on their covers this month. My only choice this week was to make a peach cake. This is one of my all-time favorite cakes. It comes from *The Cake Bible* cookbook, by Rose Levy Beranbaum. I have wanted to buy this book for years, but could never bring myself to open my wallet wide enough. This week it fell into my hands when a friend who was a chef in a former life loaned it to me. Maida Heatter wrote in her forward to the book, "If you ever bake a cake, this book will become your partner in the kitchen." In her master's thesis Beranbaum proved that sifting dry ingredients together is not any better than mixing them in the mixing bowl before adding the wet ingredients. Rarely is a master's thesis this valuable. Stunned and happy to learn this, I've amended all my recipes.

Preheat oven to 350° F and place oven rack in lower third of the oven. You will need one 10" cast iron skillet, which you won't need to butter. A cast iron skillet is ideal because you can melt the butter and brown sugar in it on the stove top, and it really caramelizes the topping during baking. If you don't have a cast iron skillet, I suggest getting one, because you can cook many types of food in it and cast iron skillets aren't very expensive. You can substitute a 10" springform pan, but you will need to wrap the outside with heavy duty aluminum foil to prevent it from leaking.

Fruit Topping

2 10-ounce cans of sliced peaches, [or three fresh peaches if you are lucky enough to have them]
14 pitted sweet cherries (or the maraschino type)
4 tablespoons unsalted butter
½ cup light brown sugar, firmly packed
¼ cup pecan halves

1. Drain the fruit and place on paper towels to absorb excess moisture.

2. Melt the butter in the skillet on the stove over medium heat. Stir in the brown sugar until moistened and remove from the heat.

3. Place the peach slices around the outer rim of the pan in a pinwheel configuration.

4. Place the cherries in the center and surround them with a smaller pinwheel of peach slices.

5. Tuck the pecans into any gaps between the fruit, or make up your own design.

Cake

3 large egg yolks
½ cup sour cream
1 teaspoon vanilla
1½ cups sifted cake flour
¾ cup sugar
¾ teaspoon baking powder
¼ teaspoon baking soda
¼ teaspoon salt
9 tablespoons room-temperature unsalted butter

1. In a medium bowl, lightly combine egg yolks, vanilla, and ⅛ cup sour cream.

2. In a large mixing bowl, combine the dry ingredients and mix on low speed for 30 seconds to blend.

3. Add softened butter and the remaining sour cream. Mix on low speed until dry ingredients are moistened. Increase to medium speed and beat for 1½ minutes to aerate and develop cake's structure. Scrape down the sides.

4. Gradually add egg mixture to batter in 3 batches, beating for 20 seconds after each addition to incorporate ingredients and strengthen structure. Scrape down the sides. Scrape batter (it will be thick) into the fruit-lined skillet, smoothing evenly with a spatula.

5. Bake for 40 to 50 minutes or until golden brown and a cake tester comes out clean and the cake springs back when pressed lightly in the center. Run a small metal spatula around sides and invert immediately onto a serving plate. Leave the skillet in place for 1 to 2 minutes before lifting it. If any fruit has stuck to the skillet, simply use a small spatula to place it back on the cake.

How to Not Go to Work

"Research is the process of going up alleys to see if they are blind." —Marston Bates, American zoologist

I am still home this week. I have been planning to take some time off for the past twelve years and I am going to do it this time. My definition of a week off work is one where I am not traveling for work or on a family trip, a week when I get up when I want and do what I want. The first January we lived here, I remember telling the department secretary that I was going to take off a whole week, when classes were over, to paint the rooms of my house. Every room, every square inch of wall and ceiling, including the trim, was screaming at me to paint them. Classes were over the last week of April and my plan was to throw open the windows and paint from dawn to dusk.

I wrote a grant proposal instead. And so it has been every year. But this year, with tenure far behind me and my new job looming, I am determined to do what I want. The plan is to rest and work on this book.

Of course our home computer crashed last week, taking down with it many chapters of this book. I had been too busy in the last month to back up my files. Life is hard when you are not very smart. My friend Val e-mails me with advice: "Quick, send it to Drive Doctors." But Wayne had already taken it to his guys, and so all I can do is wait.

This week I am going to learn how to hang out in my hammock again, with the goal of building up to twenty minutes at a stretch. What follows is a chronicle of my week off.

On Monday I wake up earlier than I do on work days. What the? I slip out of bed and into my sandals and start the tea brewing. I call for Tula and head out for my daily rounds. Our city lot is small but it takes me fifteen minutes at this time of year to inspect every plant. Tula doesn't mind because it gives her time to chase out any squirrels, bunnies, or chipmunks loitering from the night before. She can jump eight-foot fences, so we installed the electric kind. Tula can jump those as well. I am happy to report that after years of constant training, she mostly stays in the yard now, usually comes when I call her, and no longer lunges at the mail carrier. Tula is sweet and smart and loves me more than I deserve.

The early morning coolness reminds me of the mornings of my childhood, when I would trail behind my grandmother as she inspected her garden bordering Lake Erie. She would sing "Oh What a Beautiful

Morning" or the lovely old hymn "I Go to the Garden Alone." The best mornings were the ones when we found hummingbirds hanging out in her patch of tiger lilies. Something was always blooming in my grandmother's gardens. My family would arrive the day after school let out to outdoor rooms filled with white, lavender, and deep purple lilacs followed by lilies-of-the-valley and honeysuckle and then by tiger lilies and hydrangeas. The show continued until Labor Day, when we finally dragged ourselves back home, arriving deep in the night the day before school started.

In my garden, on this morning in June, the lilies are in their full glory—red, orange, white, pink, and yellow, they look like exotic birds perched on my fence. The heavenly blue morning glories have finally begun their ascent of the trellis. And tiny green tomatoes hang on some of the plants.

I spend the rest of the morning on the front porch proofing a PhD dissertation and chatting with neighbors passing by, while Wayne ferries Kat to swim team and tennis lessons. I ask Wayne to call his computer guys and he does! They promise to look at my crashed computer tomorrow.

Kat returns and I head to the local water park with her and a friend. Every summer I take Kat to this particular water park because it is just the right size for her. The slide is fun but not terrifying, the lazy river is relaxing, and the wave pool's waves are guaranteed to break just the right way at the same spot every time. I sit for five hours, only getting up when nature calls, and I manage to make it through two more pages of Amy's dissertation, which I've been dragging everywhere for the past month. I fall asleep face down on the pages, leaving a trace of Diet Pepsi drool. I hope Amy doesn't notice it.

We stay until the park is closing and the line for the water slide has dwindled. I let the girls take a last run. We all leave happy and tired. Soon I am back on my porch sipping a glass of Pinot Noir and eating roast pork and fresh green beans, courtesy of Wayne. Then he takes me for an aimless ride in the convertible.

I climb into bed early, but stay up late finishing my current book. As I drift off to sleep, to the sounds of a spectacular Midwestern thunderstorm, I remember I didn't spend any time in the hammock. I promise myself that I will be in the hammock tomorrow.

On Tuesday I start with my usual morning rounds. Today I realize the basil is ready for harvesting and I gather enough for a large batch of pesto for tonight's dinner.

I make the momentous decision to skip my Pilates class, knowing full well that in middle age even a few days off means my muscles will start to turn to mush. Instead I read the paper on the front porch.

I think about asking Wayne to call his computer guys and decide it won't do any good.

I finish the last of the first round of comments on Amy's dissertation just as she drives up in her navy blue jeep. I hand her ten pages and she hands me the whole thing, minus ten pages. It is an inch thick, at least, and I promise to re-read it by Thursday, which is only two days away. I can tell she is skeptical that I will actually have it done by then, but she doesn't say anything. I sigh, because all of my students eventually realize that I almost never finish any editing on time. We sit and talk for a bit about her job interview coming up the following week.

As Amy drives off, I put her dissertation on the top of

the pile and move the pile out of my sight. She needs to defend her dissertation in three weeks, and I will have to fit it in on my week off. At least I forced her to come to my front porch, resisting the temptation to meet her in the lab. This is a small but important step in Not Going to Work.

I decide that I'm dying to hear Kat's litany of swim team agony and get in the car, drive the mile to Starbucks for a chai (for me) and a hot chocolate (for her), and on to the pool to pick her up. She does not disappoint, telling me every last detail about the number of laps she swam, how the new coach taught her to do a breast stroke turn, how the new coach is "really strict but really nice," and the crazy number of individual medleys they had to do.

Back on the porch I take up writing again. With Amy's dissertation out of sight, I feel deliriously free and write without interruption. I guess the neighbors are sensing my need for solitude–or maybe I was a bit surly yesterday. At any rate they seem to be leaving me alone. I am shocked to realize that it is 2:30 and wander into the kitchen in search of something to snack on. Spying some very ripe bananas, I decide to make a fresh banana cake with chocolate sour cream ganache frosting that has been tempting me for a long time. I head to the market for missing ingredients. It is like a tomb and I think maybe something terrible has happened. But then I realize I am never here in the middle of the day in the middle of the week.

At home the mail lady has come and gone. A find a bill for $200 for the four tickets I got parking at my own university during the past nine months. I have a hard time remembering to transfer my damn parking tag when I am already late for work. Fortunately I love donating money to my place of work, and so I put the bill in my purse and vow not to pay it until absolutely the last second.

I spend the next two hours making the cake and the pesto for dinner. While the cake is baking, I head for the hammock. It is a little wet from last night's heavy rains and smells a bit like a camp cabin, but I climb on in. I hang in the dappled afternoon sun for what seems like a long time before I open my eyes to discover a spider dangling one inch above my nose. Only seven minutes have passed. I imagine I hear the cake buzzer and rush inside. I never make it back to the hammock.

Kat arrives home from spending the afternoon at the pool just as I finish frosting the cake. She has a friend with her and they are very excited about the cake. It looks beautiful and their appetites have been sharpened by sun and chlorine. I cut three pieces. The cake is a horrible, horrible combination of flavors. We decide the lemon zest doesn't go with the banana and the chocolate is too dark. I decide I will improve this recipe, which is from a famous pastry chef, and make a better cake. But not this week.

Kat heads off to walk Tula, two friends in tow, and to explore, on foot, the wealthy side of our town. Kat is at the same age as Lizzie when she first discovered the drop-dead gorgeous public gardens and estates on the west side of town. They are gone for two hours and return hungry and thirsty.

Wayne is inside making his delicious Italian chicken to accompany my pesto on pasta, when a car pulls into the driveway. It is my friend Albert and his wife, Kathy, who have just returned from Boston, where

Albert had prostate cancer surgery. I leap up and run to meet them, throwing my arms around Albert. They stay for dinner and I'm glad to see Albert looking and eating well. While Wayne cleans up, Albert and Kathy tell all about their trip to Costa Rica and the course he taught there. Both agree they might like it even better than their usual haunt, Hawaii. I decide that next year all of us will join Albert on his next trip to Costa Rica. Kathy and Albert stay until it is so dark that I've lit the candles on the porch. Wayne returns with Kat and friends after a long ride in the convertible to get ice cream and explore an old fort on the west side of town.

I go to bed in a state of grace, appreciating good friends and skilled surgeons.

Wednesday dawns cool and sunny—it is another day in paradise. On my morning tour of the garden, I note that the basil has rejuvenated itself overnight. The phlox have formed impressive clumps and are close to bursting into bloom. A gift from a former neighbor, they always remind me of her. I inventory the plants gifted to me by other gardeners and I am impressed at the numbers. Hostas and hellebores from Albert top the list. Recently I scored a start of Corydalis from a stranger. At the annual plant sale at the arboretum, where we are members, I asked one of the volunteers if Corydalis was available and two of them volunteered to give me some from their own yards. I laughed when they started to quarrel over which one would have the privilege of granting my request. It is a badge of honor, I've observed, for true gardeners to create their gardens through plant exchanges with friends and fellow gardeners. It is as much fun to give as to receive.

I slip into work for an hour to finish up an experiment that cannot wait (science not only never sleeps, it rarely naps). I bike down early and manage to avoid everyone but Amy, who arrives just as I am finishing up. I bike home up the huge hill with more energy than I ever have at the end of a long work day. On the way, I see something shocking but not surprising: a boy who looks about nine is manning a lemonade stand on a corner while talking on a cell phone. I can't shake the image. Will this generation be known as the Connected Generation or perhaps the Matrix Generation? What worries me is the effect all of this plugging in will have on their ability to connect deeply to other people. Will they be able to do so without technological aids?

The short bike ride inspires in me visions of a nap and I lie down on our freshly made bed. Beginning to doze off, I remember that the computer guys had promised to look at our dead computer yesterday. I ask Wayne to call them. A long time passes and I realize he hasn't done this. I ask him again. Sounding annoyed, he says, "You know, bugging them won't get it done any faster?" I reply sweetly, "But they said they would have it done yesterday?" A few minutes later, I hear him on the phone. He tells me they will know soon. I suggest that if they cannot retrieve the files, we should send the hard drive to Drive Doctors. Wayne gets miffed. I get miffed back. No chance of sleeping now that I am all miffed up. I fire up my new laptop, backing up every fifteen minutes.

I hear weird sounds at the door and somewhere in the recesses of my middle-aged brain it occurs to me that Tula is on the porch unattended. Yes, she is out there scaring my friend Gretchen. I apologize and we sit on the porch and talk for a while. Gretchen asks me to drop her at the car dealership where her car is being repaired, and I take her in the convertible, which she enjoys. On the way home I stop at the garden store I usually avoid because it is too far away and too dangerously full of exotic and lovely plants. I buy a pot of ivy for my new office and head to the lab to complete the experiment I started this morning. The results are as perfect as they can be in science and I float out to my car, realizing that through some miracle it has not been ticketed.

I celebrate by hitting the hammock. I spend a full fifteen minutes in it.

That night I go to bed grateful for data that are reproducible and lovely and for a day that has not included the addition of another parking ticket to my collection.

On Thursday I spend the day editing Amy's dissertation, which I complete two minutes before she arrives to pick it up. I celebrate with two shots—two allergy shots, one in each arm. Time in the hammock makes it all better. I forget to clock my hammock time as I hang suspended, hypnotized by birds flitting and floating through the air. I stay until dusk gathers and head inside.

That night I watch the movie *The Notebook* with Kat, and we agree it is both happy and sad. When a twelve-year-old thinks that James Garner is cool and a great actor, there is hope that she will come out of adolescence OK. I have always loved James Garner and find it interesting that even at his advanced age Kat perceives his charm. When Lizzie was the same age, we watched Hitchcock's *North by Northwest*. She said that Cary Grant reminded her of Mister Rogers. Lizzie has turned out orders of magnitude greater than just OK, but I was still taken aback at the time.

I go to bed grateful for a long and warm marriage and for the sweet sensibilities of my twelve-year-old daughter. I am also grateful that I won't have to look at Amy's dissertation again until Monday.

I make the short trek to the farmers' market on Friday to buy cardamom seeds for my chai habit. Bob, the Amish organic farmer, is selling luscious raspberries and I can't pass them by. They are the first raspberries of the season and I buy two pints. I let Kat and her friends eat them out of hand until there are just enough left to make this cake. Perhaps it is heretical to use the first of the season in a cake, but I have always thought that baking improves raspberries, intensifying their taste and fragrance.

While the cake bakes, I head for the hammock. The birds seem to recognize me and perform a particularly divine dance.

Dinner was simple and eaten *al fresco* on our porch. Afterward I receive a long-awaited phone call telling me that the quilt top I finished months before has now been quilted. I convince Wayne and Kat to drive with me to the country to pick it up. We set off in the convertible and Kat complains the whole way: it is too windy and cold in the convertible and it is too loud to conduct a cell-phone conversation. But on the way home she curls up in the back seat, under the finished quilt. We stop for frozen custard to put the perfect ending on the trip.

I crawl into bed, the windows wide open with a cool breeze coming through them, which is unusual for July in this part of the country. I reflect on my week off. I worked up to a thirty-minute respite in the hammock before the urge to move on overcame me. I discovered, once again, that being horizontal at other than nighttime induces both physiological and psychological changes that are good, even necessary ones. It's important at times to refrain from human do-ings to become human be-ings. The hammock isn't going to become my new religion, but it will be my refuge from the craziness of the world. Anyway, I'm convinced that the birds are becoming dependent on me as their audience.

Fresh Raspberry (or Blueberry) Breakfast (or Dinner) Cake

We ate this cake for dinner while still warm, with creamy vanilla ice cream. It can also be made with blueberries (a combination of the two would make a great Fourth of July treat). This recipe comes from the *Hollyhocks and Radishes* cookbook, one of my long-time favorites. My own hollyhocks are getting pretty tall but are not close to flowering yet. Not a crumb of this cake was left by the time we got up from the table. Kat's friend, who had joined us for dinner, exclaimed several times, "This is really good."

Preheat oven to 375° F and butter a 9" cake or tube pan.

Cake

2 eggs, separated
¾ cup sugar
½ cup soft vegetable shortening (Crisco)
1 ½ cups sifted cake flour
1 teaspoon baking powder
½ teaspoon salt
⅓ cup whole milk
1 teaspoon vanilla
2 cups fresh raspberries, rinsed and dried
(fresh blueberries may be substituted, but lightly flour them before adding them to batter so that they will not sink to the bottom).

1. In the small mixing bowl of an electric mixer, combine sifted flour, baking soda, and salt. Mix on low for 30 seconds; set aside.

2. In the large mixing bowl of an electric mixer, beat together egg yolks, sugar, and shortening on medium speed until well mixed (about 5 minutes).

3. Add dry ingredients and unbeaten egg whites, and mix on low speed just until mixed.

4. Add milk and vanilla, and beat on low speed just until mixed.

5. Fold in raspberries gently with a spoon.

6. Pour batter into the prepared pan and bake for 30 to 40 minutes until the center springs back to a light touch.

7. Serve warm alone, or with whipped cream, or with vanilla ice cream.

My Island Affair

"I would love to be the poet laureate of Coney Island."
—Thornton Wilder

This week, the week of the Fourth of July, I officially assume the position of department chair. I celebrate by taking three days off. I have a history of bad starts. On my first professional job I called in sick on the morning of the second day. Actually Wayne had to call in for me, because I woke up in the middle of the night vomiting violently from food poisoning. My boss told me several years later that his wife had commented at the time, "Boy you sure know how to pick 'em." I went on to work for this man for another nine years before returning to graduate school, and we remain friends and collaborators. But whenever he wants to psychologically short sheet me, he brings up me taking my second day of work off. It hadn't been my plan to make this a policy but it has turned out that whenever I start a new job, I've somehow managed to miss work the first week.

I am going to spend this Fourth of July in the Lake Erie islands. I have migrated to this spot every possible Fourth of July since 2000, the year my sister, Ann, and her husband, Alan, bought their cottage and invited us to "come on over." A cottage on an island in the middle of Lake Erie and fireworks on the lake–what could be better?

My mind goes back to that first visit in 2000. We drove the four hours to the southern shore of the lake only to learn we had missed the ferry by minutes. The ferry fairy informed us that the next ferry, the last one, was due in only two hours. Islands are coy–alluringly remote and difficult to get to. Having missed the ferry, I was suddenly desperate to see this island. So we waited, trying to cool our heels, but the July heat bouncing off the blacktop wasn't helping. When we finally boarded the ferry, we could no longer recall why we cared about going to an island in the middle of Lake Erie. The ride was ruined by the drunken revelry of a group heading to an island winery. An inebriated jerk tried to pass his bottle of cheap whiskey to Lizzie, who was fifteen at the time, but I put a stop to that.

Once we were finally deposited on the flat and rocky island, it wasn't love at first sight. We trudged the mile to Ann and Alan's cottage, dragging suitcases and a cooler. Most of the ferry passengers joined us in our pilgrimage. All of us looked like refugees, except we had nice luggage and were hauling enough alcohol to set up our own island drinking establishments. My brother, Steve, and his family showed up long after the ferry stopped running. To this day they will not reveal how they pulled this off.

Ann greeted us as we arrived at the cottage dusty, droopy, and hungry. She sat us down to a fine dinner of grilled chicken and lite beer, the drink of the natives. Suddenly I was liking this place. After dinner we wandered to the docks and a took a boat ride on the same big water where Ann, Steve, and I had spent our charmed childhood summers only fifteen miles to the north. Refreshed by the night air, all eleven of us slept well head-to-toe in the tiny cottage.

The next day dawned sunny and hot. After a big breakfast, we headed out on the boat for a day on the lake. Once the kids tired of tubing and sunshine, we dropped them off, along with the adults who were ready to bail out. Alan, Ann, and I headed back out into the surf for some fast and furious boating, which is defined as not having to stop to drag kids around in a tube or let them jump off the bow.

We had just hit the deeper waters, when Alan's fire-and-rescue radio squawked. He was on his very first shift as the weekend Emergency Medical Technician. We surmised that a holiday tourist had gone into cardiac arrest or that someone was having a minor boating problem. Through the static we thought we heard, "Terrorist–squawk–collapse." Terrorists? Collapse of what? We cut the engines and waited. "Terrace collapsed–Lonz Winery." Alan revved the motor, pointing the boat in the direction of the ferry docks and the winery at the end of the island. We made it there quickly, but as we maneuvered to tie up, the dock master waved us away. "Emergency vehicles only," he told us. I pointed to my brother-in-law, saying, "He's an EMT." Alan was pulled ashore and Ann and I went on our way, piloting the boat ourselves. Somehow we managed to dock it and we walked down the road to the cottage, where we told everyone what had happened—without really knowing what had happened.

By the time Alan returned three hours later, CNN had reported the story. We were in a tiny cottage on a small island in the middle of Lake Erie finding out on CNN what was happening on the other side of the island. Crazy. A terrace filled with happy holiday revelers had collapsed under their weight. One had died and many were hurt. Alan had helped to triage and treat the wounded, making a difference on that day.

The next day was our last on the island, and the tragedy had us all a bit worn out. Ann, Steve, and I had decided it was time to do something with our parents' ashes. Our father had been dead for twelve years, our mother for three. We debated whether to bury them together or separately, given that their marriage had not always been sanguine. Finally we decided that their happiest times, and ours, had been at our cottage in Canada on Lake Erie. So we gathered the ashes and set out by boat to Canadian waters for a sea burial a deux. We made it as far as Hen Island, a small oval of a place that just looked happy. This was it, we decided. Here our parents could be separate and together. The water was as smooth as glass and the sun was about to set when we stopped the boat to pour the ashes and say our prayers. As we pulled away from the spot, the solemn lake swallowed the sun and all was peaceful.

And so I've returned to my sister's cottage most

Fourth of July holidays since then. The winery never reopened after the terrace collapsed; Ohio bought the building and land and made it a state park. We encounter fewer drunks on the ferry these days. Usually it is just me and Kat (and her current fave friend), because Wayne and Lizzie are not island types. I am charmed by the culture of this tiny place and lately I've been thinking that, unlike Thornton Wilder, I'd prefer to be poet laureate of this island. Imagine my business cards: Jayne Robinson, Poet Laureate of Middle Bass Island. I will wax poetic about bass and lite beer and local politics (which revolve around the same). Maybe I can do a sabbatical on this rock, where cell phones only work intermittently and the day starts with tea on the deck and ends with a beer or a glass of wine on the boat.

This Fourth there were no catastrophes or ceremonies at sea—just sunshine and fireworks (and a quick trip to Hen Island to visit Mom and Dad). We had front-row floating seats for the fireworks on Ann and Alan's boat. Kat and her friend Morgan got the best seats, which are on the bow of the boat. They spread out blankets and watched the light show breaking over their sleepy heads. No traffic, no crowds, just unobstructed pyrotechnics. The fireworks were followed by a fast and furious ride over flat water as a moon river chased us back to the cottage.

Downy Yellow Cake with Milk Chocolate Buttercream Frosting

Taking the trip out to Hen Island to visit my parents made me recall my father's favorite cake combination. We always celebrated his Valentine's Day eve birthday with this cake, made in the shape of a heart (it is one of Wayne's favorite cake combinations, as well). Moist and full of flavor, the cake has a great crumb to it. And the milk chocolate buttercream is not too sweet. The islanders loved it. Both cake and frosting recipes come from *The Cake Bible*, by Rose Levy Beranbaum.

Preheat oven to 350° F and butter two 9" round cake pans and line with parchment or wax paper. Butter again and flour.

Cake

6 egg yolks (use large eggs)
1 cup milk
2 ¼ teaspoons vanilla extract
3 cups sifted cake flour
1 ½ cups sugar
1 tablespoon plus 1 teaspoon baking powder
¾ teaspoons salt
12 tablespoons (1 ½ sticks) room-temperature unsalted butter

1. In a medium bowl combine egg yolks, ¼ cup milk and vanilla; mix lightly with a fork.

2. In the large mixing bowl of an electric mixer combine the dry ingredients and mix on low speed for 30 seconds.

3. Add the butter and remaining ¾ cup of milk. Mix on low speed until the dry ingredients are moistened.

4. Increase to medium speed and beat for 1 ½ minutes. (This will aerate and develop the cake's structure.)

5. Gradually add the egg mixture in 3 batches, beating for 20 seconds after each addition. Scrape down the sides after each addition.

6. Scrape the batter into the two prepared pans. Pans will be about ½ full.

7. Bake 25–35 minutes or until a toothpick inserted into the center comes out clean and the cake springs back when pressed lightly in the center. (The cake should only start to shrink from the sides after the cakes have been removed from the oven.)

8. Let the cakes cool in the pans on racks for 10 minutes. Loosen the sides with a small metal spatula and invert onto greased wire racks. To prevent splitting, reinvert so that the cakes are top-side-up and cool completely before frosting.

Milk Chocolate Buttercream Frosting

1 pound milk chocolate (any type but Lindt offers a smooth texture and caramel undertone).
8 ounces dark chocolate (bittersweet or extra bittersweet)
1½ cups (2 ½ sticks) room-temperature unsalted butter

1. Break the chocolate into pieces and place into the top of a double boiler on low heat so water is hot but not simmering. The water must not touch the bottom of the double boiler.

2. Stir occasionally just until chocolate is melted. Stir until smooth and set aside to cool until no longer warm to the touch. (Or melt in the microwave, stirring every 15 seconds and remove before it is fully melted.)

3. In the large bowl of an electric mixer beat the butter at medium speed and beat in cooled chocolate until uniform in color.

4. If the frosting is not stiff enough simply place the bowl in the refrigerator and take out every 10 minutes, and stir, until it is the right consistency.

Cake Assembly

1. Place one cake layer, right-side-up, on cake plate or stand that has been prepared by placing 4 strips of waxed paper, overlapping, around the edges. Make sure the cake is touching the paper all the way around.

2. Frost the top of this layer and then place the other layer, also right-side-up, on top.

3. Frost the sides and top of the entire cake.

4. Remover wax paper strips by carefully pulling out from under the cake.

Dog Days of July (again)...Home Free

"The best way to keep children home is to make the home atmosphere pleasant—and let the air out of the tires."
—Dorothy Parker

I wish I had thought to let the air out of Lizzie's tires before she headed north to find her bliss in Canada. But she is due back today, a full two weeks earlier than planned. She and her best friends, Erin and Zoe, had set out to experience the WWOOF-ing life, working on two different organic farms in Ontario.

I spent the day killing time (and weeds) waiting for the girl to wheel her Volvo into the driveway. When I was a kid, I always wanted to make it to home base, to be home free. It is only in the games we play as children that we can ever know we are really home free. But life does offer us brief moments of feeling safe and free from trouble. One of those moments is when someone we love returns from a journey safe and sound. I am happiest when all of my family's feet are under the same old dining room table.

Lizzie arrived just as I ran out of weeds to whack. We embraced for a long time and then she headed to her room to recover from the day's journey.

Later we gathered for dinner, with cake for dessert of course. Erin and Zoe joined us and between bites of lasagna we were treated to a lively recounting of the last seven weeks of their lives. Their early weeks were spent at a nonprofit, self-help employment resource center in Ontario, where they labored in organic gardens, a bike repair shop, a café, and art studios, with people who were learning to help themselves. The principal of the center provided access to tools and hospitality to all. They worked hard and loved it

Reluctantly they left for their second site. This WWOOF site billed itself as an "Ecospiritual Sanctuary for Conscious Living" replete with gardens, orchards, fields, and a magical forest for walking and wild-crafting. The objective of the center was to "empower students to fulfill their highest potential as architects of peace." Sounded great.

Unfortunately the three of them became little more than indentured servants, living in leaky tents, rising at 5 AM for drum circle, and then doing hard labor lifting heavy crates of jars for the new-age potions under preparation. A new-age couple ran the place, the male-half a Fabio look-alike. He advocated eating only "living" food and told stories about those who lived by simply inhaling their own breath, aka "Breathitarians."

Erin did a fantastic riff on this, mimicking the amazing new-age Fabio, "Why would you want to put *dead* food into your *living* body?," she asked. "Well, I want to put *cake* into my living body," she said. The three of them had tired quickly of wet-tent living, raw foods, and hard labor. They told of their escape to a nearby town to inhale pizza. On another day, while selling the herbal potions at a local fair, Lizzie snuck off to a booth selling elephant ears. She bought this "dead" food and hid behind a dumpster to avoid getting busted. Eventually, emboldened by the sugary dead food, they confronted their captors with their thoughts on how they were being treated. All agreed it was best to part ways, and the girls packed up and headed home.

Just as they were nearing the end of their stories, the tornado siren went off. We headed to the basement, cake in tow. We watched the All-Star game, and Lizzie and Kat debated whose baby blankie was in the worst shape, until the all-clear signal released us. We live in tornado alley where blankies still come in handy once in a while.

Later, when I walked by the door to the third floor, I could hear Lizzie with Erin and Zoe; they were laughing and talking as if they hadn't just spent seven weeks living on top of one another.

Home is where everything starts, yet it means different things to different people. For me it represents security, perhaps because I moved too many times growing up. Or maybe my passion for security began when I was in college. Two weeks into a summer term, the bursar's office informed me that my tuition check had bounced. When I phoned home to ask my parents what had happened, they mentioned that they couldn't afford to keep me in college that summer. I guess it was a moot point that they had already known this when they waved goodbye to me two weeks previously.

I left college and returned home. I lied about my age to get a job in a nightclub, Big Al's, where I sang and danced cabaret-style, serving drinks between shows. I came home from work one day to find my mother sitting in the driveway sobbing, with the Elton John song "Don't let the Sun Go Down on Me" playing on the radio. Between sobs, she said that she and my father were in debt and our house was going to be sold at a sheriff's auction. My mother was never the same after that. To her, homes equaled status and she spent her life pining for a bigger, better home. The mistake my mother made was believing that home is a place. A house is a place but a home is about people. Strife and contention in a family can't be counteracted with marble floors and crystal chandeliers. For years I was afraid to buy a house, afraid it would tie me down and it wouldn't last. But I have been more fortunate—I have both a house and a home, one humble, the other glorious.

The day after Lizzie & Co's return from Canada, I headed to Chicago to attend a seminar for new department chairs. I called it Chair Camp, much to my dean's distaste. The first session reminded me that my new life as department chair would be all about meetings and budgets and nothing about the things I really care about. The leader of the afternoon session kept repeating, "As chairs, you will have little authority but lots of influence." It took me a while to figure out why he was saying this. He himself is a dean and therefore does not want chairs to have authority. After this revelation, I was much more skeptical about what he was telling us and stopped hating Chair Camp.

After the first day's brainwashing, I retreated to my room on the fifteenth story of a luxury hotel on Miracle Mile. I flopped on the bed and turned on the TV, which offered cable and new movies. At home TV is not allowed in bedrooms and we don't have cable, so this was a luxury. As the sun set outside my window, I tried to figure out what movie I was watching, a game that always reminds me of my father who reveled in tuning into a movie half-way through it and unraveling the plot.

The leading man was a down-and-out boxer (Russell Crowe) and he had a sweet, long suffering wife (Rene Zellweger). Eventually I figured out it was *Cinderella Man*, a movie I had made a note to see (I lost the note). It is a true story in which Crowe plays James J. Braddock, the boxer who challenged Max Baer for the heavyweight championship during the Great Depression. Braddock was forced to go on the dole to support his wife and kids as he pursues the title. He is trying for the title for the sake of his children, to earn enough money to "put a little distance between my kids and the street." All parents want to put a little distance between their kids and the street. E-mail may have replaced letters and TV the fine art of conversation, but nothing will ever replace home.

I couldn't wait to get home. Tied down, but home free.

After Lizzie returned from her trip, we were finally able to open a package from her friend Emmy that had arrived shortly after she left. Inside were some clothes for Lizzie and a note for us. Here is the note:

Wayne and Jayne Anderson,

Just so you know, you have the most thoughtful, kindest, unafraid person for a daughter that I've ever met. It seems you have raised her in a way that has taught her to not be afraid of life.

I wish I could have met the two of you. Hope all is well forever!

Emmy

Tangerine Cake with Brown Sugar Icing

Both of my daughters consume several goods at highly abnormal levels. Guava juice and canned mandarin oranges are two that come to mind. When I found this recipe, I couldn't resist the description of it offered by Mrs. Chard in the *Hollyhocks and Radishes* cookbook. Mrs. Chard ran a fruit and vegetable stand in the Upper Peninsula of Michigan for decades. All the recipes in this book are simple and simply wonderful. Here are Mrs. Chard's comments that sold me on the cake before tasting it: "A most unusual cake, it has no shortening but is quite moist, and turns a rich, caramel color when baked. My neighbor describes it best: 'It's a real good traveling cake.'" I took their word for it, not only making it for Lizzie's homecoming, but also making a second one that traveled with us to Middle Bass Island. A wide range of guests sampled it and I saw many come back for more.

Lizzie's reaction, when I made it for her homecoming, was to pronounce it "moist and good." Breathitarians of the world take a deep breath and begin to salivate!

Preheat oven to 350° F and butter a 9" x 13" baking dish or pan.

Cake

2 eggs
2 cups sugar
2 cups flour
2 teaspoons baking soda
1 teaspoon salt
1 teaspoon vanilla
2 11-ounce cans mandarin oranges, drained
1 cup chopped pecans or walnuts

1. In the small bowl of an electric mixer, combine flour, baking soda, and salt. Mix on low speed for 30 seconds; set aside.

2. In the large bowl of an electric mixer, cream together eggs and sugar until light.

3. Beat flour mixture into the egg and sugar mixture on low speed just until mixed.

4. Add remaining ingredients and beat until well mixed.

5. Pour into prepared pan.

6. Bake 40 minutes or until the center springs back when lightly touched.

7. Serve plain or dusted with powdered sugar. But if you have a big sweet tooth, as we do, spread the cake with Brown Sugar Frosting when it is still warm.

Brown Sugar Frosting

½ cup brown sugar
½ cup white sugar
2 heaping tablespoons flour
1 cup water
⅓ cup butter
1 teaspoon vanilla

With a whisk, combine all the ingredients in a medium saucepan over medium heat. Stirring constantly, boil until slightly thickened. Cool and drizzle over cake.

Northern Michigan Sandcastles

"No one can grant you happiness. Happiness is a choice we all have the power to make. There is always cake." —Jimmy Tock, from *Life Expectancy*, by Dean Koontz

Sandcastles are a good example of Wabi-Sabi, which is the Japanese aesthetic that calls for the appreciation of things imperfect, incomplete, and ephemeral. You will know Wabi-Sabi when you see it. It might be a rusted gate smothered with morning glory blooms that will fade by four o'clock or a fine china cup with a crack in it or a sandcastle made by little hands that will wash away in the evening tide or storm.

During the twenty years we vacationed on a particular beach on a particular bay in northern Michigan, my children built many a sandcastle. Some were humble, some spectacular, but all were incomplete, ephemeral. I wish I had a photo of every one of them because we can no longer inhabit that particular beach. The cottage we have always rented now has new owners who, loving it as much as we did, wish to spend all summer on that strand of sand. I don't blame them, but Kat does. The Reed cottage was set in a little stand of pines that opened to a perfect crescent of sugar-sand beach on Grand Traverse Bay stretching a mile in either direction. It is an amphitheater of sand and water, the bluest water east of Maui. In a single day I could count a bevy of blues, from aquamarine to indigo. I've made lists of the shades of blue I've observed there.

The house was humble and a bit dingy from neglect, but all you had to do was look out the window to forgive the imperfection. I loved to stand at the kitchen sink and watch my lovely little daughters and their cousins or friends wind their way up from the beach along the sandy path, yelling, "Mom, I'm hungry. Mom, come see the sandcastle I built." I loved the sound of the screen door slamming shut as they headed back to the beach. For two weeks every year we stumbled from cottage to beach, carrying nothing and staying for a few minutes or a few hours. If we went to town, we were sure to get back to the beach for the sunset.

Lizzie and her cousin Caroline spent many a happy hour playing restaurant, dubbing their fine eating establishment *La Reed Cabin*. They made and served us a wide range of delicacies. Nights were spent playing board games. We had drawn closer by the end of the two weeks and sand and sun had polished all of our sharp edges. The new owners have scoured out every imperfection and turned the cabin into a showplace, even installing satellite TV. My kids were a bit taken aback, claiming they even missed the daddy longlegs. We are here again, in the same corner of the world but in a different cottage.

This new cottage is down the way, around the point. But it isn't the same. This is a cool enough cottage, known as the sandcastle because of its architecture, but a beach of boulders is tough on the toes and makes for a dangerous game of Frisbee. We've been rescued by Tom and Helen, our friends who live in the cottage next to our old cottage, who've invited us to hang out on their beach. Sadly, it turns out that braving boulders was a better idea than finding out that the new owners of "our" cottage had installed loud speakers on the beach. They play Top 40 music all day, even when they are not on the beach. This has caused Tom and Helen to mutter under their breath constantly and say almost mean things. Still we managed to have a good time with our usual trips to the beach, aerobic water games, dune hikes, and boat rides across diamond-studded sapphire bays. Nights brought bonfires on the beach and board games. This year's book to steal from each other, because we only brought one copy, was *The Time Traveler's Wife*.

My brother, Steve, and his son, Conor, joined us for part of the week and created the usual chaos. One bedtime found us rushing to their room in response to Steve screaming like someone in a B-grade horror film. The cause of his distress turned out to be the discovery of a desicated animal of some kind under his pillow. And I mean totally, completely desicated—it appeared to have been left in one of those fruit dryers. Two days later I screamed after noticing what appeared to be another dessicated rodent under my bed. Conor had put it there. It was better than the time we had a raccoon scratching at the front door.

The trouble with traditions is that they can be broken. I wanted my kids to have the deep and lovely experience of spending time on big water. The Great Lakes are inland seas, a truth often lost on those who live on the real ocean. I wanted to instill in my kids a sense of awe and love for the natural world. As a child I spent all summer every year at my grandparents' cottage high above the shores of the Ontario side of Lake Erie. The cottage was really a large summer home, with six bedrooms and an equal number of porches. From Memorial Day to Labor Day it was filled with family and visitors. When I was a senior in high school the house was sold, and later torn down to save the house behind it from encroaching erosion. I still dream of that house and wish I could revisit it for just one day.

Our time on the big lake was wonderful, in spite of all the changes. We returned home to steamy weather and the season's first tomato. After the bikes and kayak and luggage were unloaded and stored away, we gathered in the kitchen for the ritual eating of the first tomato. I cut the golden red orb into quarters and we all grabbed one, passed the salt shaker, made a wish, and toasted to summer.

And so we have come full circle, another trip around the sun and another crop of tomatoes. I do not know what wishes Wayne, Lizzie, and Kat made over their slice of tomato, but mine was that next year a new cottage drops into our lives so we can start the magic all over again. I even know which cake I will make at the new cottage. It is going to be cherry clafouti.

Michigan Sour Cherry Pudding Cake

Two days before leaving for the cottage I got an e-mail from Williams-Sonoma announcing the "season's most memorable dessert," a cake in the shape of a sandcastle. For my convenience, they were selling the bundt cake pan ($29.95) to shape the cake, the square cake plate ($65.00) to display the cake, and the double-lemon cake mix to make the cake ($14.00). The e-mail continued, "For the finishing touch, scatter brown sugar about the base, give it a simple glaze, or fill the center with berries or ice cream. Our Square Cake Stand will present your masterpiece with panache."

I personally think sandcastles are best when made of sand on a spectacular beach, with young children playing the architects.

Clafouti is a rustic French dessert made of fresh fruit and thick batter. Part cake and part pudding, it is perfect for a vacation dessert, especially when the vacation is taking place in the heart of cherry country, the region that supplies 75 percent of the country's tart cherries. (It can also be made with, peaches, plums, blueberries, or whatever.) This traditional dessert, from the Limousin area of France, is usually cooked with the cherries unpitted. If you choose to do it this way, remember to warn those who are going to eat it.

I made it with pitted sour cherries from the Leelanau peninsula of Michigan, the epicenter of the cherry empire. I purchased them at the little stand at the end of our lane.

This serves six and can be eaten right out of the oven, but I prefer it cool or even cold.

Preheat oven to 350° F and butter a 9" glass pie plate or tart dish. Dust with 1 teaspoon sugar. This cake can be served right out of the oven, but I prefer it cool or even cold.

Cake

3 cups pitted fresh sour cherries (canned or frozen may be substituted)
3 tablespoons Cognac
½ cup sugar
¾ cup whole milk
¼ cup heavy cream
3 large eggs
1 teaspoon vanilla extract
⅔ cup all-purpose flour
Pinch of salt
Confectioners' sugar for dusting

1. Stir together cherries and cognac,let marinate for at least 15 minutes, and then strain out the cherries and reserve the cognac.

2. Blend milk, cream, eggs, remaining sugar, vanilla, salt, and flour in a blender on high speed for 1 minute, scraping down sides halfway through. (Or beat with a whisk in a bowl until well mixed.)

3. Pour ½ cup of the batter into the prepared pie plate. Arrange the cherries evenly over the batter; drizzle with the Cognac. Pour remaining batter over cherries.

4. Bake until the top is puffed and golden brown and batter is set (about 45 to 60 minutes).

5. Dust with confectioners' sugar. Serve with whipped cream or ice cream to make it extra special.

Epilogue

"Science is but another word for hope; and hope stands on tippy toes looking for healing, looking for cures, searching for the ideal."
—Emanuel Cleaver, Congressman (D-MO), speaking in January 2007 during a debate in the House of Representatives on stem cell funding

Is it possible that the world is less safe than when I started this journey? Hamas bombs Israel and Israel graciously returns the favor, millions of barrels of crude oil ooze in slow motion onto the beaches of the Gulf Coast, and millions of people have lost their jobs or homes or both. I know that pain from my childhood. We turn on the TV, and our choices are crime, reality, and talent shows. We have been told the "inconvenient truth." We know that future generations may ask why we didn't do something when we had the chance. Will we be sitting on the couch watching "So You Think You can Dance" when the world begins to burn? Or will sanity be restored?

And what of my family?

My young friend Ethan's question "Are you happier or better for eating cake every week?" has been answered with a resounding Yes. Do I continue to research and make a different cake every week? Well, we still have Cake Day at our house, just not every week. We continue to eat cake often, and certainly when we need it, and on special occasions I still make cakes of importance. On Election Day 2008, when our country took the historic leap and elected an African American man for president, I was in the kitchen at 6 AM concocting a towering chocolate chiffon cake with mocha icing. It turned into a Celebration Cake that we shared with everyone on our block gathered at our house when the state of Ohio was called for Obama.

We have given birth to a tradition that is alive and well. Not long after we completed the Year of Cake, Kat called me from home three times while I was in the car to ask if she could bake a cake with her friends. I said yes and arrived to find them making a red velvet cake. I hovered a bit during the making and baking, surprised to see that she knew exactly what to do. She buttered and floured the pans, mixed the eggs, and pulled out the sifter to dust the cake with powdered sugar. I commented on her competency. "Mom, I learned all this from you," she reminded me. When she left to have dinner at a friend's house, she took the cake with her. We are spreading the cake gospel.

My dearly loved mother-in-law, Bernie, passed away in late November 2008, right after Thanksgiving. She had made the annals of the Cleveland Clinic (not that it was a goal) by surviving back-to-back brain surgeries at age eighty-five. Bernie spent the last year of her life under the doting care of her husband. My father-in-law tended to her every need, charting her blood sugar three times a day as only an engineer would do. They spent eighty years together, meeting when she was five and he was seven, forsaking all others, which makes theirs one hell of a love story.

The world has lost a grand and lovely soul—a Steel Magnolia who never complained, Bernie also never backed down when something important popped up. More than forty years ago she stood up to the 75,000 women in her city's chapter of Church Women United. Bernie, at the end of her term as president, was about to pass on the job to the person next in line, her friend Bertha Birdsong. But this supposedly Christian organization passed over Birdsong because she was an African American. Bernie tried and failed to change their minds, and so she resigned from Church Women United. Bernie lost a lot of friends over this, but when the dust had settled, her friendship with Bertha was intact. I like to imagine Bernie and Bertha smiling as Barack H. Obama took his oath of office.

Wayne has been a rock for his father and all of us during this hard time. In addition to his well-established head-hunting business, Wayne now has his own radio spot on an NPR affiliate out of Miami University helping people to find or change jobs. His is a skill sorely needed in today's economy. He was there helping those who lost their jobs when GM made the last truck in our city. And he continues to serve as my much-appreciated personal career coach. He's the best there is. I keep urging him to launch an interactive Web site, where he will answer people's thorny job-related quandaries confidentially and in real time (sample questions: "How, exactly do I tell my coworkers and boss to go to hell without offending them?" or "Should I put a prison record on my resume?") For Christmas Wayne surprised me with the classic white KitchenAid mixer of my dreams. Eggnog and cakes have never been so easy. OK, I admit I've been silly to wait this long to buy one of those gleaming and gorgeous workhorses.

Shortly after we finished our year of cake our Lizzie was diagnosed with Multiple Sclerosis. The diagnosis was traumatic for all of us, changing the way we view ourselves, our future, and the world. How can life and health be so fragile and yet so resilient at the same time? Now twenty-four, Lizzie is back at Pitt, in graduate school, studying for her master's in social work. In addition, she is a doula in training, a skill she plans to offer to women with disabilities. Lizzie lives in a personal state of ferocious and beautiful frugality. She is generous in spirit and in her relations with people, but frugal with money and things. I marvel at her devotion to her ideals as well as her kindness and beauty. I have a lot to learn from her, but some of it I'm afraid is not teachable. Lizzie has a very special talent for living a creative, meaningful, and inclusive life. To me, her life is lyrical.

I've had the great fortune of lunching with Bernard Kuchner, the foreign minister of France and founder of Doctors without Borders, who was out and about crusading for health care without borders. Kuchner does not believe that health itself is a human right, but he does believe that access to affordable health care is. Amen. And with the changes in health care in our country, it will be tougher for insurance companies to discriminate against Lizzie because of her pre-existing condition. Life is a pre-existing condition.

Did eating cake help during the Dark Day of Diagnosis and those that followed? It did. When faced with such difficult news, we humans cling to the bits of faith and tradition that have informed our lives, hoping to cobble together a life raft. Our particular life raft included cake.

On the traumatic day when we learned that our daughter has MS, we slogged our way through the cold rain and pain until, at the end of the day, we found ourselves at a Whole Foods Market. I wandered the aisles in a daze, not in the least hungry, and eventually found myself in front of the bakery case. I fixated on a vegan chocolate fudge cake, which we bought and ate over the following three rainy days. During that time, Lizzie received massive infusions of steroids and we moved her to a healthier apartment. I kept staring at the non-stop rain through the windows of our hotel and the windows of Lizzie's new apartment. It seemed to be mimicking my tears and drumming despair, and I remembered how it had rained on the best days of my life—my wedding day and the days I gave birth to Lizzie and Kat. I had little choice but to go with the hypothesis that the rain was a positive omen, signaling that everything was going to be OK. I gently remind myself of this whenever the ugly undertow of worry tugs.

In addition to the potent MS treatments, Lizzie is following a gluten-free and mostly vegan diet. Vegan cakes are pretty easy and quite good. Gluten-free cakes are perhaps the ultimate challenge in cake-making. I'm working on it. Below you'll find the gluten-free cake I made for her birthday this year. It is delicious and gorgeous.

Kat, now sixteen, is in full bloom—zany, smart, gorgeous and equally dedicated to her friends, her music, and cross-country running. She confessed her love of chemistry and math to me, which made my heart soar. She tells me of her desire to study science, of the neuro and political kind, and to work at the UN. "Is that possible?" she asks. "Of course," I tell her. The world needs individuals (lots of them) who do science and care about people. She wants to be a neuroscientist because she thinks the mind is the most amazing thing of all. It would be great to finally understand the brains of politicians, but I don't think that is what she has in mind. While she certainly has the math and science abilities required for such a career, I'm wondering if she's baiting me.

I predict Kat may end up in advertising (like my mother), where she will have the greatest opportunity to influence (manipulate) the brains of others. I have a great deal to learn from a sixteen-year-old who has come to the realization, on her own, that neuroscience is the future.

By the way, a new cottage came to us, at the last minute, on Craig's List. Hard to imagine, but it was even sweeter than the Reed Cottage where we logged twenty years of family togetherness. We summered at our new place for two years but now feel the call of the wider, wilder world. This past summer we trekked the streets of Toronto and the trails along the

Georgian Bay. Next summer we will be in Paris, where I am to teach a class on how infectious disease has influenced history. I am not certain where life will take us after that.

As for me, I am surviving my stint as department chair. The department has grown and prospered, for which I can take only a morsel of credit. But I am starting to plan what I will do after my turn is over. A sabbatical is calling me from the end of this meeting-filled tunnel, and I've informed my dean that I will require a raise to fund an angst-induced facelift. My friend and colleague Albert is cancer-free and the same lovable PITA (pain in the ass) as always.

My sabbatical plan is to head as far away as possible and hide out in someone's lab. Will I be able to handle six months away from my family, never having been absent from them for more than six days? Will they come with me? Will I eat cake alone on some other continent? The purpose of sabbaticals is to allow professors to recharge and refocus their scholarship. I will definitely need to be recharged after six years of administration. I am thinking of how to refocus my research, how to involve myself in the terrible puzzle that is MS.

In the months following Lizzie's diagnosis, I logged hundreds upon hundreds of hours reading everything I could get my hands on about MS and writing to the scientists all over the world who are working on the disease. Every single one of those scientists responded—science never sleeps and it does find cures. How I would love to be part of a cure for this monster of a disease. And with science no longer under a political gag order in our country, perhaps we can find that cure in the stem cells that are no longer going to be under lock-and-key. My prediction: geeks will be chic and science unbound. I hope the next book I write will be about the cure for MS, but in the meantime I can donate proceeds from this book to the cause.

There is much to hate in this world, and too much to love. It is important in this information-filled life to choose carefully who and what you listen to. I choose to listen to those with messages of hope, the Jane Goodalls of the world. Thanks for listening. And remember that when life gets you down, there is always a slice of hope close by, whether it be angel, pound, chocolate, or chiffon.

Towering Hope Chocolate Walnut Torte (gluten-free)

Sweet (not too) and special! It is over four inches high! Hope made visible. Frosting isn't needed, but a dusting of powdered sugar is a divine idea. The absence of flour makes it gluten-free. Another hit adapted from *Maida Heater's Book of Great Chocolate Desserts*.

Adjust rack ⅓ up from bottom of the oven, and preheat oven to 350° F. This torte requires an angel food cake pan, 10 inches across and 4 ¼ inches deep, the kind with a removable inner core. Do not butter the pan.

Cake

7 ounces semisweet chocolate
8 ounces (2 ¼ cups) walnuts
12 large eggs, separated (to equal 1⅔ cups egg whites, scant cup of egg yolks)
1 cup granulated sugar
¼ teaspoon salt

1. Separate eggs and allow egg whites to come to room temperature.

2. Grind the nuts to a rather fine consistency, but do not let them become oily. They do not need to be finely powdered, but they must remain dry; set aside.

3. Place the chocolate in the top of a double boiler over hot water on moderate heat. Cover until the chocolate is partially melted, then uncover and stir until completely melted.

4. Remove top of pan and set aside for the chocolate to cool slightly.

5. In a small bowl of an electric mixer,beat the egg yolks with ½ cup of the sugar at high speed for 2 minutes (do not let the mixture become very thick).

6. On low speed mix in the chocolate, which may be warm but must not be hot.

7. Gradually add about half of the nuts (reserve the remaining nuts).

8. Remove the bowl from the mixer and set aside.

9. Place the egg whites (at room temperature) in the large bowl of the electric mixer, and add the salt.

10. With clean beaters, beat until the whites barely hold a soft shape. Reduce speed to moderate and gradually add the reserved ½ cup of sugar. Next, at high speed, continue to beat until the whites hold a firm shape; do not let them get stiff and dry.

11. With a rubber spatula, fold one large spoonful of the whites into the chocolate mixture; fold in a second large spoonful.

12. Now transfer the chocolate mixture to a mixing bowl that is larger than the large bowl of the electric mixer.

13. Add about ⅓ of the remaining whites and slightly fold the two mixtures together with a large rubber spatula. Do not be too thorough. Then add the remaining nuts and egg whites and gently and carefully fold them all together.

14. Turn the batter into the unbuttered 10-inch tube pan, handling gingerly to avoid losing the air that has been beaten into it.

15. Smooth the top, and bake for 1 hour and 15 minutes. During the baking, the top of the cake will rise in a dome shape, but it will become almost level with the top of the pan when it is done.

16. Remove pan from oven and invert the pan, suspending it on the neck of a bottle. A beer bottle works well.

17. Allow cake to cool completely in this inverted position.

18. Remove cake from the pan: Carefully insert the blade of a firm knife (with an approximately 6-inch blade) between the cake and the side walls of the pan, all the way to the bottom of the pan, pressing the knife blade firmly against the pan in order to not cut into or crush the sides of the cake. With short up and down strokes, in a sawing motion, cut all the way around the cake.

19. Release the cake from the sides of the pan by pulling up on the tube and/or placing your hands under the bottom of the pan and pushing the bottom up. Now carefully cut the cake from the bottom of the pan using the same technique in step 18.

20. Cover the cake with a flat serving plate and invert

onto the plate. Remove the bottom of the pan.

21. Sprinkle the top of the cake with powdered sugar.

22. Serve alone or with whipped cream.

Bibliography

"When baking, follow directions. When cooking, go by your own taste." —Laiko Bahrs

A Taste of Avon Lake: Favorite Recipes from the Avon Lake United Church of Christ and Jack-n-Jill Nursery School. Avon Lake, Ohio: 2001.

Berenbaum, Rose Levy. *The Cake Bible*. New York: William Morrow and Company, 1988.

Blanchard, Melinda and Robert Blanchard. *At Blanchard's Table: A Trip to the Beach Cookbook*. New York: Clarkson Potter, 2003.

Corriher, Shirley O. *CookWise: The Hows and Whys of Successful Cooking, The Secerts of Cooking Revealed*. New York: William Morrow and Company, 1997.

Eberly, Carole. *Potato Chip Cookies and Tomato Soup Cake: Recipes of Americana*. East Lansing, Michigan: Eberly Press, 1992.

Eckley, Mary. *The New McCall's Cookbook*. New York: Random House, 1973.

Heatter, Maida. *Maida Heatter's Book of Great Chocolate Desserts*. New York: Alfred A. Knopf, 1981.

Hewitt, Jean. *New York Times Natural Food Cookbook*. New York: Avon, 1992.

Mickelson, Bonnie Stewart. *Hollyhocks and Radishes: Mrs. Chard's Almanac Cookbook*. Bellevue, Washington: Pickle Point Publishing, 1989.

Milton, Jane. *Mexican: Healthy Ways with a Favourite Cuisine*. London: Hermes House, 2001.

Pappas, Lou Seibert. *Bread Baking*. Concord, California: Nitty Gritty Books, 1975.

Stewart, Martha. *The Martha Stewart Cookbook: Collected Recipes for Every Day*. New York: Clarkson Potter, 1995.

The Rocky River Methodist Church Cookbook. Rocky River, Ohio: 1962.

Yankee Magazine's Church Suppers and Potluck Dinners Cookbook. Edited by Andrea Chesman. New York: Villard, 1992.

Acknowledgments

Each book has a beginning moment. This one was inspired by a line in a book by Dean Koontz, a bit of sweet irony. Thank you, Dean, for your kind words, your letters, your great books, and your love of dogs. And, yes, to answer your question, there will be cake in the future.

It is a certainty that I would not have written this book if it were not for my wonderful daughters. Lizzie and Kat you continue to amaze me with your sweet and savvy ways, and I give thanks for you every day. Wayne, my dear husband of many decades, you have always provided the humor life demands. You are responsible in many ways for all the successes I have had in life, including this one—thank you, thank you, thank you. And I thank Garrison Keillor for replying to Wayne's letter asking for advice about how to support my desire to become a writer. Keillor, displeased with Wayne's attitude, admonished him with the line: "boogars on you." This has saved us many a marital fight.

I thank the rest of my family, my sister, Ann Huber, and brother, Steve Robinson, and my nieces and nephews for their support and a lifetime of family fun, on the island and off.

I must say thank you to my in-laws, Bob and the late Bernie Anderson, for being world-class grandparents. They kept my daughters in fancy shoes and made every holiday at their home on the shores of Lake Erie special. I thank Bernie, in particular, for her white cake, which has become a treasured family heirloom.

My own parents, the late Willard and Marion Robinson, were with me in spirit on every Cake Day during our Year of Cake. I extend to them my deepest thanks for always accepting their three children for exactly who we are. If every parent could do as they did, life for all children would be one piece of cake after another (although, mom, you really should have baked more cakes). And I thank them too for teaching me that we all have the duty to help those in need. I will be donating a percentage of the proceeds of this book to fund research aimed at eradicating Multiple Sclerosis—transforming it into a disease that people once had.

I must not fail to thank my neighbors and friends on our block. All of you who reside here inspire and sustain me, and I promise more cake to come. You are the village that everyone hopes to find.

A special thanks to my former student Christina Hester, who is now my teacher and cheerleader, and to all my students, past and future, who have filled my work with joy (Tracy, I'm working on a Pearl Harbor Day cake just for you).

We all need mentors and editors, and if we are lucky they also become friends. Wolfgang Dietz Bauer, my PhD advisor and editor for life, you have been the best mentor and friend I could have imagined.

And thanks to those friends whose work made this book a living reality. I must thank Erin Johnson for her whimsical artwork and her laugh that always leaves me feeling like I've just gotten off a roller coaster. I am so thankful for my book designer, Ellyn Miller, whose calm countenance, talent, and attention to detail made up for my lack of all of these things. And thank you too, Ellyn, for sharing the story of your first birthday cake in your native land, a story that deserves its own book. I thank Penny Schreiber for editing portions of this book. A special thanks to Dene Berman, my trusted friend and confidante, who provided the clue that allowed me to complete this journey.

Finally, to all who consumed the many cakes I have baked over the years: thank you very much. May sweetness follow you all, wherever you may go. Please don't hesitate to spread the gospel of cake. Let us all eat cake!

Jayne Robinson
Dayron, Ohio
November 2010

Meet Jayne

Jayne Robinson is professor and chair of the biology department at the University of Dayton. She is married to Wayne Anderson, entrepreneur, and they have two lovely and amazing daughters, Lizzie and Kat. Robinson is also a mother to all of the students who have come through her lab, patiently guiding them into the mysterious world of scientific research. By day, Robinson explores the secret lives of microbes in her quest to vanquish the evil ones among them. She is addicted to shiny new hypotheses, particularly those which can be proven through experimentation. But what she has learned about love, parenting, and family life has come through not-so-scientific experimentation on her husband and children. Robinson believes in the salvation that emanates from the small and simple acts and pleasures of daily life. Cake is the latest of her unscientific experiments and it has been a wholly successful one.